C# Multithreaded and Parallel Programming

Develop powerful C# applications to take advantage of today's multicore hardware

Rodney Ringler

PUBLISHING

BIRMINGHAM - MUMBAI

C# Multithreaded and Parallel Programming

First published: December 2014

Production reference: 1171214

Published by Packt Publishing Ltd.
Livery Place
35 Livery Street
Birmingham B3 2PB, UK.

ISBN 978-1-84968-832-1

www.packtpub.com

Credits

Author
Rodney Ringler

Reviewers
Ahmed Ilyas
Allen LeVan
Danijel Malik
Doug Ortiz
Philip Pierce
Abhishek Ranka

Acquisition Editor
James Jones

Content Development Editor
Akshay Nair

Technical Editor
Dennis John

Copy Editor
Laxmi Subramanian

Project Coordinator
Mary Alex

Proofreaders
Bridget Braund
Martin Diver
Paul Hindle

Indexers
Monica Ajmera Mehta
Rekha Nair
Tejal Soni

Graphics
Sheetal Aute
Ronak Dhruv
Abhinash Sahu

Production Coordinator
Melwyn D'sa

Cover Work
Melwyn D'sa

About the Author

Rodney Ringler has 25 years' experience developing multitasking and parallel applications, with the last 10 focused on C# and .NET. He graduated cum laude from Clemson University with a BS degree in Computer Engineering. He then worked for 12 years in the fiber optic manufacturing industry on C-based real-time multitasking process control systems, where he went from being a developer to a project manager to an IT architect. After this, he spent 8 years running his own application development and hosting company focused on both .NET and open source technologies. He then spent several years as a consultant, working with companies in the retail, software, and manufacturing industries.

Currently, Rodney works as a senior .NET developer at a manufacturing company based in Charlotte, NC, and takes .NET and object-oriented programming classes at Central Piedmont Community College.

In his spare time, Rodney enjoys life in Lake Wylie, SC, with his wife and four children.

I would like to thank my lovely wife, Rachel, and our four wonderful children, Matt, Amanda, Caroline, and Dave, for all of their patience and support while I spent many nights and weekends working on this project. I would also like to thank my parents, Fred and Joyce Ringler, for all their help, encouragement, love, and support.

I would like to offer one last thank you to all of the people at Fellowship Hall, especially Mike and Mahala, who helped save my life and taught me that miracles do happen as long as you show up and do your part.

About the Reviewers

Ahmed Ilyas has a BEng degree from Edinburgh Napier University, Scotland, where he majored in software development. He has 15 years of professional experience in software development.

After leaving Microsoft, he ventured into setting up his own consultancy company, offering the best possible solutions for a variety of industries and providing real-world answers to those problems. He only uses the Microsoft stack to build these technologies and bring in the best practices, patterns, and software to his client base to enable long-term stability and compliance in the ever-changing software industry. He is keen on improving the experience of software developers around the globe as well as pushing the limits of technology to enable the developers themselves to become better.

He was awarded the title MVP in C# three times by Microsoft for providing excellence and independent real-world solutions to problems that developers face.

The breadth and depth of knowledge he has obtained comes not only from his research, but also from the valuable wealth of information and research at Microsoft; the motivation and inspiration come from his knowledge of the fact that 90 percent of the world is using at least one or the other form of Microsoft technology.

Ahmed has worked for a number of clients and employers. His great reputation has resulted in a large client base for his consultancy company, Sandler Ltd., UK, and Sandler Software, USA, which includes clients from different industries, right from media to medical and beyond. Some clients have included him on their approved contractors/consultants list, including ICS Solutions Ltd., who have placed him on their DreamTeam portal, and CODE Consulting/EPS Software (www.codemag.com), based in USA.

He has also been involved in the past in reviewing books for Packt Publishing and wishes to thank them for the great opportunity once again.

> I would like to thank the author/publisher of this book for giving me the great honor and privilege of reviewing the book. I would also like to thank my client base and especially Microsoft Corporation and my colleagues over there for enabling me to become a reputable leader as a software developer in the industry, which is my joy, passion, and pride.

Allen LeVan has had a long and successful career in IT, working for small shops and some of the largest companies in the world. Recently, he acquired a degree in game programming from the University of Advancing Technology after getting transferred from Arizona State University, where he studied computer science. He relocated to Los Angeles to pursue his goal of working in the video game industry.

> I would like to thank my instructors at UAT and ASU; my career services advisor at UAT, Joel Walton; and the project coordinators I worked with at Packt Publishing during the course of this book.

Danijel Malik is a solutions architect who works for a company called SSW in beautiful Sydney, Australia. In his career, which includes more than 10 years of professional experience, he worked on desktop, mobile, and web projects — many of them at the enterprise level. He is now a specialist for Application Lifecycle Management (ALM) and is recognized as a Microsoft MVP for Visual Studio ALM. Besides that, he is a Microsoft Certified Solutions Developer (MCSD) for the Web.

Danijel worked for numerous clients ranging from the manufacturing sector to medical services to taxes. Although he is very passionate about bleeding edge technologies, he always looks for quality first. He is a strong believer that applications must be robust, resilient to errors, and should perform well; after all, he has spent years writing software running on multiple threads and delivering great UX to users.

Doug Ortiz is an independent consultant whose skillset encompasses multiple platforms such as .NET, SharePoint, Office, and SQL Server.

He holds a Master's degree in Relational Databases and has over 20 years of experience in information technology, half of which are with .NET and SharePoint. His roles have ranged from architecture, implementation, administration, disaster recovery, migrations, and development and automation of information systems within and outside of SharePoint. He is the founder of Illustris, LLC, and can be reached at dougortiz@illustris.org.

The following are the interesting aspects of his profession:

- He has experience integrating multiple platforms and products
- He helps organizations gain a deeper understanding and value of their current investments in data and existing resources, turning them into useful sources of information
- He has improved, salvaged, and architected projects by utilizing unique and innovative techniques

His hobbies include practicing yoga and scuba diving.

Philip Pierce is a software developer with 20 years of experience in mobile, web, desktop, and server development; database design and management; and game development. His background includes developing AI for games and business software, translating AAA games between various platforms, developing multithreaded applications, and creating patented client-server communication technologies.

He has won several hackathons and has won several prizes including Best Mobile App at the AT&T Developer Summit 2013 and a runner-up prize for Best Windows 8 App at PayPal's Battlethon, Miami. His most recent project was converting Rail Rush and Temple Run 2 from the Android platform to Arcade platforms.

Philip has worked on many software development books, including *Multithreading in C# 5.0 Cookbook*, *NGUI for Unity*, and another book on NGUI for Unity (scheduled to be published in December 2014), all by Packt Publishing.

Philip's portfolios can be found at http://www.rocketgamesmobile.com and http://www.philippiercedeveloper.com.

Abhishek Ranka is a graduate from Vellore Institute of Technology. He is currently working as a software developer with an MNC. He has profound knowledge of Microsoft technologies. His area of expertise is standalone and multithreaded Windows applications and he has over 7 years of hands-on experience. He is frolicsome and free-minded. He loves taking trips.

www.PacktPub.com

Support files, eBooks, discount offers, and more

For support files and downloads related to your book, please visit www.PacktPub.com.

Did you know that Packt offers eBook versions of every book published, with PDF and ePub files available? You can upgrade to the eBook version at www.PacktPub.com and as a print book customer, you are entitled to a discount on the eBook copy. Get in touch with us at service@packtpub.com for more details.

At www.PacktPub.com, you can also read a collection of free technical articles, sign up for a range of free newsletters and receive exclusive discounts and offers on Packt books and eBooks.

https://www2.packtpub.com/books/subscription/packtlib

Do you need instant solutions to your IT questions? PacktLib is Packt's online digital book library. Here, you can search, access, and read Packt's entire library of books.

Why subscribe?

- Fully searchable across every book published by Packt
- Copy and paste, print, and bookmark content
- On demand and accessible via a web browser

Free access for Packt account holders

If you have an account with Packt at www.PacktPub.com, you can use this to access PacktLib today and view 9 entirely free books. Simply use your login credentials for immediate access.

Instant updates on new Packt books

Get notified! Find out when new books are published by following @PacktEnterprise on Twitter or the *Packt Enterprise* Facebook page.

Table of Contents

Preface

Welcome to C# *Multithreaded and Parallel Programming*. This book will take you through all of the ways to perform multithreaded and concurrent programming using the C# programming language and the .NET Framework. We will start with a description of what concurrent and parallel programming is, why it is important, and when you should implement it. We will then go through the different classes provided by the .NET Framework and the different design patterns commonly used when developing multithreaded applications.

Most modern machines have dual-core processors. This means that the present-day computer has the ability to multitask. Using multiple cores means your applications can process data faster and be more responsive to users. However, to fully exploit this in your applications, you need to write multithreaded code.

This will take us on a journey from the BackgroundWorker component, the Thread class, the Task Parallel Library, to the async and await keywords. We will also explore common design patterns such as Pipelining, producer-consumer, and the IAsyncResult interface.

Using the concurrent and parallel classes provided by .NET allows you to easily write powerful multithreaded applications. In the latest version of .NET, Microsoft has added the Task Parallel Library and the async keyword to make concurrent programming functionality much easier than using threads.

We will cover all aspects of developing multithreaded applications using the latest version of .NET in this book.

What this book covers

Chapter 1, Understanding Multiprocessing and Multiple Cores, covers the evolution of computer hardware from single-processor systems to multiprocessor and multiple-core systems. It will also discuss how the Windows Scheduler allots time to threads. This chapter then discusses design considerations for concurrency, how to take advantage of multiprocessor/multiple core systems, and the expected performance improvements these designs can realize. During this chapter, we will walk through a simple single-threaded and then multithreaded example to show how performance is improved.

Chapter 2, Looking at Multithreaded Classes – BackgroundWorker, enables us to examine the basics of multithreaded programming with the BackgroundWorker class. We will go through a WPF example showing how we can update a UI while processing is going on in the background. This chapter will discuss the basics of coordinating work between multiple processes and the concept of concurrency.

Chapter 3, Thread Class – Heavyweight Concurrency in C#, allows us to examine and work with the Thread class and namespace. We will learn how to create threads, coordinate between threads, share data between threads, and stop threads. This chapter will explore the idea of heavyweight concurrency versus lightweight concurrency, which will be explained in detail later in the book. We will focus on manually using and coordinating multiple threads in an application.

Chapter 4, Advanced Thread Processing, explains in detail the concept of heavyweight concurrency and working with multiple threads using the Thread class. This chapter will further expand the image processing application to demonstrate how to coordinate between threads and wait on threads to complete by avoiding deadlocks, locking, and error handling. This chapter will leave the reader with a clear understanding of how to develop applications with multiple threads and have complete control over their execution and interaction.

Chapter 5, Lightweight Concurrency – Task Parallel Library (TPL), introduces the Task Parallel Library and the next evolution of multithreaded programming in C#/.NET. Now that we have a full understanding of how to develop, manage, and control applications with many threads, we will learn how to take advantage of the Parallel namespace in .NET to do a lot of the heavy lifting for us. We will introduce the idea of lightweight concurrency by leveraging the Parallel classes that .NET now provides. This will allow us to focus more on designing an efficient and powerful application and less on coordinating individual threads.

Chapter 6, Task-based Parallelism, enables us to examine the Task Parallel Library and task parallelism. A task is an asynchronous set of operations that can be run concurrently with other tasks. We will examine designing an application as a series of tasks that can be performed in parallel. With the help of examples, we will demonstrate how to create, manage, and coordinate tasks. We will further examine additional topics with the Task Parallel Library and task parallelism. We will learn how to perform exception handling when running multiple tasks, how to schedule tasks under certain conditions, and how to cancel running tasks before they complete when needed.

Chapter 7, Data Parallelism, explores the concept of data parallelism. We will see how to perform the same operations on elements of a collection concurrently using the Task Parallel Library. The Parallel class has the For and ForEach loops, and we will show examples of each to demonstrate how they handle concurrent data processing. We will convert our image processing application from heavyweight to lightweight concurrency using the Task Parallel Library instead of the Thread class.

Chapter 8, Debugging Multithreaded Applications with Visual Studio, teaches us how to take full advantage of Visual Studio 2012 to debug our multithreaded applications. We will demonstrate using the Threads view, and the Tasks, Parallel Stacks, and Parallel Watch windows. We will finish with debugging our image processing application.

Chapter 9, Pipeline and Producer-consumer Design Patterns, helps us explore two of the most popular parallel patterns for development—Pipelining and producer-consumer. In Pipelining, we will see how to accomplish a parallel task where a simple parallel loop will not work due to data dependencies. The producer-consumer pattern allows a producer, which is generating results, to run along with the consumer so that the consumer can consume the results concurrently. We will expand our image processing application to implement these two patterns in combination.

Chapter 10, Parallel LINQ – PLINQ, details the benefits and functionality provided by Parallel LINQ (PLINQ). We will see how PLINQ speeds up traditional LINQs by separating the data source into sections and executing the query on each section. We will also discuss what kind of queries to use PLINQ for because not all queries will run faster using PLINQ.

Chapter 11, The Asynchronous Programming Model, explains the Asynchronous Programming Model (APM), which is a design pattern that is based on classes implementing the IAsyncResult interface. We will see how to begin and end asynchronous operations and use delegates to call methods asynchronously. This chapter will also cover the new async and await keywords and how to use them to implement an asynchronous design in your custom classes.

What you need for this book

For this book, you will need a working knowledge of C#, .NET, and Visual Studio, and a desire to learn all of the different methods and techniques .NET provides to improve application performance through parallel multithreaded techniques.

Who this book is for

This book is intended for developers who have a working knowledge of C# and the .NET Framework. We assume that you understand the basics of C# programming and the Visual Studio development environment.

This book is for developers looking to expand their toolbox with all of the techniques and methods available in .NET to develop and transition the existing code into multithreaded and concurrent programs. If you are looking for ways to increase the performance and scalability of your applications using today's multiple CPU and multicore processors, then this is the book for you.

This book is also designed for developers with knowledge of the original multithreaded techniques used in the earlier versions of .NET and who want to update their knowledge with all of the new classes that the latest versions of .NET provide, most notably the Task Parallel Library and the async and await keywords. If you need to update older applications with today's latest .NET parallel techniques, then this is a good guide for you.

Conventions

In this book, you will find a number of styles of text that distinguish between different kinds of information. Here are some examples of these styles, and an explanation of their meaning.

Code words in text, database table names, folder names, filenames, file extensions, pathnames, dummy URLs, user input, and Twitter handles are shown as follows: "This will require us to work with the `BackgroundWorker` component."

A block of code is set as follows:

```
        private void setFishesVisibility(System.Windows.Visibility
    pbValue)
        {
            // Change the visibility of the controls
            //related to the fishes game.
            imgFish1.Visibility = pbValue;
            imgFish2.Visibility = pbValue;
```

```
        imgFish3.Visibility = pbValue;
        txtFishGame.Visibility = pbValue;
        btnGameOver.Visibility = pbValue;
    }
```

New terms and **important words** are shown in bold. Words that you see on the screen, in menus or dialog boxes for example, appear in the text like this: "Create a new WPF application C# project in Visual Studio (**File** | **New** | **Project** | **Visual C#** | **WPF Application**)."

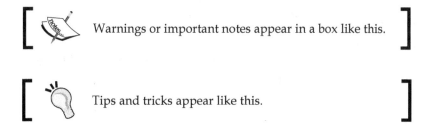

> Warnings or important notes appear in a box like this.

> Tips and tricks appear like this.

Reader feedback

Feedback from our readers is always welcome. Let us know what you think about this book—what you liked or may have disliked. Reader feedback is important for us to develop titles that you really get the most out of.

To send us general feedback, simply send an e-mail to feedback@packtpub.com, and mention the book title via the subject of your message.

If there is a topic that you have expertise in and you are interested in either writing or contributing to a book, see our author guide on www.packtpub.com/authors.

Customer support

Now that you are the proud owner of a Packt book, we have a number of things to help you to get the most from your purchase.

Downloading the example code

You can download the example code files for all Packt books you have purchased from your account at http://www.packtpub.com. If you purchased this book elsewhere, you can visit http://www.packtpub.com/support and register to have the files e-mailed directly to you.

Errata

Although we have taken every care to ensure the accuracy of our content, mistakes do happen. If you find a mistake in one of our books—maybe a mistake in the text or the code—we would be grateful if you could report this to us. By doing so, you can save other readers from frustration and help us improve subsequent versions of this book. If you find any errata, please report them by visiting http://www.packtpub.com/submit-errata, selecting your book, clicking on the **Errata Submission Form** link, and entering the details of your errata. Once your errata are verified, your submission will be accepted and the errata will be uploaded to our website or added to any list of existing errata under the Errata section of that title.

To view the previously submitted errata, go to https://www.packtpub.com/books/content/support and enter the name of the book in the search field. The required information will appear under the **Errata** section.

Piracy

Piracy of copyright material on the Internet is an ongoing problem across all media. At Packt, we take the protection of our copyright and licenses very seriously. If you come across any illegal copies of our works, in any form, on the Internet, please provide us with the location address or website name immediately so that we can pursue a remedy.

Please contact us at copyright@packtpub.com with a link to the suspected pirated material.

We appreciate your help in protecting our authors, and our ability to bring you valuable content.

Questions

You can contact us at questions@packtpub.com if you are having a problem with any aspect of the book, and we will do our best to address it.

1
Understanding Multiprocessing and Multiple Cores

Taking into consideration the fact that we know how to develop C# applications and can make the software do *what* we need it to, this book focuses on how we can make our C# applications perform their tasks more efficiently and faster by taking advantage of today's powerful hardware.

In the *old days*, computers had a single CPU that could run one software thread at a time. With sophisticated scheduling logic and fast clock and bus speeds, they were able to make it appear that multiple software threads were running at the same time, but this was just an illusion. A single CPU system with one core in the CPU can only execute one thread's instruction every clock cycle. A computer has a clock that controls the execution of the CPU. Each time the clock counts one unit, the CPU executes an instruction. In this model, there is limited need to develop applications that use multiple software threads. It can still be useful for UI responsiveness so that a long-running task does not *freeze* the user interface. We will discuss this more in *Chapter 2, Looking at Multithreaded Classes – BackgroundWorker*. So, multithreaded applications allow software applications to be more responsive to the user but not to process tasks faster.

We must understand some fundamentals related to the multiprocessing capabilities offered by modern computers. We will have to consider them in order to develop applications that take full advantage of parallel processing features. In this chapter, we will cover many topics to help us understand the new challenges involved in parallel programming with modern hardware. Upon reading it and following the exercises, we shall benefit in the following ways:

- Begin a paradigm shift in software design
- Understand the techniques needed to develop a new generation of applications
- Have an idea of the performance improvements we can achieve using parallel programming with C# using Gustafson's and Amdahl's laws
- Perform accurate response-time estimation for critical processes

Mono-processor systems – the old gladiators

The **mono-processor** systems use old-fashioned, classic computer architecture. The microprocessor receives an input stream, executes the necessary processes, and sends the results in an output stream that is distributed to the indicated destinations. The following diagram represents a mono-processor system (one processor with just one **core**) with one user and one task running:

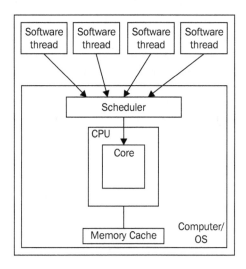

This working scheme is known as **input-processing-output (IPO)** or **single instruction, single data (SISD)**. This basic design represents a **von Neumann machine**, developed by the outstanding mathematician, John von Neumann, in 1952.

Single core – only one warrior to fight against everybody

These days, systems with a single processing core, with just one logical processor, are known as **single core**.

When there is only one user running an application in a mono-processor machine and the processor is fast enough to deliver an adequate response time in **critical** operations, the model will work without any major problems.

For example, consider a robotic servant in the kitchen having just two hands to work with. If you ask him to do one task that requires both his hands, such as washing up, he will be efficient. He has a single processing core.

However, suppose that you ask him to do various tasks—wash up, clean the oven, prepare your lunch, mop the floor, cook dinner for your friends, and so on. You give him the list of tasks, and he works down the tasks. But since there is so much washing up, it's 2 p.m. before he even starts preparing your lunch—by which time you get very hungry and prepare it yourself. You need more robots when you have multiple tasks. You need multiple execution cores and many logical processors.

Each task performed by the robot is a critical operation, because you and your friends are very hungry!

Let's consider another case. We have a mono-processor computer and it has many users connected, requesting services that the computer must process. In this case, we have many input streams and many output streams, one for each connected user. As there is just one microprocessor, there is only one input channel and only one output channel. Therefore, the input streams are enqueued (**multiplexing**) for processing, and then the same happens with the output streams, but the order is inverted.

Doing a tiny bit of each task

Why does the robot take so long to cook dinner for you and your friends? The robot does a tiny bit of each task and then goes back to the list to see what else he should be doing. He has to keep moving to the list, read it, and then starts a new task. The time it takes to complete the list is much longer because he is not fast enough to finish multiple tasks in the required time. That's **multiplexing**, and the delay is called **von Neumann's bottleneck**. Multiplexing takes additional time because you have just one robot to do everything you need in the kitchen.

Systems that provide concurrent access to multiple users are known as **multiuser** systems.

If the processor is not fast enough to deliver an adequate response time in every critical operation requested by each connected user, a bottleneck will be generated in the processor's input queue. This is well known in computer architecture as von Neumann's bottleneck.

There are three possible solutions to this problem, each consisting of upgrading or increasing one of the following:

- The processor's speed, by using a faster robot. He will need less time to finish each task.

- The processor's capacity to process instructions concurrently (in parallel), that is, adding more hands to the robot and the capability to use his hands to do different jobs.

- The number of installed processors or the number of processing cores, that is, adding more robots. They can all focus on one task, but everything gets done in parallel. All tasks are completed faster and you get your lunch on time. That is multitasking.

No matter which option we pick, we must consider other factors that depend particularly on the kind of operations performed by the computer and which could generate additional bottlenecks. In some cases, the main memory access speed could be too slow (the robot takes too much time to read each task). In other cases, the disks' subsystem could have bad response times (the robot takes too much time to memorize the tasks to be done), and so on. It is important to make a detailed analysis of these topics before making a decision to troubleshoot bottlenecks.

Moreover, sometimes the amount of data that needs to be processed is too large and the problem is the transfer time between the memory and the processor, that is, the robot is too slow to move each hand. Poor robot! Why don't you buy a new model?

In the last few years, every new microarchitecture developed by microprocessor manufacturers has focused on improving the processor's capacity to run instructions in parallel (a robot with more hands). Some examples of these are the continuous duplication of processing structures such as the **Arithmetic and Logic Unit (ALU)** and **Floating Point Unit (FPU)**, and the growing number of processing cores that are included in one single physical processor. Hence, you can build a super robot with many independent robots and many hands. Each sub-robot can be made to specialize in a specific task, thus parallelizing the work.

Computers used as servers, with many connected users and running applications, take greater advantage of modern processors' capacity to run instructions in parallel as compared to those computers used by only one user. We will learn how to take full advantage of those features in the applications that are developed using the C# programming language. You want the robot to get your lunch on time!

Multiprocessor systems – many warriors to win a battle

Systems with multiple processors are a solution to von Neumann's bottleneck, but it is first necessary to know their detailed features in order to set aside some myths about them. They do not offer an immediate performance improvement for all applications! The dilemma is that systems with multiple processors are not always the most appropriate solution to a performance problem.

There are two basic procedures to distribute tasks in systems with multiple processors:

- **Symmetrical multiprocessing (SMP)**: Any available processor or core can execute tasks. The most used and efficient one is **n-way symmetrical multiprocessing**, where n is the number of installed processors. With this procedure, each processor can execute a task isolated from the rest and also when a particular software is not optimized for multiprocessing systems. You have eight robots in the kitchen. When a robot is free, he goes back to the list to see what else he should be doing and starts working on the next task (8-way symmetrical multiprocessing).

- **Asymmetrical multiprocessing (AMP or ASMP)**: Usually, one processor acts as the main processor. It works as a manager and is in charge of distributing the tasks to the other available processors, using different kinds of algorithms for this purpose. You have nine robots in the kitchen. One of them is in charge of task distribution (the manager robot). He is always reading the list and watching the other robots work (the worker robots are the processors dedicated to run tasks). When a robot is free, the manager robot tells him what to do next.

The robots are expensive! You do not want to waste a robot to distribute the tasks. You would rather have robots that are independent. You want robots arranged similar to a symmetrical multiprocessing scheme.

The n-way symmetric multiprocessing procedure achieves the best performance and the best resources usage, where n can be two or more processors. With it, every available processor can execute tasks in an absolutely dynamic way. This is the reason why most multiprocessing systems use this approach.

A symmetric multiprocessing system with many users connected or numerous tasks running provides a good solution to von Neumann's bottleneck. The multiple input streams are distributed to the different available processors for their execution, and they generate multiple concurrent output streams, as shown in the following diagram:

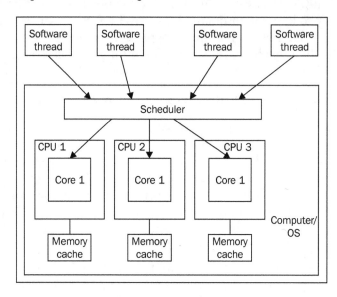

But what if there is so much washing up that it takes a single robot several days to complete? A bottleneck will be generated again. Are his hands as fast as necessary? Are his legs too slow? Is he a lazy robot?

We have to take into account that if the response time of a processor to a user's request is not quick enough, a bottleneck will be generated again. However, it can also be generated by other problems along the performance waterfall. We must delve deeper into the process in order to understand these potential performance issues.

Therefore, while the number of users or the number of tasks being executed in a multiprocessing system increases, it is more likely to run out of processing capacity, among other things. If this happens, each user's tasks being executed will take longer to run, and for that reason, the response time will worsen.

Under these circumstances, there are two possible approaches to keep the response time untouched:

- **Replacing the existing processors with new ones (buying super robots)**: In order to apply this solution, there should be processors with better performance ratios than the ones that are currently used, or with more execution cores (to achieve a greater degree of parallelism). They also have to be compatible with the motherboard and with the sockets used by them. The great disadvantage of this approach is that the old processors are thrown out. It is also expensive.

- **Adding new processors to work with the existing ones (buying new robots to help the existing ones)**: In order to apply this solution, there should be free sockets on the motherboard.

Multiple core processors and hyperthreading

We have discussed multiple- and single-CPU computer systems. Now, let's take a look at multiple core CPU's and hyperthreading. A multiple core CPU has more than one physical processing unit. In essence, it acts like more than one CPU. The only difference is that all cores of a single CPU share the same memory cache instead of having their own memory cache. From the multithreaded parallel developer standpoint, there is very little difference between multiple CPUs and multiple cores in a CPU. The total number of cores across all of the CPUs of a system is the number of physical processing units that can be scheduled and run in parallel, that is, the number of different software threads that can truly execute in parallel.

There is a slight performance bottleneck with having multiple cores in a CPU versus having multiple CPUs with single cores due to the sharing of the memory bus. For most applications, this is negligible.

For the parallel developer trying to estimate performance gains by using a parallel design approach, the number of physical cores is the key factor to use for estimations.

This diagram shows three physical CPUs each having two logical cores:

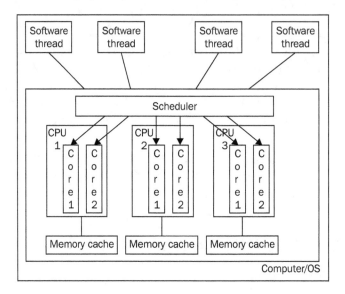

The following diagram shows a CPU with four logical cores, each having its own memory and then shared memory between them:

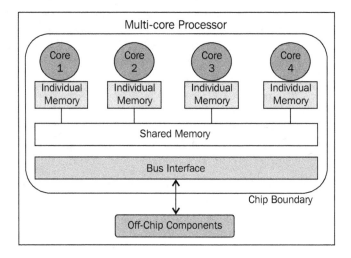

Next, let's discuss hyperthreading. This is a proprietary simultaneous multithreading (SMT) technology, which Intel has developed, that allows a single physical core in a CPU to have multiple logical cores. Each of these logical cores is called a **hardware thread** and can be scheduled separately by the **operating system (OS)** scheduler.

The OS has to implement SMT to be able to take advantage of hyperthreading technology, but today, most operating systems do. Even though each hardware thread (logical core) appears as a separate core for the OS to schedule, only one logical core per physical core can execute a software instruction at a time. Hyperthreading is explained in the following diagram:

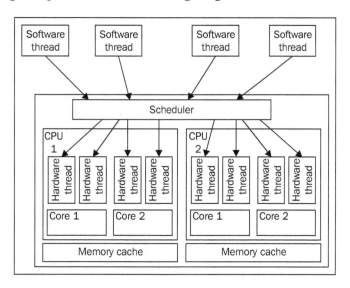

This is important to realize when you examine your computer hardware and estimate performance gains of a parallel application. For our examples of performance estimations using Amdahl's and Gustafson's laws, we will only be counting physical cores because technically logical cores, in a single physical core, cannot execute instructions during the same clock cycle.

Taking advantage of multiple execution cores

One of the techniques to improve the processing capacity consists of increasing the microprocessors' working frequency (**overclocking**), which raises the number of instructions capable of processing in the same period. This technique has been used for many years and has evolved from the legendary 8086/8088 with its poor 4.77 MHz (megahertz) to the many GHz (gigahertz) of modern microprocessors.

Nevertheless, microprocessor manufacturers are increasingly facing difficulties in raising the frequencies because the manufacturing process becomes more complex and the generated heat is difficult to dissipate in an efficient and inexpensive way.

Consider our robot instance again. You want to buy a single robot, but want him to clean the oven in 5 seconds. That is possible, but he needs plutonium as an energy source because he must move his arms and legs at a very high speed. Besides, he needs an ambient temperature of 50F (5 degrees Fahrenheit) or -15C (-15 degrees Celsius). Why? Well, because metals moving at very high speeds generate heat. You do not want a burnt robot. Moreover, plutonium is very expensive. Something similar happens with modern microprocessors.

Therefore, the other alternative is to develop new microarchitectures; incorporating first duplicated, and then quadruplicated processing structures, and so on. In this way, there are many subprocessors in one single microprocessor's package. These subprocessors are known as **execution cores** or **processing cores**.

Microprocessors with multiple execution cores, also known as **multicore**, offer many complete execution cores that are interconnected in a single package. Their physical look is very similar to a conventional single core microprocessor. Nevertheless, they are equivalent to something like two or more microprocessors inside a single piece of silicon, as well as many pieces of silicon interconnected under the same physical package. Of course, we are avoiding a full discussion of the deep technical issues.

At present, most available modern computers have microprocessors with at least two execution cores (dual core). Therefore, they are computers with multiprocessing capabilities.

Ever since the rise of multiple execution cores, the possibilities of combining the communication architectures, the different cores owned, and shared resources have continued to multiply. As with everything in life, in each possibility, there is a trade-off between manufacturing costs and performance. For this reason, a new land appeared in the microprocessor world.

In some cases, each execution core includes L1 and L2 cache memories. Caches can be divided up into levels with smaller, faster caches accessed first, and slower, larger ones accessed next. An architecture can employ as many caches as it wants, but typically you will see two levels. This allows the architecture to house often-used data in a cache with lower latency for faster retrieval.

In other cases, L2 cache memories are shared between two or more cores. Therefore, each core will have access to the whole L2 cache.

The greater the number of resources included in each core and the fewer the resources shared with the others, the greater the processing speed achieved by each core. On the other hand, sharing resources between cores benefits applications not optimized for multiprocessing because they use a single execution core.

The robots' communications interface must be as efficient as possible, since you want the robots to do many different tasks.

Achieving efficient external memory accesses is one of the most important matters with these microarchitectures. The communication with external memory has a great overhead with respect to time, compared to the internal core speed. When we design the most critical algorithms for our applications, we must minimize the external memory access in order to achieve the best performance. It is one of the main subjects to consider in designing applications that will be developed with parallelism in mind.

There are two options available to speed up the tasks done by the robots, taking into account the washing-up example:

- Divide the washing-up into parts corresponding to the number of robots available, and have the robots do their own portion of the global task
- Have a big pile of washing-up, and have each robot pick items up from that pile when they have room in their sinks to do that washing-up

The internal bus is very important, because it transports data between the different execution cores. Many microprocessors use one or more dedicated buses for that task with very high working speeds, while others establish those communications through the **Front Side Bus** (**FSB**), which is a less efficient way. When the microprocessor has more than two cores, the architecture could be any possible merger between the known architectures for single-and dual-core microprocessors. There are some microprocessors built by two pairs of cores, each one using a dedicated bus for the data interchange between both the cores, but with both pairs talking through the FSB.

When we are optimizing applications to take full advantage of these microarchitectures, one of the things that we should minimize is the information going through the FSB. Besides, we must consider this in evaluating the optimized application's efficiency. If we don't, we will probably draft wrong conclusions about them and we will try to optimize already maximized performances (according to the underlying hardware architecture).

A system with asymmetric multiprocessing based on many independent physical processors has many FSBs to access external memory, one for each physical processor. However, a system with a microprocessor having multiple cores has to share the FSB that acts as a great single door to the outside world and to the external memory. Therefore, the tasks to coordinate the activities in the execution cores require additional time to avoid conflicts in the shared FSB. This is an important difference between multiprocessing using independent physical microprocessors and multiple cores in one physical microprocessor.

The probability that an FSB will become a bottleneck is very high when applications are not optimized to take full advantage of cache memories included in each core. Therefore, when the software is running over these microarchitectures, it should avoid frequent accesses to the main memory.

Besides, many asymmetric multiprocessing systems use duplicated communication channels with the main memory. This feature is not available in many multicore microprocessors. It makes it nearly impossible to predict the performance of applications in completely different system architectures. However, designing them with parallelism in mind will take full advantage of any feature present in the system.

Nowadays, microprocessors with multiple execution cores are widespread. However, we can find many of them arranged in an n-way asymmetric multiprocessing system such as an 8-core system with two physical quad-core microprocessors. It is a very attractive setup in high-end workstations and servers.

In the coming years, microprocessors are going to include more and more processing cores. Modern operating systems are already optimized to take advantage of their parallel processing capabilities. We must optimize our applications to take full advantage of them.

Analyzing the microarchitectures used in modern microprocessors is a topic for an entire book. However, we needed some knowledge about them in order to understand the parallel processing capabilities that are useful for our goals.

Do not expect plutonium robots! They are still too expensive to maintain.

Examining our hardware

As we will see with some of the tools used to analyze a system's hardware, most count logical cores and not just physical cores. This is important to remember because of the limitation mentioned in the previous section where a CPU only executes an instruction each clock cycle for a physical core.

Let's take a second to look at some examples. First, if you are on a Windows machine (which we will assume for the examples in this book), you can right-click on the Taskbar and run the Task Manager. The following is a sample from my computer:

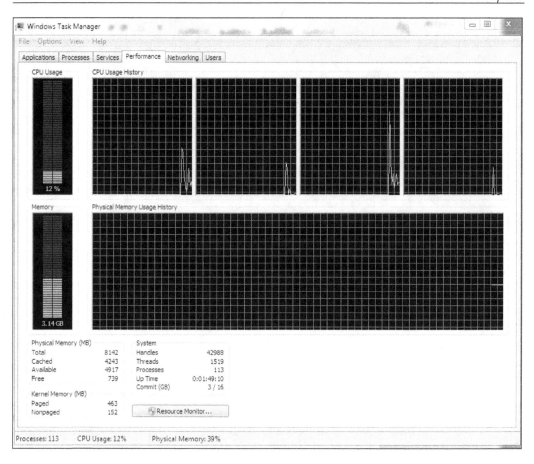

When looking at the **Performance** tab, you can see it shows four CPUs running. This would lead us to believe that my system has four CPUs in it. But in fact it actually has one CPU that has two cores (physical) with each having two **hardware threads** (logical cores). So, the Task Manager in Windows shows us how many logical cores are there in our system. This is the number of schedulable hardware threads the system scheduler can utilize.

 CPU-Z is a handy utility to analyze the hardware of a computer in order to find information about a computer. You can download this free software from `http://www.cpuid.com/`.

Here is the output from CPU-Z for my computer:

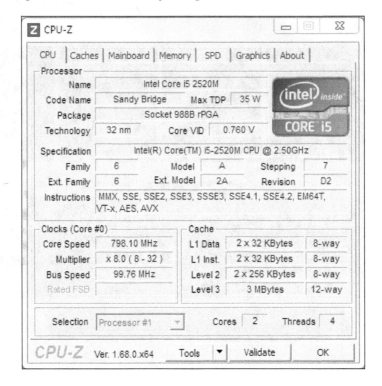

As you can see from the bottom of the CPU-Z output, I have **1** CPU with **2** cores and **4** hardware threads. It is important to understand how many CPUs, physical cores, and hardware threads a system has so you can properly estimate performance gains from parallel development. In the next sections, we will examine several methods to predict this performance gain based on the number of physical cores. This will also help you understand the gains possible by "throwing more hardware" at a software application designed with parallelism.

OS scheduler operations

So far we have been discussing hardware and the number of CPUs, hardware cores, and logical cores; now, let's transition to software threads and the OS. A software application or service can run in one or many processes and threads. Typically, a **software application** has a user interface and is run by a user of the computer, while a **software process** is run by the OS and runs in the background. Both of these are types of software that are being executed by the computer they are running on.

Each **application** or **service** in turn has one or several processes that they actually execute inside. **Processes** are the running objects of an application or service. Also, each process has one or many execution threads (or software threads). The **threads** are the items that the scheduler schedules on the cores. I know this might seem confusing but it is important to understand the hardware from the ground up and how many physical cores can execute a software instruction, and the software from the top-down to each software thread that executes on a core.

The **scheduler** for an operating system is the subsystem of the OS that manages all of the software threads currently running and allocates execution time on the cores (both physical and logical) of the computer. Execution time is divided up in machine cycles, and a **machine cycle** is a tick of the computer's clock.

The scheduler determines which software threads run on which core (physical) each clock cycle. So, during each clock cycle in a computer, each core can execute an instruction of a software thread. Remember that using hyperthreading technology, the scheduler treats each logical core as a physical core. But in actuality, in each clock cycle, each physical core executes a single software thread's instruction.

Also important in our parallel development and estimation of performance gains is that we are assuming in our estimates that all hardware cores are available to our software application each clock cycle. In reality, most computers have many processes running at a given time and utilize some of the execution time of a core.

In Windows, the Task Manager provides some useful information to see what is running and consuming hardware resources. We have already looked at the **Performance** tab. Now, let's look at the **Processes** tab:

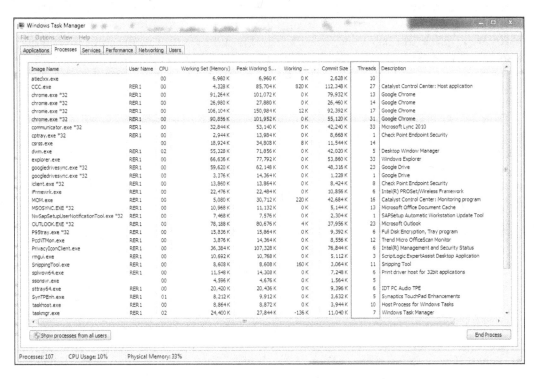

This tab in the Task Manager shows various information about the processes running on a Windows computer. As you can see from the **Threads** column in the preceding screenshot, some processes have many threads of execution at any given time.

You can go to the **View** menu and select **Select Columns** to change which columns of information are displayed by the Task Manager for each process.

Designing for concurrency

Now that we have an understanding of today's hardware capabilities (multiple processors, multiple physical cores, and multiple logical cores (hardware threads)) and OS schedulers, let's discuss how to take advantage of this in our software development.

We know that our hardware has the ability to execute multiple instructions at the same time. As we will see in later chapters, .NET provides several classes and libraries that allow us to develop software that runs in multiple threads instead of a single software thread. The question is then, when does it make sense to develop our software to run in multiple threads concurrently and what kind of performance gains can we expect?

When designing for concurrency, we should look at a high-level abstraction of the application's requirements. Look at what functions the application performs and which functions can operate in parallel without affecting other functions. This will help us decide how to determine the amount of parallel operations we can design into the application. We will discuss in detail the .NET classes to implement both heavyweight concurrency (the `Thread` class) and lightweight concurrency (Task Parallel Library) in later chapters; but for now, we need to determine what and how much of our application can happen in parallel.

For example, if the application takes a list of items and encodes each item into an encrypted string, can the encoding of each item be run in parallel independent of the encoding of another item? If so, this "function" of the application is a good candidate for concurrency. Once you have defined all of the high-level functions an application must perform, this analysis will determine the amount of parallelism that the application can benefit from.

The following is a simple example of a parallel design where some of the functions operate sequentially and others in parallel. As we will see in the next section, once we can define how much of the application functions concurrently versus sequentially, then we can understand the performance gains we can expect.

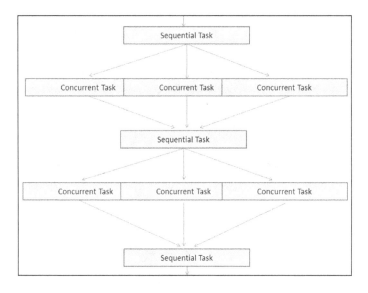

A lot of parallel designs employ some sort of pipelining design where some sequential work is performed, then some parallel work, then some sequential work, and so on. The preceding diagram shows a simple model for a pipeline design. Another popular concurrent design pattern is the **producer-consumer** model, which is really just a variation on the pipeline model. In this design, one function of the application *produces* an output that is *consumed* by another function of the application. The following is a diagram of this design pattern. In this example, each function can operate in parallel. The **Load Image** function *produces* image files to be *consumed* by the **Scale Image** function. The **Scale Image** function also produces thumbnail images to be consumed by the **Filter Image** function, and so on. Each of the function blocks can run in multiple concurrent threads because they are independent of each other:

The following diagram illustrates the sequential operation:

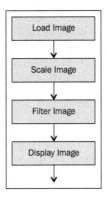

The following diagram illustrates the parallel pipeline design:

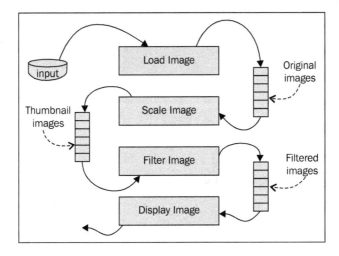

Estimating performance improvements

One of the most common mistakes in designing or upgrading systems with multiple processors is making linear projections in their processing speed. It is very common to consider that each additional processor in the system will increase the performance in a way that is directly proportional to its processing capacity.

For instance, when we have a system with just one processor, and if we add three more, we will not have four times the performance. This is because each time we add a processor, the time they dedicate to coordinate their work and the task assignment process increases. Therefore, because of the increased processing power spent on managing tasks, their performance will not increase linearly.

The additional robots added to the kitchen must talk among themselves to coordinate their work.

The coordination costs and the performance increment depend upon a number of factors including the following:

- **The operating system and its management procedures to coordinate and distribute processes and threads among multiple processors**: This is the robots' accuracy in assigning the appropriate task to the most capable robot model for that particular task.

- **The level of optimization to run multiple processors offered by applications**: This is one of the most relevant points, even when we are using an n-way symmetric multiprocessing scheme. In this book, we will learn to reach high levels of optimizations for concurrency in our software. This can be correlated to the robots' abilities to work with other robots on the same tasks.

- **The microprocessors' microarchitecture**: This corresponds to how fast the robots move their hands and legs, and do similar tasks.

- **The speed of the memory subsystem shared by the microprocessors**: This is the robots' communications interface.

- **The speed of the I/O buses shared by the microprocessors**: This is the robots' efficiency and precision in managing their hands and legs to do each task (mopping the floor and cooking, for example).

All these items represent a problem when we design or upgrade a machine, because we need answers to the following questions:

- How many microprocessors do we need when the number of users increases? How many robots do you need according to the number of friends/tasks?

- How many microprocessors do we need to increase an application's performance? How many robots do you need to accelerate the wash-up time?

- How many microprocessors do we need to run a critical process within a specific time period? How many robots do you need to clean the oven in 5 minutes?

We need a reference, similar to the one offered in the following table, in which we can see the coordination cost and the relative performance for an increasing number of processors:

Number of processors	Coordination cost		Relative performance	
	In relative processors	In percentage	In relative processors	In percentage
1	0.00	0%	1.00	100%
2	0.09	5%	1.91	95%
3	0.29	10%	2.71	90%
4	0.54	14%	3.46	86%
5	0.84	17%	4.16	83%
6	1.17	19%	4.83	81%
7	1.52	22%	5.48	78%
8	1.90	24%	6.10	76%
9	2.29	25%	6.71	75%
10	2.70	27%	7.30	73%
11	3.12	28%	7.88	72%
12	3.56	30%	8.44	70%
13	4.01	31%	8.99	69%
14	4.47	32%	9.53	68%
15	4.94	33%	10.06	67%
16	5.42	34%	10.58	66%

Number of processors	Coordination cost		Relative performance	
17	5.91	35%	11.09	65%
18	6.40	36%	11.60	64%
19	6.91	36%	12.09	64%
20	7.42	37%	12.58	63%
21	7.93	38%	13.07	62%
22	8.46	38%	13.54	62%
23	8.99	39%	14.01	61%
24	9.52	40%	14.48	60%
25	10.07	40%	14.93	60%
26	10.61	41%	15.39	59%
27	11.16	41%	15.84	59%
28	11.72	42%	16.28	58%
29	12.28	42%	16.72	58%
30	12.85	43%	17.15	57%
31	13.42	43%	17.58	57%
32	14.00	44%	18.00	56%

This table was prepared taking into account an overall average performance test with many typical applications well optimized for multiprocessing, and the most modern processors with multiple execution cores used in workstations and servers. These processors were all compatible with AMD64 or EMT64 instruction sets, also known as x86-64. We can take these values as a reference in order to have an idea of the performance improvement that we will see in optimized applications.

As shown in the previous table, the coordination cost grows exponentially as the number of processors or cores increases. The following graph shows the relative performance versus the number of processors:

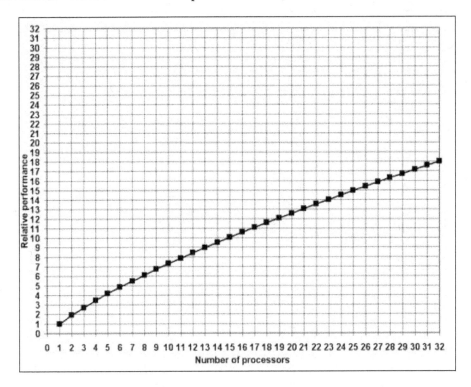

As we can see in the preceding screenshot, the relative performance grows logarithmically as the number of processors or cores increase.

The following are the formulas used to calculate the values presented in the table and the graphs:

Coordination cost = 0.3 x logarithm (number of processors) x (number of processors - 1)

Relative performance = number of processors - coordination cost

The percentages are the result of the division between the coordination cost or the relative performance and the total number of microprocessors installed.

Nowadays, the problem is that without many concurrent users, multiple processor systems have not proved to be as useful as expected. The use of machines equipped with more than one processor in workstations used by just one user is meaningful only when the applications executed are designed to work with multiple processors.

Most applications designed for a single user are not optimized to take full advantage of multiple processors. Therefore, if the code is not prepared to use these additional processors, their performance will not improve, as was explained earlier.

But, why does this happen? The answer is simple. The process to develop applications that take full advantage of multiple processors is much more complex than traditional software development (this book will show how to make this task much easier). With the exception of specialized applications requiring a lot of processing capacity and those dedicated to resolving complex calculations, most applications have been developed using a traditional, linear programming scheme.

Nevertheless, the release of physical microprocessors with multiple logical execution cores lead to the widespread availability of multiprocessing systems and an urgent need to take full advantage of these microarchitectures.

A system with multiple processors can be analyzed and measured by the following items:

- **Total number of processors and their features**: This is the total number of robots and their features.

- **Processing capacity (discounting the coordination overload)**: This is the robots' speed at working on each task (without communicating).

- **Microarchitecture and architecture**: This is the number of execution cores in each physical microprocessor and the number of physical microprocessors with each microarchitecture. These are the subrobots in each robot, the number of hands, legs, and their speed.

- **Shared memory's bus bandwidth**: This is the maximum number of concurrent communications that the robots can establish.

- **I/O bus bandwidth**: This is the robots' efficiency, precision, and speed in managing their hands and legs concurrently to do each task.

Bandwidth between processors

This bus allows the processors to establish a fluid communication between them. It is also known as the **inter-processor bus**. In some microarchitectures, this bus is the same as the FSB. It competes with the outputs to the microprocessors' outside world and therefore steals available bandwidth. The great diversity in microarchitectures makes it difficult to foretell the performance of the applications optimized for multiprocessing in every running context that is possible in the modern computing world.

We are considering neither the storage space nor the amount of memory. We are focused on the parameters that define the operation and the performance of multiple processors.

Amdahl's law

Amdahl's law is one of the two laws of parallel optimization that is used to help determine the expected performance gains with parallel computer designs, for both hardware and software.

Amdahl's law is a formula to help estimate the performance gains to be expected in an application given the amount of the application that is executed concurrently and the number of physical cores in the machine.

Gene Amdahl is a computer architect who in 1967 presented his algorithm to compute the maximum expected performance improvement that can be expected when part of a system is written for parallelism. The algorithm calculates the expected speedup as a percentage.

This law takes into account the number of physical cores of execution, N, the percentage, P, of the application that is concurrent, and the percentage, B, that is serial. The time it takes to process when N cores are being used is as follows:

$T (N) = T(1) \ x \ (P + 1/Nx(1-N))$

So, the maximum speedup (N) would be calculated as:

$Speedup \ (N) = T(1)/T(N) = T(1)/T(1)(B+1/N(1-P)) = 1/(P+1/N(1-P))$

So, Amdahl's law states that if, for example, 50 percent of an application is run sequentially, 50 percent is concurrent, and the computer has two cores, then the maximum speedup is:

$Speedup = 1/((1-.50)+.5/2) = 1.333$

So, if the task took 100 execution cycles sequentially, then it will take 75 cycles with 50 percent concurrency because *75 (work units) x 1.33333 (percentage speedup) = 100 (work units)*.

The following graph shows the predicted speed increase of an application based on the number of additional processors and the percentage of the code that can run in parallel:

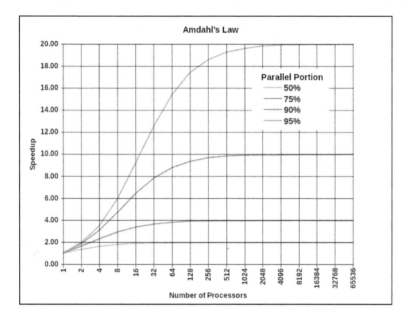

This law allows you to be able to estimate the performance gain of concurrency and to determine if the benefits are worth the extra complexity it adds to development, debug, and support. The extra costs of development, debug, and support have to be considered when developing a parallel software application.

Gustafson's law

Gustafson's law tries to address a shortfall of Amdahl's law by factoring in the scale of a problem. Gustafson was under the assumption that the problem size is not fixed but grows (scales). Amdahl's law calculates the speedup of a given problem size per the number of execution cores. Gustafson's law calculates a scaled speedup.

Gustafson's law is: $S(P) = P - a * (P - 1)$ where S is the speedup percentage, P is the number of processing cores, and a is the percentage of concurrency of the application:

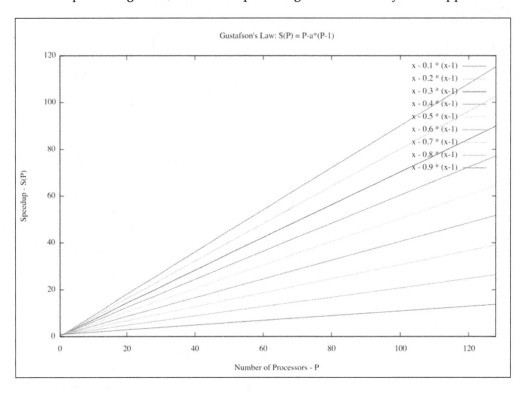

You will notice that the curves for a given percentage of concurrency do not level off in Gustafson's calculation versus Amdahl's.

Summary

We learned a lot in this chapter about multiprocessor and multicore hardware architectures and how the operating system scheduler manages them. We also learned how to design a software application for parallel operation and the performance gains we can expect from this. This chapter prepared us for the rest of the book and showed us the possibilities today's hardware can give the software developer if they are aware of the potential that multiple CPUs and multiple cores bring.

Now that we've learned about the principles of multiprocessing and multiple cores, we're ready to learn the main components of a parallel program, the processes and the threads, which is the topic of the next chapter.

2
Looking at Multithreaded Classes – BackgroundWorker

C# offers a variety of ways to create and control threads in our applications. There are the `Thread` and `ThreadPool` classes, the **Task Parallel Library** (**TPL**), the `Async` methods, and the `BackgroundWorker` component. The `BackgroundWorker` is the original way of doing multiple things at once in C# and, to many, it has become passé and `Tasks` and `Threads` are now the preferred method. But for simple multithreaded needs, `BackgroundWorker` is an extremely handy and easy-to-use way to accomplish multiple things at once.

In this chapter, we will study this component in detail, and we will begin developing multithreaded applications that take full advantage of multiprocessing. After reading this and following the exercises, we shall:

- Develop applications that are able to execute tasks in the background while keeping alive the graphical user interface, offering the user a more real-life experience
- Learn to create independent threads using a simple component
- Understand the differences between synchronous and asynchronous execution
- Develop applications that are able to show the progress of their many concurrent running tasks in the graphical user interface
- Learn to start and cancel background tasks
- Develop applications capable of launching multiple background tasks when necessary

Getting started with the BackgroundWorker component

Since the introduction of .NET 2.0 (C# 2005), a new component has become a part of Visual C# that simplifies the execution of tasks in independent threads, separated from the main thread. It is the BackgroundWorker component (System. ComponentModel.BackgroundWorker), and it allows us to begin working with many threads and taking advantage of parallelism with very little effort.

One of the main advantages of components in C# and the .NET working environment is the possibility to define their properties, values, and events in design time without the need to write lots of code.

Unfortunately, the BackgroundWorker component is not a **Windows Presentation Foundation (WPF)** component. As you can see in the following screenshot, in a Windows Form application, it is available in **Toolbox** under **Components**:

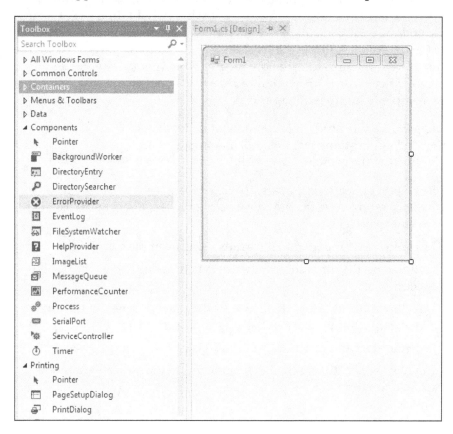

In a WPF application, it is not available, as shown:

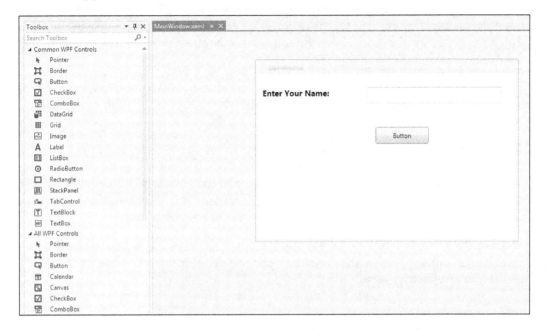

This does not mean that it is not available in WPF. It just means that you will need to implement it completely in code instead of being able to manipulate it in the **Designer** view. To declare a `BackgroundWorker` instance in WPF, we simply add the following `using` statement:

```
using System.ComponentModel;
Then we declare it in the code.
BackgroundWorker Worker = new BackgroundWorker();
```

Historically, multithreaded programming terrified developers because of the extreme complexity of the code needed to initialize, coordinate, stop, and free those threads.

The easiest way to begin experimenting with multithreading in .NET and learn the basic principles is to use the `BackgroundWorker` component. It allows us to define certain properties in design time (in Windows Forms) and introduce the code for the `DoWork` event handler. It represents an easy and rapid way to generate a new thread, independent of the main thread (the one that runs the main application's flow), and without having to use more flexible or more complicated methods.

The work to be done and run in a new thread is programmed in the DoWork event handler of BackgroundWorker. To understand how it works, let's look at an example to see it in action and experience the difference between the code running in the same thread (the application's main thread) and in another thread.

Imagine that we must create a CodeBreaker application. There is a code of four Unicode characters, and we want to break it by a brute-force attack. Therefore, we must loop through each Unicode character until we have a match, then move on to the next character, and so on.

However, as the application will take some time to break the code, we do not want to get caught by a guard during the hacking process. Therefore, we will add some pictures that will simulate a Fishes game, present in the *How to do it* section under the *Simple example without a BackgroundWorker object* section. We must be able to hide our hacking application and show the Fishes game by clicking on a button.

First, we are going to build a new C# application, and we will program a classic linear programming loop with some processing in order to run the code in the same thread (the application's main thread):

 We need a computer with at least two cores or two microprocessors installed in order to achieve significant results for the forthcoming experiments, and for the examples in the rest of this book.

Simple example without a BackgroundWorker object

We will start this WPF chapter by first creating a single thread version of our CodeBreaking application. This will give us a starting point and show us the limitations of running everything on a single thread. We will then refactor our application to use two threads, and then many threads, to show the improved performance and capabilities.

As mentioned before, we will be doing all of this in a WPF application instead of Windows Forms. This will require us to work with the BackgroundWorker component entirely in code instead of being able to use it at design time.

Downloading the example code

You can download the example code files for all Packt books you have purchased from your account at http://www.packtpub.com. If you purchased this book elsewhere, you can visit http://www.packtpub.com/support and register to have the files e-mailed directly to you.

How to do it

The following are the steps that we need to perform:

1. Create a new WPF application C# project in Visual Studio (**File** | **New** | **Project** | **Visual C#** | **WPF Application**).

2. The IDE will create a very simple application with MainWindow.xaml and MainWindow.xaml.cs files. We will name our project CodeBreaker:

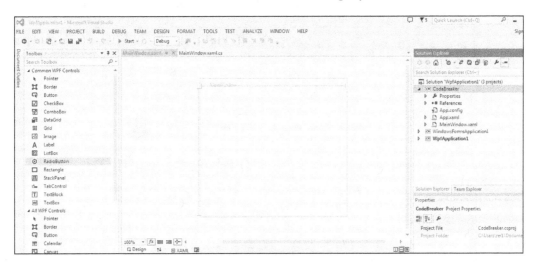

3. Open MainWindow.xaml in the designer, and add the following controls:

   ○ Two images showing a skull and an agent (imgSkull and imgAgent).

   ○ Three images showing three fish (imgFish1, imgFish2, and imgFish3).

   ○ Four textblock elements with their Text property set to "#1","#2","#3", and "#4" (txtNumber1, txtNumber2, txtNumber3, and txtNumber4 respectively).

   ○ Four labels with their Text property set to "*" (txtOutput1, txtOutput2, txtOutput3, and txtOutput4).

- ° One textblock element with its `Text` property set to `"CodeBreaker (Single-threaded)"`.

- ° One textblock with its `Text` property set to `"Fishes Game!!!"`.

- ° One button with its `Text` property set to `"Start"` (btnStart). This is the button that will run the main loop, which will find the code.

- ° One button showing with its `Text` property set to `"Hide"` (btnHide). This button must hide all the controls related to the CodeBreaker and show the Fishes game. You will click on this button when the guard is coming!

- ° One button with its `Text` property set to `"Game over"` (btnGameOver). This button must hide all the controls related to the Fishes game and show the CodeBreaker again. You will click on this button when the guard has gone and you will feel safe to continue breaking the code!

The controls mentioned here are shown in the following screenshot:

4. In the `MainWindow.xaml.cs` code file, add the following line in the
    `public partial class MainWindow : Window` definition to declare
    two private variables:

    ```
    // The simulated code to be broken
       private string Code;
       // The list of Labels of the characters to be broken.
       private List<TextBlock> OutputCharLabels;
    ```

5. Add the following method, `SimulateCodeGeneration`, to our `MainWindow`
    class. This will simulate the code that must be broken:

    ```
    private void SimulateCodeGeneration()
    {
        // A Random number generator.
        Random loRandom = new Random();
        // The char position being generated
        int i;

        Code = "";
        for (i = 0; i <= 4; i++)
        {
            // Generate a Random Unicode char for each of
            //the 4 positions
            Code += (char)(loRandom.Next(65535));
        }
    }
    ```

6. Add the following procedure, `setFishesVisibility`. This will change the
    visibility of the controls related to the Fishes game:

    ```
    private void setFishesVisibility(System.Windows.Visibility
    pbValue)
    {
        // Change the visibility of the controls
        //related to the fishes game.
        imgFish1.Visibility = pbValue;
        imgFish2.Visibility = pbValue;
        imgFish3.Visibility = pbValue;
        txtFishGame.Visibility = pbValue;
        btnGameOver.Visibility = pbValue;
    }
    ```

7. Add the following procedure, `setCodeBreakerVisibility`. This will change the visibility of the controls related to the CodeBreaking procedure:

```
private void setCodeBreakerVisibility(System.Windows.
Visibility pbValue)
    {
        // Change the visibility of the controls related to
the CodeBreaking procedure.
        imgSkull.Visibility = pbValue;
        imgAgent.Visibility = pbValue;
        txtCodeBreaker.Visibility = pbValue;
        txtNumber1.Visibility = pbValue;
        txtNumber2.Visibility = pbValue;
        txtNumber3.Visibility = pbValue;
        txtNumber4.Visibility = pbValue;
        txtOutput1.Visibility = pbValue;
        txtOutput2.Visibility = pbValue;
        txtOutput3.Visibility = pbValue;
        txtOutput4.Visibility = pbValue;
        btnStart.Visibility = pbValue;
        btnHide.Visibility = pbValue;
    }
```

8. Add the following procedure, `showFishes`. This will show the Fishes game and will hide everything related to the CodeBreaking procedure:

```
private void showFishes()
{
// Hide all the controls related to the code
// breaking procedure.
setCodeBreakerVisibility(System.Windows.Visibility.Hidden);
// Change the window title
this.Title = "Fishing game for Windows 1.0";
// Make the fishes visible
setFishesVisibility(System.Windows.Visibility.Visible);

}
```

9. Add the following procedure, `showCodeBreaker`. This will hide the Fishes game (implying you do not want to play), and will show everything related to the CodeBreaking procedure. You need this in order to break the code:

```
private void showCodeBreaker()
    {
        // Hide all the controls related to the fishes
        // game
        setFishesVisibility(System.Windows.Visibility.Hidden);
```

```
// Change the window title
this.Title = "CodeBreaker Application";
// Make the code breaker controls visible
setCodeBreakerVisibility(System.Windows.Visibility.
```
Visible);

```
    }
```

10. Add the following function, `checkCodeChar`. This will return `true` if the received character and position matches the one in the code. This will help us in our simulation, and we can then replace it with a real decoder:

```
private bool checkCodeChar(char pcChar, int piCharNumber)
{
    // Returns a bool value indicating whether the
piCharNumber position of the code is the pcChar received.
    return (Code[piCharNumber] == pcChar);
}
```

11. Add the following code in the MainWindow constructor (after `InitializeComponent()`):

```
// Generate a random code to be broken
SimulateCodeGeneration();
// Create a new list of Label controls that show the
characters of the code being broken.
OutputCharLabels = new List<TextBlock>(4);
// Add the Label controls to the List
OutputCharLabels.Add(txtOutput1);
OutputCharLabels.Add(txtOutput2);
OutputCharLabels.Add(txtOutput3);
OutputCharLabels.Add(txtOutput4);
// Hide the fishes game and show the CodeBreaker
showCodeBreaker();
```

12. Open the `Click` event in the button `butGameOver` and enter the following code:

```
// Hide the fishes game and show the CodeBreaker
showCodeBreaker();
```

13. Open the `Click` event in the button `butHide`, and enter the following code:

```
// Hide the CodeBreaker and show the fishes game
showFishes();
```

14. Open the `Click` event in the button `butStart`, and enter the following code:

```
// This code will break the simulated code.
// This variable will hold a number to iterate from 1
to 65,535 - Unicode character set.
int i;
// This variable will hold a number to iterate from 0
to 3 (the characters positions in the code to be broken).
int liCharNumber;
// This variable will hold a char generated from the
number in i
char lcChar;
// This variable will hold the current Label control
that shows the char position being decoded.
TextBlock loOutputCharCurrentLabel;

for (liCharNumber = 0; liCharNumber < 4;
liCharNumber++)
    {
        loOutputCharCurrentLabel =
        OutputCharLabels[liCharNumber];
        // This loop will run 65,536 times
        for (i = 0; i <= 65535; i++)
        {
            // myChar holds a Unicode char
            lcChar = (char)(i);
            loOutputCharCurrentLabel.Text = lcChar.
ToString();

            //Application.DoEvents();
            if (checkCodeChar(lcChar, liCharNumber))
            {
                // The code position was found
                break;
            }
        }
    }
MessageBox.Show("The code has been decoded
successfully.", this.Title);
```

15. Build and run the application:

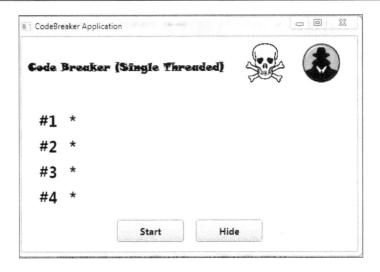

16. Click on the **Start** button. While the loop is running and the code is being broken by brute force, try clicking on the **Hide** button. You won't be able to.

How does it work?

If a guard comes past when you are trying to break the code, you will be caught because there is no way to stop the CodeBreaking once it starts until it completes.

Why? Because we do not have a multithreaded application, we lose control over the graphical user interface.

The code programmed in the btnStart click event handler runs in the main thread. Therefore, when the user clicks on this button, he or she loses control over the UI and cannot click on the other button to hide the CodeBreaker-related controls because the thread is processing the btnStart click method. Until this method finishes, nothing else can be processed.

The code is quite simple. It generates the 65,536 Unicode characters four times, and calls the checkCodeChar function in order to determine whether it is part of the code or not. It tries to display the progress showing each tested character in the window, but as it is a single-threaded application, it fails in this objective. Again, as the loop is run in the main thread of the process created when the application is executed, we lose control over the UI. We cannot move the window, change its size, or push a button. The main thread is processing the intensive loop and consuming all the processing time of a single core. Hence, it cannot show information in the main window.

For this reason, when the guard comes, you are dead. Hence, let's create a multithreaded application and save human lives!

You must comment out these lines of code because, as the BackgroundWorker object creates a new thread in which the loop is going to run, it cannot make changes to the user interface. There are mechanisms to do that, and we will learn them later.

6. Open the Click event in the button btnStart, and enter the following code:

```
// Start running the code programmed in
// BackgroundWorker DoWork event handler
// in a new independent thread and return control to
// the application's main thread
bakCodebreaker.RunWorkerAsync();
```

7. Build and run the application.

8. Click on the **Start** button. While the loop is running and the code is being broken by brute force in a new thread created by the BackgroundWorker component, try to click on the **Hide** button. It works, and while the CodeBreaker code is still working in the background, you will see the Fishes game being displayed in the window, as shown in the following screenshot:

9. Move the window, change its size, maximize it, and do anything else you want to. While you do these operations, the code programmed in the DoWork event will keep on executing in another thread.

How does it work?

We can click on the **Hide** button, and the window shows the three fish with the **Game Over** button, but the program continues processing the CodeBreaker in the other thread (the DoWork method of BackgroundWorker).

The code programmed in the DoWork event handler runs in an independent thread. Therefore, when the user clicks on the **Start** button, a new thread is created, and he or she does not lose control over the UI. While the CodeBreaker is running, the user can move the mouse cursor over other buttons, change the window size, and use other user interface components similar to the buttons.

However, we cannot see the progress of the code being broken. We will fix this issue shortly.

How does it work without blocking the UI?

After calling the RunWorkerAsync() method of BackgroundWorker, the advantage of threading begins by running the code programmed in the DoWork event handler in a new independent thread. This mechanism is known as **asynchronous execution**.

When an asynchronous method is called, it runs in an independent way and the program flow goes on with the instruction after the method call, even though the code has not finished its execution. The code in the asynchronous method runs concurrently with the main program flow.

We are going to run our last example step-by-step in order to understand the asynchronous execution and how the main thread's code goes on running.

How to do it

The following are the steps that need to be followed:

1. Open the project CodeBreaker.
2. Define a breakpoint in the line bakCodebreaker.RunWorkerAsync(); in the Click event code of btnStart.
3. Define a breakpoint in the line showFishes(); in the Click event code of btnHide.
4. Press *F5* or navigate to **Debug | Start Debugging** in the main menu.
5. Click on the **Start** button. The line with the breakpoint defined is shown highlighted as the next statement that will be executed.

6. Press *F10* or navigate to **Debug | Step Over** in the main menu a few times. As you can see, the next statement that will be executed in the main thread is not in the **DoWork** event handler of `BackgroundWorker`. It remains in the `Click` event code of `btnStart`.

7. Now, click on the **Hide** button.

8. Press *F10* or navigate to **Debug | Step Over** in the main menu a few times. As you can see, the thread created by `BackgroundWorker` keeps running while the next statement that will be executed in the main thread is not in the `DoWork` event handler of `BackgroundWorker`. It remains in the `Click` event code of `btnHide`.

How does it work?

Running the application step by step, we could not enter the code in the `DoWork` event handler of `BackgroundWorker`. However, the code was running because the CodeBreaker thread did its job. It happened because the `BackgroundWorker` object starts an asynchronous execution of the code in another thread. Therefore, the main thread continues with its next statements as if the `RunWorkerAsync()` method had completed successfully. Hence, that method does not execute code in a linear, synchronous way.

The execution flow in the main thread is synchronous. The main thread and the one created by `BackgroundWorker` run concurrently.

> Nevertheless, not everything that shines is gold. Asynchronous code execution brings many new headaches to programmers because it ends with many implicit warranties related to synchronous and linear code execution. We will be talking about them and will provide simple solutions for the most common problems.

When we worked with a single thread, we used to be the only owners of all the available elements in the programming context, the instances, the variables, the collections, the arrays, the controls that compose the graphical user interface, the components, and so on. However, when we work with multiple threads and asynchronous execution, we are sharing this world, in many ways, with strangers. Hence, there may be some code that runs concurrently, affecting the values for some variables, or accomplishing changes in the instances of the objects that we were going to work on.

For this reason, a paradigm shift in the way we approach our code is needed. We must stop thinking that we are alone with our code. The same thing happened when home computers were not connected to a network, some decades ago. They did not use a hard drive, and the user was the complete and unique owner of everything that was executed. Things such as memory swapping did not take place then. On the other side, nowadays, it would be difficult to find a modern computer without some kind of Internet connection. The antivirus, antispyware, anti-malware, and many other anti-threats that could interrupt the digital ecosystem harmony appeared. Therefore, every action in an application on a website is accompanied by those "anti-" whatever threat.

The same happens with multithreading and asynchronous execution. New threats appear and they can make the most perfectly designed code for a single thread produce completely unexpected and incomprehensible results when executed in a multithreading environment.

Many techniques must be applied in order to avoid the different problems related to concurrent programming. We are going to analyze them with concrete examples through this book, case by case.

WPF example with a synchronous BackgroundWorker

We are used to synchronous execution when we work with a single thread. This mechanism executes the next instruction once the current instruction processing is completed.

When a synchronous method is called, it runs on the same thread and the program flow goes into the method's code. Once it returns from the method with or without a result, it goes on with the instruction next to the method call. There is no code in the method left for later execution, because it finishes when it returns the control to the caller. The main program has to wait for the method to complete its execution in order to go on with the next set of instructions.

This is what happens when you debug a single-threaded application, step-by-step.

In a single-threaded application, the synchronous execution takes place as we observed in classic linear programming. When a line of code executes, nothing else runs.

However, in a multithreaded application, such as the ones using one or more `BackgroundWorker` controls, asynchronous execution comes into the picture.

[

We must master this important change in the way methods are
called and new independent threads are created on the fly, in
order to get used to parallel and concurrent programming in C#.
]

Showing progress

Users may get impatient when processes are delayed for more than a few seconds.
In such cases, they need to know how long it will take them to finish. A good
evidence of this is the replacement of messages such as *Hold on…* by animated
dialog boxes with progress bars, entertaining the users while they wait for the
process and showing them an approximate time required to finish the task.

Reporting progress is one of the main problems when we work with only one
thread and make intensive use of the processing power. Now, we will make changes
to the application to show the code as it is being decoded and report the decoding
progress for each character. This way, you will be able to decide whether to hide
the CodeBreaker when the guard is coming or wait for the process to finish.

As we work in the same thread that updates the user interface, if we send orders to
make changes in a control to show any kind of progress, it will probably show the
update whenever the main thread retrieves control (usually, when the process has
already finished). Hence, as it is not useful to watch when the process has finished,
it is necessary to update the progress report regularly.

[

As a rule, we cannot make calls to a control since the thread used
is different from the one that created it. If that happened, an
`InvalidOperationException` would be raised. In order to make
these calls safely, we must use delegates and asynchronous calls,
known as **callbacks**.
]

The `BackgroundWorker` component offers a straightforward way to report progress
and simplifies updating any control in the user interface that shows this progress,
without any need to use delegates or asynchronous calls (callbacks). The last two are
indeed much more complex ways to achieve the same results.

In order to show the progress of an operation using the `BackgroundWorker`
component, we must assign the `true` value to its `WorkerReportsProgress` property.
Its type is `bool`, and it tells whether the code executed in the new thread will report
some kind of progress or not. If the value is `true`, the `BackgroundWorker` component
will trigger the `ProgressChanged` event handler.

This event facilitates updating the user interface. Therefore, it allows changes to control values, without having to consider the problems generated when we want to do it from a thread different from the one that created the control (the application's main thread).

We are going to make some changes to our second example to take advantage of the features offered by the `BackgroundWorker` component to report progress in the user interface without delegates or callbacks. This way, we will be safe from the guards.

How to do it

The following are the steps that need to be followed:

1. Open the project `CodeBreaker`.

2. Add four `ProgressBar` controls to `frmMain` (pgbProgressChar1, pgbProgressChar2, pgbProgressChar3, and pgbProgressChar4).

3. Register the `ProgressChanged` event handler in the `MainWindow` constructor:

    ```
    bakCodebreaker.ProgressChanged += bakCodebreaker_ProgressChanged;
    ```

4. Set the `WorkerReportsProgress` property of `bakCodebreaker` to true.

5. Add the following lines of code to the `setCodeBreakerVisibility` procedure. This will change the visibility of the new controls related to the progress of the CodeBreaking procedure:

    ```
    // Change the visibility of the controls related to the
    // progress of the CodeBreaking procedure
    pgbProgressChar1.Visibility = pbValue;
    pgbProgressChar2.Visibility = pbValue;
    pgbProgressChar3.Visibility = pbValue;
    pgbProgressChar4.Visibility = pbValue;
    ```

6. Add the following lines of code in the form class declaration to declare a new private variable:

    ```
    // The list of ProgressBar controls that show the
    // progress of the character being decoded
    private List<ProgressBar> prloProgressChar;
    ```

7. Add the following code in the form constructor (after `InitializeComponent()`):

    ```
    // Create a new list of ProgressBar controls that show
    // the progress of each character of the code being
    // broken
    prloProgressChar = new List<ProgressBar>(4);
    // Add the ProgressBar controls to the list
    ```

```
prloProgressChar.Add(pgbProgressChar1);
prloProgressChar.Add(pgbProgressChar2);
prloProgressChar.Add(pgbProgressChar3);
prloProgressChar.Add(pgbProgressChar4);
```

8. Add a new class file to the project and call it CodeBreakerProgress.
   The new CodeBreakerProgress class will have properties that will help
   provide many values related to the progress to update the user interface.
   Add the following code to the class.

```csharp
public class CodeBreakerProgress
{
    // The char position in the 4 chars code
    private int priCharNumber;
    // The Unicode char code
    private int priCharCode;
    // The decoding process percentage completed
    private int priPercentageCompleted;

    public int CharNumber
    {
        get
        {
            return priCharNumber;
        }
        set
        {
            priCharNumber = value;
        }
    }

    public int CharCode
    {
        get
        {
            return priCharCode;
        }
        set
        {
            priCharCode = value;
        }
    }

    public int PercentageCompleted
    {
```

```
       get
       {
           return priPercentageCompleted;
       }
       set
       {
           priPercentageCompleted = value;
       }
    }
}
```

9. Open the `DoWork` event in `bakCodebreaker` of `BackgroundWorker`, and enter
    the following code at the beginning, before the `for` loop:

    ```
    // This variable will hold a CodeBreakerProgress
    // instance
    CodeBreakerProgress loCodeBreakerProgress = new
    CodeBreakerProgress();
    // This variable will hold the last percentage of the
       iteration completed
    int liOldPercentageCompleted;

    liOldPercentageCompleted = 0;
    ```

10. Now, in the same event, add the following code before the `if`
    `(checkCodeChar(lcChar, liCharNumber))` line:

    ```
    // The percentage completed is calculated and stored in
    // the PercentageCompleted property
    loCodeBreakerProgress.PercentageCompleted = (int)((i * 100) /
    65535);
    loCodeBreakerProgress.CharNumber = liCharNumber;
    loCodeBreakerProgress.CharCode = i;

    if (loCodeBreakerProgress.PercentageCompleted >
    liOldPercentageCompleted)
        {
            // The progress is reported only when it changes with
    regard to the last one (liOldPercentageCompleted)
            bakCodebreaker.ReportProgress(loCodeBreakerProgress.
    PercentageCompleted, loCodeBreakerProgress);
            // The old percentage completed is now the
            // percentage reported
            liOldPercentageCompleted = loCodeBreakerProgress.
    PercentageCompleted;
        }
    ```

11. Now, in the same event, add the following code before the `break;` line:

```
// The code position was found
loCodeBreakerProgress.PercentageCompleted = 100;
bakCodebreaker.ReportProgress(loCodeBreakerProgress.
PercentageCompleted, loCodeBreakerProgress);
```

12. Open the `ProgressChanged` event in the `bakCodebreaker` of `BackgroundWorker` and enter the following code (this is the code that will be run when the `ReportProgress` method is called):

```
// This variable will hold a CodeBreakerProgress instance
CodeBreakerProgress loCodeBreakerProgress =
(CodeBreakerProgress)e.UserState;

// Update the corresponding ProgressBar with the percentage
received in the as a parameter
prloProgressChar[loCodeBreakerProgress.CharNumber].Value =
loCodeBreakerProgress.PercentageCompleted;
// Update the corresponding Label with the character being
processed
OutputCharLabels[loCodeBreakerProgress.CharNumber].Text =
((char)loCodeBreakerProgress.CharCode).ToString();
```

13. Build and run the application.

14. Click on the **Start** button and you will see the progress bars filling up, showing how the process advances from 0 to 65,535 Unicode characters and the characters being tested. This is shown in the following screenshot. Now you have more information to decide whether to hide the application or not.

While the code is being broken, the UI can be used because the CodeBreaking is being done in a separate thread.

If the CodeBreaking runs too fast on your system, to see what is going on, add the following line before the `if (checkCodeChar(lcChar, liCharNumber))` statement.

```
System.Threading.Thread.Sleep(1);
```

This will add a 1-millisecond wait between each character being checked.

How does it work?

The code programmed in the loop reports the progress only if the percentage completed increased by a unit or more. Otherwise, we would be triggering 65,536 events in order to report only 100 different percentages. That would not make sense and add extra burdensome processing. That would be very inefficient and would make the loop take longer to complete its execution.

Canceling a BackgroundWorker thread

Executing a time-consuming process in an independent thread allows us to work concurrently while showing its progress. One of the advantages of doing this is the possibility of allowing the user to go on using the controls in the graphical user interface without the restrictions of single-threaded applications. For example, perhaps he or she wants to cancel the CodeBreaking process instead of letting it finish.

The `BackgroundWorker` component simplifies the task of canceling the execution of the code running in the thread it creates without a lot of programming effort.

To do this, we must assign the `true` value to the `WorkerSupportsCancellation` property of `BackgroundWorker`. It is a `bool` value and tells whether the code executed in the new thread will support cancellation through a call to the `CancelAsync()` method of `BackgroundWorker`. This method simply assigns the `true` value to the `BackgroundWorker` property `CancellationPending`. Hence, the code being executed in the `DoWork` event handler must regularly check this property's value to determine whether it has to go on working or not.

Hiding the CodeBreaking does not stop the CodeBreaking process. So, we can still get caught if someone hacks into our computer and sees the process. Therefore, it is very important to provide the application with a fast cancellation procedure.

How to do it

We are going to make some changes to our example to allow the user to cancel the loop at any time without delegates or callbacks, using the features provided by the BackgroundWorker component:

1. Open the project CodeBreaker.

2. Set the WorkerSupportsCancellation property of bakCodebreaker to true.

3. Add a button control btnStop. Set its Text property to "Stop".

4. Add the following line of code to the procedure, setCodeBreakerVisibility. It will change the visibility of the new button:

   ```
   // Change the visibility of the new stop button
      btnStop.Visibility = pbValue;
   ```

5. Open the DoWork event in bakCodebreaker and enter the following code before the line lcChar = (char) (i) in the beginning of the for loop (the code now adds support for a premature cancellation):

   ```
   if (bakCodebreaker.CancellationPending)
   {
       // The user requested to cancel the process
       e.Cancel = true;
       return;
   }
   ```

6. Open the Click event in the button btnStart and add the following lines of code at the beginning (the code now disables the **Start** button and enables the **Stop** button):

   ```
   // Disable the Start button
   btnStart.IsEnabled = false;
   // Enable the Stop button
   btnStop.IsEnabled = true;
   ```

7. Set the IsEnabled property of the btnStop button to false in the constructor. Hence, the button will be disabled when the application starts.

8. Open the Click event in the btnStop button and enter the following code:

   ```
   // Disable the Stop button
   btnStop.IsEnabled = false;
   // Enable the Start button
   btnStart.IsEnabled = true;

   //Call the CancelAsync method to cancel the
   // process.
   bakCodebreaker.CancelAsync();
   ```

9. Build and run the application.

10. Click on the **Start** button. Now click on the **Stop** button. The CodeBreaker will cancel its execution. The thread created by the `BackgroundWorker` component will stop running. The result is shown in the following screenshot:

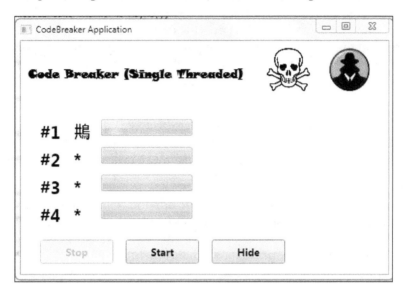

11. Now, click on the **Start** button and let the CodeBreaking complete.

How does it work?

Earlier, you could avoid the guards, and now you are able to stop the CodeBreaking in case spies hack your system!

We can now develop an application that is able to execute a time-consuming task in the background, while keeping the graphical user interface alive. This offers the user a more real-life experience and we can offer the user the possibility of starting and stopping the process whenever they want to. We have done all of this using the `BackgroundWorker` component features.

However, the application has a defect. When we click on the **Start** button and let the process finish, the **Stop** button will not be shown disabled. Additionally, we cannot see the final code on the screen. We must create a remedy for this.

Working with multiple BackgroundWorker components

We can work with many `BackgroundWorker` components in order to run many concurrent threads. Usually, we will use the `Thread` class to run many threads at once, but the `BackgroundWorker` class provides us an easy way to do this as well. As we learned in the previous chapter, the performance results will depend upon the number of cores or processors available in the computer in which we run the application and how busy each core is with other threads of execution.

Using the real algorithms, the process of breaking the four Unicode characters code is very intensive and requires more time than expected. Breaking the code must take the minimum time possible. So far, we have been using multithreading to have a more responsive application, but now, we must make execution of the CodeBreaking process much faster.

We are going to take the code presented in our previous examples and divide it into four `BackgroundWorker` components. With this example, we will learn how multiple `BackgroundWorker` components coexist and create new independent threads, and hence achieve an incredible performance enhancement.

How does it work?

The steps that need to be followed are as follows:

1. Open the project `CodeBreaker`.

2. Add three new `BackgroundWorker` components (`bakCodeBreaker2`, `bakCodeBreaker3`, and `bakCodeBreaker4`) to create four independent threads. This is done in the declaration section of the `MainWindow` class. Next, set the `True` value for their properties `WorkerReportsProgress` and `WorkerSupportsCancellation` in the class constructor.

3. Add a new class to the project and call it `CodeBreakerParameters`. The `CodeBreakerParameters` class will have properties that will help provide many values that will be available as parameters for the four `BackgroundWorker` components:

    ```
    public class CodeBreakerParameters
    {
        // The first char position in the 4 chars code to
        // process
        private int priFirstCharNumber;
        // The last char position in the 4 chars code to
        // process
    ```

```csharp
        private int priLastCharNumber;
// The maximum number of the Unicode character
private int priMaxUnicodeCharCode;

public int FirstCharNumber
{
    get
    {
        return priFirstCharNumber;
    }
    set
    {
        priFirstCharNumber = value;
    }
}

public int LastCharNumber
{
    get
    {
        return priLastCharNumber;
    }
    set
    {
        priLastCharNumber = value;
    }
}

public int MaxUnicodeCharCode
{
    get
    {
        return priMaxUnicodeCharCode;
    }
    set
    {
        priMaxUnicodeCharCode = value;
    }
}
}
```

4. Again, add another new class file. This one will be called `CodeBreakerResult`. The new `CodeBreakerResult` class will have properties that help in providing many values as parameters for the four `BackgroundWorker` components' `RunWorkerCompleted` events:

```
public class CodeBreakerResult
{
    // The first char position in the 4 chars code to
    // process
    private int priFirstCharNumber;
    // The last char position in the 4 chars code to
    // process
    private int priLastCharNumber;
    // The part of the broken code
    private string prsBrokenCode;

    public int FirstCharNumber
    {
        get
        {
            return priFirstCharNumber;
        }
        set
        {
            priFirstCharNumber = value;
        }
    }

    public int LastCharNumber
    {
        get
        {
            return priLastCharNumber;
        }
        set
        {
            priLastCharNumber = value;
        }
    }

    public string BrokenCode
    {
        get
        {
            return prsBrokenCode;
```

```
            }
            set
            {
                prsBrokenCode = value;
            }
        }
    }
```

5. Open the `Click` event in the `btnStart` button and add the following lines of code before the line `bakCodebreaker.RunWorkerAsync();` (now the code will set the parameters for the four `BackgroundWorker` components and will run them asynchronously):

```
// Start running the code programmed in each
// BackgroundWorker DoWork event handler in a new
// independent thread and return control to the
// application's main thread
// First, create the CodeBreakerParameters for each
// BackgroundWorker and set its parameters
CodeBreakerParameters loParameters1 = new
CodeBreakerParameters();
CodeBreakerParameters loParameters2 = new
CodeBreakerParameters();
CodeBreakerParameters loParameters3 = new
CodeBreakerParameters();
CodeBreakerParameters loParameters4 = new
CodeBreakerParameters();
loParameters1.MaxUnicodeCharCode = 32000;
loParameters1.FirstCharNumber = 0;
loParameters1.LastCharNumber = 0;
loParameters2.MaxUnicodeCharCode = 32000;
loParameters2.FirstCharNumber = 1;
loParameters2.LastCharNumber = 1;
loParameters3.MaxUnicodeCharCode = 32000;
loParameters3.FirstCharNumber = 2;
loParameters3.LastCharNumber = 2;
loParameters4.MaxUnicodeCharCode = 32000;
loParameters4.FirstCharNumber = 3;
loParameters4.LastCharNumber = 3;
bakCodebreaker.RunWorkerAsync(loParameters1);
bakCodebreaker2.RunWorkerAsync(loParameters2);
bakCodebreaker3.RunWorkerAsync(loParameters3);
bakCodebreaker4.RunWorkerAsync(loParameters4);
```

6. Now, in the same aforementioned event, remove the line `bakCodebreaker.RunWorkerAsync();`.

7. Open the `Click` event in the `btnStop` button and add the following lines of code (now the code will cancel the four `BackgroundWorker` components, `bakCodebreaker` and the three `BackgroundWorker` components added in the following lines):

   ```
   bakCodebreaker2.CancelAsync();
   bakCodebreaker3.CancelAsync();
   bakCodebreaker4.CancelAsync();
   ```

8. Now, we will create generic procedures to handle the following programmed events of `BackgroundWorker` components, receiving the same parameters as the corresponding event handler:

   ° `DoWorkProcedure` for the `DoWork` event

   ° `RunWorkerCompletedProcedure` for the `RunWorkerCompleted` event

   ° `ProgressChangedProcedure` for the `ProgressChanged` event

9. Paste the `DoWork` event handler code of `bakCodebreaker` in a new private procedure and then make the following changes as shown:

   ```
   private void DoWorkProcedure(object sender, DoWorkEventArgs e)
   ```

10. Add the following variable definitions at the beginning:

    ```
    // This variable will hold the broken code
    string lsBrokenCode = "";
    CodeBreakerParameters loCodeBreakerParameters =
    (CodeBreakerParameters)e.Argument;
    ```

11. Replace the line `int liTotal = (int)e.Argument;` with the following (now the event handler procedure needs more parameters, and so we create a class to manage them):

    ```
    int liTotal = loCodeBreakerParameters.MaxUnicodeCharCode;
    ```

12. Replace the line that defines the first loop with the following (now the loop takes into account the parameters received through a `CodeBreakerParameters` instance):

    ```
    for (liCharNumber = loCodeBreakerParameters.FirstCharNumber;
    liCharNumber <= loCodeBreakerParameters.LastCharNumber;
    liCharNumber++)
    ```

13. Replace the pending cancellation check with the following line (we use the `sender` parameter typecast because the same procedure is employed by the four `BackgroundWorker` components):

```
if (((BackgroundWorker)sender).CancellationPending)
```

14. Replace the call to the `ReportProgress` method by the following line (again, we use the `sender` parameter typecasted for generalization):

```
((BackgroundWorker)sender).ReportProgress(loCodeBreakerProgress.
PercentageCompleted, loCodeBreakerProgress);
```

15. Replace the call to the `ReportProgress` method when the `checkCodeChar` function returns `true` with the following line:

```
((BackgroundWorker)sender).ReportProgress(loCodeBreakerProgre
ss.PercentageCompleted, loCodeBreakerProgress);
```

16. Replace the line `e.Result = lsBrokenCode;` with the following lines (now we must return more than one result; therefore, we use an instance of the `CodeBreakerResult` class created earlier):

```
// Create a new instance of the CodeBreakerResult class
// and set its properties' values
CodeBreakerResult loResult = new CodeBreakerResult();
loResult.FirstCharNumber = loCodeBreakerParameters.
FirstCharNumber;
loResult.LastCharNumber = loCodeBreakerParameters.
LastCharNumber;
loResult.BrokenCode = lsBrokenCode;
// Return a CodeBreakerResult instance in the Result
// property
e.Result = loResult;
```

17. Enter the following code to create the new `RunWorkerCompleted` procedure:

```
private void RunWorkerCompletedProcedure(object sender,
RunWorkerCompletedEventArgs e)
{
    if (!e.Cancelled)
    {
        // Obtain the CodeBreakerResult instance
        // contained in the Result property of e
        // parameter
        CodeBreakerResult loResult = (CodeBreakerResult)
e.Result;
        int i;

        // Iterate through the parts of the result
```

```
            // resolved by this BackgroundWorker
            for (i = loResult.FirstCharNumber; i <= loResult.
    LastCharNumber; i++)
                {
                    // The process has finishes, therefore the
                    // ProgressBar control must show a 100%
                    prloProgressChar[i].Value = 100;
                    // Show the part of the broken code in the
                    // label
                    OutputCharLabels[i].Text = loResult.BrokenCode[i -
    loResult.FirstCharNumber].ToString();
                }
        }
```

18. Enter the following code to create the new `ProgressChangedProcedure` procedure:

```
        private void ProgressChangedProcedure(object sender,
    ProgressChangedEventArgs e)
        {
            // This variable will hold a CodeBreakerProgress
            // instance
            CodeBreakerProgress loCodeBreakerProgress =
    (CodeBreakerProgress)e.UserState;
            // Update the corresponding ProgressBar with the
    percentage received as a parameter
            prloProgressChar[loCodeBreakerProgress.CharNumber].Value =
    loCodeBreakerProgress.PercentageCompleted;
            // Update the corresponding Label with the character being
    processed
            OutputCharLabels[loCodeBreakerProgress.CharNumber].Text =
    ((char)loCodeBreakerProgress.CharCode).ToString();
        }
```

Now, you have to program the code for the three additional event handlers of the four `BackgroundWorker` components. As we have used procedures, we will use the same code for the four `BackgroundWorker` components:

1. Add the following code in the four `BackgroundWorker` components' `DoWork` event handlers:

   ```
   DoWorkProcedure(sender, e);
   ```

2. Add the following code in the four `BackgroundWorker` components' `ProgressChanged` event handlers:

   ```
   ProgressChangedProcedure(sender, e);
   ```

3. Add the following code in the four `BackgroundWorker` components'
    `RunWorkerCompleted` event handlers:

    ```
    RunWorkerCompletedProcedure(sender, e);
    ```

4. Build and run the application.

5. Click on the **Start** button and let the process finish. You will see that all four
    characters are being decoded at the same time concurrently. If you have
    a machine with four cores in it, you will see all four cores being utilized
    simultaneously and much improved performance:

And here is how it looks once it is completed:

How does it work?

Now, your CodeBreaking procedure is very fast! Each character of the code is being decoded in parallel.

As we have seen, it is easy to split a process into many threads using the features provided by the `BackgroundWorker` component. The results of the execution of the previous example will depend on the number of cores or processors available in the computer. The ideal situation is to start as many `BackgroundWorker` components as the number of cores available. This way, we can achieve the best performance for each thread and take the CPU usage to around 95 percent. Of course this will vary and we will not always know the number of cores on a target machine. As we will see in future chapters, there are ways to use the **Task Parallel Library** (TPL) to achieve maximum concurrency on machines when we do not know the number of cores on a machine ahead of time.

Now, we do not need to run many instances of an application to take advantage of parallel processing capabilities. Using the `BackgroundWorker` component and everything we have learned so far, we can quite easily split a process into many threads.

However, we had to make some important changes to the code because we needed to generalize the behavior of four `BackgroundWorker` components without writing the same piece of code four times. This is called **refactoring** and should also be done when developing software to minimize redundant code.

We created new classes to pass parameters and obtain results because we needed many parameters and many results. As you can see, with typecasting, C# offers us excellent alternatives to generalize the code.

The key was the `sender` parameter. Remember that this parameter, available in the event handlers, offers a reference to the component (the `BackgroundWorker`) that triggers the event. Typecasting the `sender` parameter to a `BackgroundWorker` component, we could generalize the code in the different event handlers and create procedures for each one.

There were many changes. But once the code patterns are practiced and learned, it will be easier to work with concurrent programming structures. This will be especially important when working with the TPL.

As of now, the application uses four `BackgroundWorker` components, and hence four independent threads not including the main thread. It does not give the user a message about the end of the CodeBreaking global process.

Exploring other examples

Try adding another `BackgroundWorker` to show a message box telling the user the process has finished, or disabling the **Stop** button and enabling the **Start** button, when the four `BackgroundWorker` components complete their work. You can use the `IsBusy()` function.

You can use the **Process Explorer** to view the running threads for the example and monitor its activities. You can download and install **Process Explorer** from `http://download.cnet.com/Process-Explorer/3000-2094_4-10223605.html`, if you do not already have it loaded. This is a very handy utility and will allow you to really dissect what is happening with the different threads in your application. The following is a sample of Process Explorer running alongside our `CodeBreaker` application.

Apply all the things we have learned in the previous chapter. Also, use the Windows Task Manager. You will have a better understanding of the differences between multiple processes and multithreaded applications when monitoring the application running concurrently with the four `BackgroundWorker` threads, in a computer with a quad-core microprocessor and using the Process Explorer.

Before the **Start** button is pressed, these are the threads and information you should see for this application:

After the **Start** button is pressed, these are the threads and information you should see for this application:

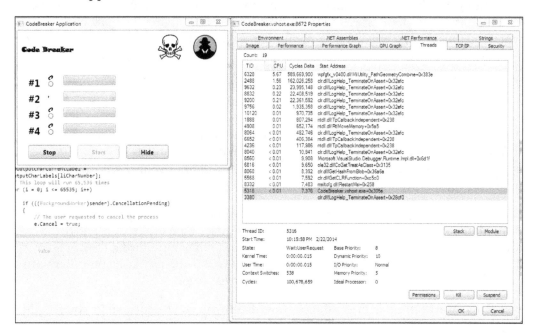

Monitor the application using one, two, three, and four threads running concurrently.

Enhance the application using the patterns we have learned in the previous example using only one `BackgroundWorker` component. Change the code to add the possibility to start and stop the threads running in each `BackgroundWorker` component.

Monitor the application starting and stopping one, two, three, and four threads running concurrently, and pay attention to what happens with the threads' activities and CPU usage in the Process Explorer.

Run the application in different computers with different microprocessors and use the Process Explorer to monitor their behavior and measure their performance.

Summary

We learned a lot in this chapter about working with threads using the BackgroundWorker component. Specifically, we covered the following:

- Developing applications that are able to create background threads using the BackgroundWorker component and showing the progress of execution by taking advantage of the methods provided by this component

- Programming the threads' code to be executed by BackgroundWorker

- Understanding the differences between synchronous and asynchronous execution and how they are related to threads

- Reporting the progress of multiple threads in the user interface

- Starting and canceling threads created using BackgroundWorker instances

- Launching multiple threads using many BackgroundWorker components

- Creating the various event handlers of the BackgroundWorker component in code

Now that we've learned a simple way to create many threads in a C# application using the BackgroundWorker component, we're ready to do these things using a much more flexible but more complex technique — the Thread class — which is the topic of the next chapter.

3
Thread Class – Heavyweight Concurrency in C#

In the previous chapter, we examined the `BackgroundWorker` component and how to use it to achieve performance gains by multithreading our application. This component is useful but has many limitations. In order to have very precise control over the concurrently running threads in our applications, we can use the `Thread` class instead.

In this chapter, we will study this class in detail and develop more complex multithreaded applications that take full advantage of the multiprocessing capabilities of today's hardware.

We will use the terms **heavyweight concurrency** and **lightweight concurrency** throughout this book. Let's take a minute to reflect on what we mean by this. When we use the `Thread` class, as we will see in this and the next chapter, we will develop multithreaded applications through heavyweight concurrency. This means that it is up to us to create, coordinate, and manage the different threads in our application. It will also be up to us to know how many processing cores the hardware has that runs our application in order to maximize the multithreading efficiency of our application. We use the term heavyweight concurrency to describe this kind of multithreaded development because it takes extra code and work on the developer's part to achieve maximum benefits. We have to create the threads, coordinate the interaction of the threads, manage when threads have completed, and so on.

Later in the book, we will study the `Task` class and **Task Parallel Library** (**TPL**). This library is a recent addition to the .NET framework and takes multithreading application development to the next level. Using these classes allows the developer to achieve the maximum benefits of multithreading an application with much less effort.

TPL handles thread creation, coordination, and management for you. Developing using the TPL classes is referred to as lightweight concurrency because it takes less effort by the developer. There are some downsides, as we will see, to using these classes because much of the multithreaded work is handled for you and may not be done exactly how you want it to be.

So, depending on your application and expertise, there are times when both heavyweight concurrency and lightweight concurrency are the right solution. The key is to understand both and know when to use each.

For now, we will focus on heavyweight concurrency and the `Thread` class. After reading this chapter and following the exercises, we shall be able to:

- Develop applications with great control over multiple running threads, offering exciting performance enhancements
- Learn how to create independent and very flexible threads using a very powerful class
- Find out how to start, control, and coordinate multiple threads
- Discover how to send parameters to and retrieve data from threads
- Learn how to share data between many threads
- Find out how to combine asynchronous and synchronous execution in order to have exhaustive control over the running threads and their tasks
- Develop applications capable of launching multiple threads when necessary

Creating threads with the Thread class

So far, we have used the `BackgroundWorker` component to create new threads independent of the main application thread. The applications can respond to UI events while processing continues and take full advantage of multiple cores, thus running faster. However, there are some restrictions when we must control and coordinate the execution of many threads that are not intended to just run in the background. Now, let's learn how to use the `Thread` class to make an application capable of taking full control of the synchronous and asynchronous execution of concurrent threads. The `Thread` class is just what it sounds like, a class that allows you to create separate threads of execution for your process to run.

We can work with many instances of the Thread class (System.Threading.Thread) in order to run many concurrent threads with more control capabilities than the ones created using the BackgroundWorker component. As we learned in the previous chapter, the performance results will depend upon the number of cores or processors available in the computer on which we run the application. However, the Thread class offers many fine-tuning capabilities to help us achieve the desired performance using multithreading.

The Thread class does a great job of offering great flexibility while offering a simple way to initialize, coordinate, run, stop, and free multiple threads.

Let's get started with an encryption program

To demonstrate how to use the Thread class, we are going to create a simple WPF application that takes text messages and encrypts and decrypts them. The customers of this application are working with a new cellular phone capable of sending SMS (text messages) with access to the complete Unicode character set. The cellular phone is a single-core device. The application has to work in a very fast and efficient encryption engine capable of encrypting the incoming text messages and leaving them in an output queue. This engine is going to run on a huge server with many multi-core processors. They want it to use a very fine-tuned multithreading application capable of working with as many threads as there are available cores in the computer on which the engine is being executed. So, the application will have to be smart enough to detect the number of cores and create that many threads. In this way, it uses the full capabilities of the hardware, but doesn't create extra threads that will not further enhance performance.

How to do it

First, we are going to build a new C# WPF application, and we will define and test the methods to encrypt and decrypt a string:

1. Create a new C# project using the WPF application template in Visual Studio. Use SMSEncryption as the project's name.

2. Open `MainWindow.xaml` in the designer mode, add the following controls, and align them as shown in the following screenshot:

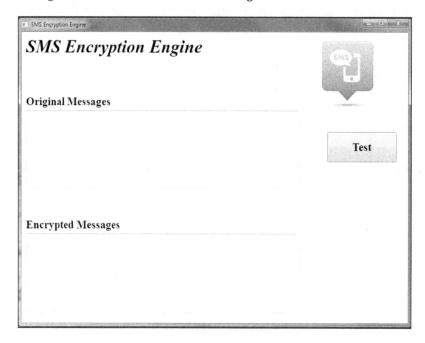

-   ○ One image showing a text message graphic called `imgTextMessage`.
-   ○ Three textboxes with their `Text` property set to `SMS Encryption Engine`, `Original Messages`, and `Encrypted Messages`.
-   ○ Two textboxes with their `Names` property set to `txtOriginalSMS` and `txtEncryptedSMS`, and their `AcceptsReturn` property set to `true`.
-   ○ One button control named `butTest` with its `Text` property set to `Test`. This is the button that will test the encryption and decryption methods.

3. Next, add a class file called `EncryptionProcedures` that has two static methods, one called `Encrypt` and the other called `Decrypt`.

4. The `Encrypt` method will encrypt the string received as a parameter and return a string containing the resulting encoded message with unrecognizable characters. Add the following code for this method:

```
public static string Encrypt(string psText)
{
        string lsEncryptedText;
        string lsEncryptedTextWithFinalXOR;
        // A Random number generator
```

```
        Random loRandom = new Random();

        // The char position being encrypted
        int i;
        char loRandomChar;

        // Debug
        // Show the original text in the Immediate Window
        System.Diagnostics.Debug.Print("Original text:" +
psText);

        lsEncryptedText = "";
        for (i = 0; i <= (psText.Length - 1); i++)
        {
            loRandomChar = (char)(loRandom.Next(65535));
            // Current char XOR random generated char

            // Debug
            // Show the random char code (in numbers)
generated in the Immediate Window
            System.Diagnostics.Debug.Print("Random char
generated:" + ((int)loRandomChar).ToString());

            lsEncryptedText += ((char)(psText[i] ^
loRandomChar)).ToString();
            // Random generated char XOR 65535 - i
            // It is saved because we need it later for the
decryption process
            lsEncryptedText += ((char)(loRandomChar ^ (65535 -
i))).ToString();
            // Another random generated char but just to add
garbage to confuse the hackers
            loRandomChar = (char)(loRandom.Next(65535));
            lsEncryptedText += loRandomChar.ToString();

            // Debug
            // Show how the encrypted text is being generated
in the Immediate Window
            System.Diagnostics.Debug.Print("Partial encryption
result char number: " + i.ToString() + ": " + lsEncryptedText);

        }

        lsEncryptedTextWithFinalXOR = "";
        // Now, every character XOR 125
        for (i = 0; i <= (lsEncryptedText.Length - 1); i++)
        {
            lsEncryptedTextWithFinalXOR += ((char)
(lsEncryptedText[i] ^ 125)).ToString();
        }
```

```
        // Debug
        // Show how the encrypted text is being generated in
the Immediate Window
        System.Diagnostics.Debug.Print("Final encryption
result with XOR: " + lsEncryptedTextWithFinalXOR);

        return lsEncryptedTextWithFinalXOR;

}
```

5. The `Decrypt` method will decrypt the encrypted string received as a parameter and return a string with the resulting decoded message:

```
        public static string Decrypt(string psText)
        {
            // The decrypted text to return
            string lsDecryptedText;

            // The char position being decrypted
            int i;
            // The random char
            char loRandomChar;

            lsDecryptedText = "";
            for (i = 0; i <= (psText.Length - 1); i += 3)
            {
                // Retrieve the previously random generated char
XOR 125 XOR 65535 - i (but previous i)
                loRandomChar = (char)(psText[i + 1] ^ 125 ^ (65535
- (i / 3)));
                // Char XOR random generated char
                lsDecryptedText += ((char)(psText[i] ^ 125 ^
loRandomChar)).ToString();
            }

            return lsDecryptedText;
        }
```

6. Open the `Click` event handler method for the button, `butTest`, and enter the following code:

```
        private void butTest_Click(object sender,
RoutedEventArgs e)
        {
            // The encrypted text
            string lsEncryptedText;

            // For each line in txtOriginalSMS TextBox
            int lineCount = txtOriginalSMS.LineCount;
            for (int line = 0; line < lineCount; line++)
```

```
        {
            lsEncryptedText = EncryptProcedures.
Encrypt(txtOriginalSMS.GetLineText(line));
            // Append a line with the Encrypted text
            txtEncryptedSMS.AppendText(lsEncryptedText +
Environment.NewLine);
            // Append a line with the Encrypted text decrypted
to test everything is as expected
            txtEncryptedSMS.AppendText(EncryptProcedures.
Decrypt(lsEncryptedText) + Environment.NewLine);
        }
    }
```

7. Build and run the application.

8. Enter a short text in the textbox labeled `Original SMS Messages`, and click on the **Test** button. The encrypted message will appear in the textbox labeled `Encrypted SMS Messages`. The decrypted message will also become visible in the bottom textbox, but this will be the result of decrypting the encrypted message to test the algorithm.

9. The results will look similar to the following screenshot:

How it works

In this program, we have created the `Encrypt` and `Decrypt` methods that take a `String` value and encrypt and decrypt it, respectively. The encryption algorithm uses a random number generator and many **Exclusive OR (XOR)** operations. It also adds garbage in the text in order to confuse potential hackers.

 Remember that in C#, the XOR operation is specified by the `^` operator and can be applied to numbers. Thus, we needed many typecastings to `char` type, and then we called the `ToString()` method.

One of the most exciting properties of the XOR operation is the possibility of returning to the original value when it is applied twice. For example, consider the following lines of code:

```
int liOriginalValue = 120;
int liFirstXOR = liOriginalValue ^ 250;
int liSecondXOR = liFirstXOR ^ 250;
```

The value assigned to `liSecondXOR` will be the same as is in `liOriginalValue`, that is, `120`.

As the encryption algorithms use the complete Unicode character set, with 65,536 possible characters, the resulting text is unreadable and very confusing, as it is not limited to the classic 256-character set.

Creating an application with threads

As we have tested the decryption of the previously encrypted message, we are sure it is working fine. We are now going to run the encryption algorithm in a new thread created using the `Thread` class.

We want to use the `Thread` class to have tight control over the execution of the different processing threads in our application. First, we need to make the encryption function run in just one thread. Later, we will align the threads with the number of cores in our hardware to ensure maximum efficiency. So, for now, we will change the application we previously built so that the encryption logic runs in a separate thread from the main application. This will begin to give us control over when and how we encrypt the text messages.

How to do it

Now, we are going to make some changes to the application, and we will encrypt the messages in a new independent thread created and configured using the Thread class:

1. Open the SMSEncryption project.

2. Add a button control (butRunInThread). Set its Text property to Run in a Thread.

3. Since we are going to use the Thread class, we need to add a Using statement so that our application can find this class from the .NET framework. Add the following line of code at the beginning (as we are going to use the System. Threading.Thread class):

   ```
   using System.Threading;
   ```

4. Add the following line in the MainWindow code-behind file, MainWindow. xaml.cs class definition to declare three new private variables:

   ```
   // The thread
   private Thread proThreadEncryption;
   // The string list with SMS messages to encrypt (input)
   private List<string> prlsSMSToEncrypt;
   // The string list with SMS messages encrypted (output)
   private List<List<string>> prlsEncryptedSMS;
   ```

5. Add one button control named butRunInThread with its Text property set to Run in a Thread. This is the button that will test the encryption and decryption methods running in a separate thread from the main thread.

6. Open the Click event method for the butRunInThread button and enter the following code to run the encryption process in a new thread created using the Thread class:

   ```
   private void butRunInThread_Click(object sender, RoutedEventArgs
   e)
           {
               // Prepare everything the thread needs from the UI
               // For each line in txtOriginalSMS TextBox
               prlsSMSToEncrypt = new List<string>(txtOriginalSMS.
   LineCount);

               // Add the lines in txtOriginalSMS TextBox
               int lineCount = txtOriginalSMS.LineCount;
               for (int line = 0; line < lineCount; line++)
               {
                   prlsSMSToEncrypt.Add(txtOriginalSMS.
   ```

```
GetLineText(line));
            }
            // Create the new Thread and use the
ThreadEncryptProcedure method
            proThreadEncryption = new Thread(new ThreadStart(Threa
dEncryptProcedure));

            // Start running the thread
            proThreadEncryption.Start();

            // Join the independent thread to this thread to wait
until ThreadProc ends
            proThreadEncryption.Join();

            // When the thread finishes running this is the next
line that is going to be executed
            // Copy the string List generated by the thread
            foreach (string lsEncryptedText in prlsEncryptedSMS)
            {
                // Append a line with the Encrypted text
                txtEncryptedSMS.AppendText(lsEncryptedText +
                Environment.NewLine);
            }
        }
    }
```

7. Now, we need to create the `ThreadEncryptProcedure` that will run in a separate thread and encrypt the text message. Enter the following code to create this procedure.

```
    private void ThreadEncryptProcedure()
        {
            string lsEncryptedText;

            //Initialize the encrypted array to the size of the
array to encrypt.
            prlsEncryptedSMS = new List<string>(prlsSMSToEncrypt.
Count);

            // Line of text message to encrypt
            string lsText;

            // Iterate through each string in the prlsSMSToEncrypt
string
            for (int i = 0; i < prlsSMSToEncrypt.Count; i++)
            {
                lsText = prlsSMSToEncrypt[i];
```

```
            lsEncryptedText = EncryptProcedures.
Encrypt(lsText);

                // Add the encrypted string to the List of
encrypted strings
                prlsEncryptedSMS.Add(lsEncryptedText);
            }
        }
```

8. Build and run the application.

9. Enter or copy and paste a long text in the Textbox labeled Original SMS Messages and click on the **Run in a Thread** button. The encrypted message will appear in the Textbox labeled Encrypted Messages. However, the code runs in a different thread. The results will be similar to what is shown in the following screenshot:

How it works

Now, when the user clicks the **Run in a Thread** button, the encryption runs in a new thread, but with synchronous execution. We create the thread and then we start the thread with the `proThreadEncryption.Start();` command. Since it is a synchronous operation, we then wait on the thread to complete operation with the `proThreadEncryption.Join();` command. So, in a separate thread, the `ThreadEncryptProcedure` runs and encrypts the text message string into a list of strings.

When the thread running the `ThreadEncryptProcedure` completes, the main thread, which was waiting on the thread to complete by executing the `Join` command, continues and takes the encrypted list of strings and displays them in the bottom textbox.

The `Thread.Join` method tells the issuing thread to wait here until the thread completes. As we are not using a `BackgroundWorker` component, which simplified UI decoupling, we must do that work in code.

The following lines declare the two private string lists that will work as an input (`prlsSMSToEncrypt`) and as an output (`prlsEncryptedSMS`) for the new independent thread:

```
private List<string> prlsSMSToEncrypt;
private List<List<string>> prlsEncryptedSMS;
```

When started, the thread will execute the code in the `ThreadEncryptProcedure` (without parameters). This procedure is private and resides in the same class as the two aforementioned private string lists. Thus, the code in the `ThreadEncryptProcedure` can access these two variables to take the input strings, encrypt them, and add them to the output string list. Instead of working against the UI controls, we decouple the UI and avoid the problems related to multithreading with the UI.

`ThreadEncryptProcedure` does a very simple task without touching the UI controls. For each string in the input string list (`prlsSMSToEncrypt`), it encrypts the string and adds it to the output string list (`prlsEncryptedSMS`).

When the user clicks on the **Run in a Thread** button, the following lines prepare everything the thread needs from the UI:

```
prlsSMSToEncrypt = new List<string>(txtOriginalSMS.
LineCount);

            // Add the lines in txtOriginalSMS TextBox
            int lineCount = txtOriginalSMS.LineCount;
            for (int line = 0; line < lineCount; line++)
            {
                prlsSMSToEncrypt.Add(txtOriginalSMS.
GetLineText(line));
            }
```

First, we create a new instance of `List<string>`. As mentioned earlier, we pass the number of items (capacity) as a parameter in order to optimize the execution, using the `LineCount` property for the lines in the `txtOriginalSMS` textbox.

Then, we use the `Add` method to add all the strings to our new `List<string>` instance. Now, we have everything the thread needs as an input in a private `List<string>`, which it can access without problems.

 Mastering the use of lists, arrays, and collections is a must when working with multithreading.

This is a very simple way to share data with a new independent thread without complications. However, we must be very careful, as we must learn more things in order to change data in the same variables accessed from many threads.

When we access variables from multiple threads, they must be of thread safety types. **Thread safety types** are those that are safe for multithreaded operations. If you have any doubt about a type, you can check whether it is of a thread safety type or not in the C# documentation. It offers a section describing the thread safety, as shown in the following screenshot for the Int32 type:

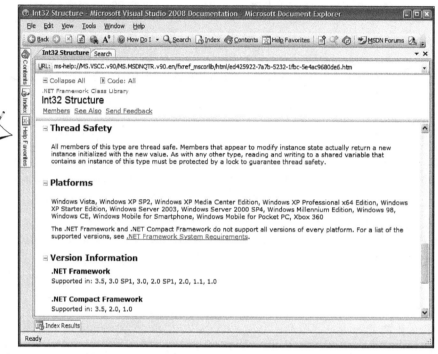

The following line declared the proThreadEncryption variable with the Thread type:

```
private Thread proThreadEncryption;
```

When the user clicks on the **Run in a Thread** button, the following lines create an instance of the Thread class specifying the method it must execute in the new thread when it is started. In order to accomplish this, we use the ThreadStart delegate because we do not need to send parameters or other data to the thread for initialization purposes:

```
proThreadEncryption = new Thread(new
  ThreadStart(ThreadEncryptProcedure));
```

Once the thread is created, it does not start running the code in the specified `ThreadEncryptProcedure` until we call the `Start()` method. Since we do not want to send parameters to the procedure, we use the `Start()` method:

```
proThreadEncryption.Start();
```

This method tells the scheduler to start running the code in the new independent thread with an asynchronous execution. However, as it is executed asynchronously, we lose control over the time when the code in the thread begins running. It can be 100 milliseconds, 200 milliseconds, or 2 seconds.

In this case, we do not want to start an independent thread and lose control over its execution time, but we want to start it with a synchronous execution and wait, in the main thread, until it finishes. In order to do so, we call the `Join` method in the next line:

```
proThreadEncryption.Join();
```

It makes the new thread run the `ThreadEncryptProcedure` code. Once it finishes its execution, it returns control to the main thread and goes on with the next statement.

 It works as if we were calling a classic method, but in another thread.

Separating the code in a new thread using the `Thread` class is easy if we follow this simple code pattern.

Since it was joined with the main thread, the statements after the call to the `Join` method are executed as soon as the thread finishes its execution. These lines collect the encrypted strings generated in the `prlsEncryptedSMS` string list and append them, one per line, in the `txtEncryptedSMS` textbox:

```
foreach (string lsEncryptedText in prlsEncryptedSMS)
{
    txtEncryptedSMS.AppendText(lsEncryptedText +
    Environment.NewLine);
}
```

As the thread stores the results of its processing in a private variable, which is also accessible from the main thread, we can use it to show the results in the UI controls.

This is a very simple way to retrieve data from threads, leaving the results in a variable, accessible from both the main and the secondary threads.

This is one of the main advantages of threads over processes. It is very easy to share data between threads without much effort.

Sharing data between threads

So far, we have used the BackgroundWorker component and the Thread class to execute code in independent threads. The Thread class allows us to have great control over the thread while the BackgroundWorker component offers a very simple way to update the UI without using complicated delegates or callbacks. How can we combine this component and this class in an application to make it faster to complete while keeping the UI responsive?

If we want to work with a BackgroundWorker component to show some feedback or progress to the UI controls, while one or more threads created using the Thread class is running, we must find a way to share data between threads.

We made something like that in our last example. However, we must use some techniques in order to avoid confusion between the different ways in which this useful component, BackgroundWorker, and this flexible and powerful class, Thread, work.

 We can do it using the Thread class, but there is a BackgroundWorker component ready to help us. Thus, let's be pragmatic and use the best of both worlds.

How to do it

Now, we are going to make some changes to the application, adding a BackgroundWorker component to display progress. In order to accomplish that, we must share data between two threads:

1. Open the SMSEncryption project.

2. Add a label control (lblNumberOfSMSEncrypted). Set its Text property to 0. Add another label control, and set its Text property to Number of Messages Encrypted.

3. Add a BackgroundWorker component (bakShowEncryptedStrings) to create a new independent thread capable of talking to the UI, as we learned in the previous chapter. Declare the following variable in the MainWindow.xaml.cs file:

```
private BackgroundWorker bakShowEncryptedStrings = new
BackgroundWorker();
```

4. In order for the program to recognize the `BackgroundWorker` class, you will also need to add the following:

```
using System.ComponentModel;
```

5. Set the following properties of the `BackgroundWorker` component in the `MainWindow` constructor.

6. Add the following lines in the `MainWindow` class definition to declare three new private variables:

```
// The number of the last encrypted string
    private int priLastEncryptedString;
// The number of the last encrypted string shown in the UI
private int priLastEncryptedStringShown;
// The number of the previous last encrypted string shown in
the UI
private int priOldLastEncryptedStringShown;
```

7. Add the following line of code at the beginning of `ThreadEncryptProcedure`:

```
priLastEncryptedString = 0;
```

8. Add the following line of code after the line `prIsEncryptedSMS`. `Add(lsEncryptedText);` in `ThreadEncryptProcedure`:

```
priLastEncryptedString++;
```

9. Register the `DoWork` event handler in the `MainWindow` constructor for the `BackgroundWorker` component `bakShowEncryptedStrings`:

```
        //Register the DoWork  event handler.
        bakShowEncryptedStrings.DoWork +=
bakShowEncryptedStrings_DoWork;
```

10. Now, enter the following code in the `bakShowEncryptedStrings_DoWork` method:

```
// Initialize the last encrypted string shown
priLastEncryptedStringShown = 0;
// Initialize the last encrypted string shown before
priOldLastEncryptedStringShown = 0;
// The iteration
int i;
// The last encrypted string (saved locally to avoid changes
in the middle of the iteration)
int liLast;
```

```
// Wait until proThreadEncryption begins
while ((priLastEncryptedString < 1))
{
    // Sleep the thread for 10 milliseconds)
    Thread.Sleep(10);
}


while (proThreadEncryption.IsAlive || (priLastEncryptedString
        > priLastEncryptedStringShown))
{
    liLast = priLastEncryptedString;
    if (liLast != priLastEncryptedStringShown)
    {
        ((BackgroundWorker)sender).ReportProgress(liLast);
        priLastEncryptedStringShown = liLast;
    }
```

```
// Sleep the thread for 1 second (1000 milliseconds)
    Thread.Sleep(1000);
}
```

11. Register the `ProgressChanged` event handler in the `MainWindow` constructor for the `BackgroundWorker` component `bakShowEncryptedStrings`:

```
//Register the DoWork  event handler.

bakShowEncryptedStrings.ProgressChanged +=
bakShowEncryptedStrings_ProgressChanged;
```

12. Open the `ProgressChanged` event in the `BackgroundWorker` `bakShowEncryptedStrings`, and enter the following code:

```
// The iteration
int i;
// Show the number of SMS messages encrypted by the
concurrent proThreadEncryption thread.
lblNumberOfSMSEncrypted.Content =
priLastEncryptedString.ToString();
// Append each new string, from
priOldLastEncryptedStringShown to the received parameter in
e.ProgressPercentage - 1.
```

```
                    for (i = priOldLastEncryptedStringShown;
                        i < (int)e.ProgressPercentage; i++)
                    {
                        // Append the string to the txtEncryptedSMS
TextBox

                        txtEncryptedSMS.AppendText(prlsEncryptedSMS[i]
                        + Environment.NewLine);


                    }
                    // Update the old last encrypted string shown
                    priOldLastEncryptedStringShown =
priLastEncryptedStringShown;
```

13. Open the `Click` event in the `butRunInThread` button and enter the following code before the line `proThreadEncryption.Start();` (we must start the `BackgroundWorker` component before we start the encryption thread):

```
        // Start the BackgroundWorker with an asynchronous execution
        bakShowEncryptedStrings.RunWorkerAsync();
```

14. Next, we need to comment out the `proThreadEncryption.Join();` line because we do not want the main thread to wait on the encryption routine to finish. We will also comment out lines after this that display the encrypted text message once the encryption thread finishes. We will be doing this through the `BackgroundWorker` processing and will explain this in the following code snippet:

```
            // Join the independent thread to this thread to wait
until ThreadProc ends
            //proThreadEncryption.Join();

            // When the thread finishes running this is the next
line that is going to be executed
            // Copy the string List generated by the thread
            //foreach (string lsEncryptedText in prlsEncryptedSMS)
            //{
            //     Append a line with the Encrypted text
            //     txtEncryptedSMS.AppendText(lsEncryptedText +
            //       Environment.NewLine);
        //   }
```

15. Try running the application before commenting out these lines after the `Join` method but leave the `proThreadEncryption.Join();` command uncommented. You will create a race condition that may throw a null exception error for the variable, `prlsEncryptedSMS`. If the main thread tries to use this variable to display the encrypted text message before the encryption thread finishes the first line, then this variable will still be null. Since both the main thread and the encryption thread are running in parallel, we cannot ensure this will not happen.

16. Now, let's build and run the application with those lines commented out.

17. Enter or copy and paste a very long text (with more than 5,000 lines) in the textbox labeled `Original Messages`, and click on the **Run in a Thread** button. You will see the strings representing the messages encrypted appearing in the textbox labeled **Encrypted Messages** as the number of messages that are encrypted increases. The application will look something like the following screenshot:

How it works

Now, when the user clicks on the **Run in a Thread** button, the encryption runs in a new thread, but with an asynchronous execution because we no longer tell the main thread to wait on it with the `Thread.Join()` method. At the same time, the `BackgroundWorker` component creates a new thread to give some feedback to the UI and also runs asynchronously. Thus, we have two concurrent threads with an asynchronous execution, doing completely different tasks in parallel.

This is why we added the following lines:

```
bakShowEncryptedStrings.RunWorkerAsync();
proThreadEncryption.Start();
```

First, we start the `BackgroundWorker` thread, and then the encryption thread that is created with the `Thread` class.

With these examples, we have learned and seen the differences between executing a thread in a synchronous and an asynchronous way. We must master this in order to have complete control over many concurrent threads.

We are using the `BackgroundWorker` component in order to give some feedback to the UI controls. In order to do so, the encryption thread must share data with the `BackgroundWorker` thread.

We use the same technique that we used in the previous example. However, this time, our application is operating concurrently. While the encryption thread is adding encrypted strings to the `prlsEncryptedSMS` string list, the `BackgroundWorker` thread looks at the number of the last encrypted string and calls the `ReportProgress` method, sending it as a parameter.

> Remember that too many calls to the `ReportProgress` method can generate a stack overflow exception. Because this method runs code that upgrades the textbox adding lines, it takes a lot more time than encrypting. If we have 100,000 messages to encrypt, and we make 100,000 calls to the `ReportProgress` method; it is highly probable that a stack overflow will be generated. The code in this method runs in the main thread, and for this reason, we must sacrifice some UI feedback to achieve a better overall performance and avoid exceptions.

The code in the `DoWork` and the `ReportProgress` event handlers is a little complex to account for this and not send updates for every single line encrypted.

Now, we define three new private variables:

```
private int priLastEncryptedString;
private int priLastEncryptedStringShown;
private int priOldLastEncryptedStringShown;
```

The encryption thread initializes `priLastEncryptedString` and then increments its value each time it adds an encrypted string to the `prlsEncryptedSMS` string list. This value is useful for the `BackgroundWorker` thread.

The code executed in the `DoWork` event handler by the `BackgroundWorker` thread concurrently with the encryption thread initializes `priLastEncryptedStringShown` and `priOldLastEncryptedStringShown`.

Then, it waits until the encryption thread has some results. This is necessary because both the threads are launched asynchronously, at nearly the same time. It is a `while` loop, but with a call to the `Thread.Sleep` method, with 10 milliseconds of inactivity for the thread:

```
while ((priLastEncryptedString < 1))
{
    Thread.Sleep(10);
}
```

Since the `priLastEncryptedString` variable has a value less than 1, the encryption thread has not added any value yet.

The `Thread.Sleep` method suspends the current thread (the thread in the actual context) for a specified time in milliseconds (0.001 seconds). As it suspends the thread execution, it does not consume CPU cycles. Hence, it does not waste processing power.

> Never use loops without instructions to wait for some time in a thread, because you will be wasting processing power. Instead, use the `Thread.Sleep` method when you have to pause a thread.

When the encryption thread finishes encrypting the first string, adding it to the encrypted string list, and incrementing the value of `priLastEncryptedString`, the `BackgroundWorker` thread will move on to the next part of the code in the `DoWork` event handler method. Now, it will enter in the other loop:

```
while (proThreadEncryption.IsAlive || (priLastEncryptedString
        > priLastEncryptedStringShown))
{
    liLast = priLastEncryptedString;
    if (liLast != priLastEncryptedStringShown)
    {
        ((BackgroundWorker)sender).ReportProgress(liLast);
        priLastEncryptedStringShown = liLast;
    }
    Thread.Sleep(2000);
}
```

The loop (and the `DoWork` thread) will go on running while the encryption thread is running, or while there are encrypted strings to be shown. We know when the `proThreadEncryption` thread is not running, or is not calling its `IsAlive` method. The `IsAlive` method returns either `true` or `false`.

The first line in the loop saves the value of `priLastEncryptedString` in `liLast`. This is necessary because the value is changing concurrently on another thread (the encryption thread) — we are not alone (the joys of multithreaded logic!). We must save the value to work with the captured value in the rest of the comparisons and assignments. We do not want to work with a moving target within one iteration of the loop.

If the last encrypted string is not the last string shown, we use the `sender` parameter typecast to a `BackgroundWorker` component to call the `ReportProgress` method with the last string shown as a parameter.

Once the `ReportProgress` method returns with an asynchronous event triggered to update the UI, we save the last string shown and make the thread suspend its execution for 1 second (1,000 milliseconds). This is necessary in order to avoid a probable stack overflow. Because the execution of the `DoWork` code is faster than the code programmed in the `ProgressChanged` event handler, we must give some time to the UI controls to get updated.

When we call the `Thread.Sleep` method, the current thread suspends its execution for a specified time, though the other threads keep running. That is the reason why the counter shows big steps when we run the application with several text lines. The encryption thread works without suspensions.

Thus, the `BackgroundWorker` component helps the `Thread` class to update the UI controls. The `ProgressChanged` event handler does the rest of the job.

First, it updates the number of SMS messages encrypted with the line of code:

```
lblNumberOfSMSEncrypted.Content = priLastEncryptedString.ToString();
```

It then casts the `e.ProgressPercentage` property received as a parameter to an integer in order to obtain the last encrypted string, instead of a progress percentage.

Then, it appends each new string with a loop from `priOldLastEncryptedStringShown` (the previous last encrypted string shown) to the last encrypted string received (in the `e.ProgressPercentage` property). We access the `prlsEncryptedSMS` string list in an element number that the encryption thread is not modifying (because it is already encrypted). Therefore, we can append the string to the textbox without problems:

```
for (i = priOldLastEncryptedStringShown; i < (int)
    e.ProgressPercentage; i++)
{
    txtEncryptedSMS.AppendText(prlsEncryptedSMS[i]
    + Environment.NewLine);
}
```

Finally, the string previous to the last encrypted string is now the last encrypted string shown:

```
priOldLastEncryptedStringShown = priLastEncryptedStringShown;
```

By using a `BackgroundWorker` component with some threads created using the `Thread` class, we can easily give feedback to the UI and achieve better performance with a responsive application.

At this point, we should mention that the `BackgroundWorker` component is a little like the black sheep of the family. In the .NET framework, with the advent of the `Thread` class and now the Task Parallel Library and `Async` methods (to be covered later in the book), some .NET developers consider use of `BackgroundWorker` a little passé. While it might not be the latest cool feature of .NET, it is still a very easy-to-use, helpful, and powerful component. According to me all multithreaded options in .NET have their place and the `BackgroundWorker` component is still relevant.

When we call the `Start` method, the thread is sent to the scheduler for execution. As mentioned earlier, it does not mean an immediate execution.

When we call the `Start` method for many threads, one after the other, or when combined with a `BackgroundWorker` thread as in our example, we are not sure which one is going to run faster. We cannot assume one of them will reach some statement first, because the execution speed will depend upon the processor or the core it is assigned to and its capabilities. If it needs more context switches than the other thread, it will take longer to reach the same statement.

This is one of the most important issues with concurrency. It all depends on something that we do not know how to predict sometimes. Therefore, we must consider every possible situation the code that will be executed concurrently might experience.

When we call the `Join` method, the thread is attached to the thread that calls the `Join` method and it will not execute anything else until the thread method finishes its execution. This is one of the most difficult things to achieve for programmers used to traditional linear code.

Passing parameters to threads

We have used the `BackgroundWorker` component combined with the `Thread` class to provide fast execution and UI feedback. Now, we will combine multiple `Thread` class instances with many `BackgroundWorker` components to create an application that runs as fast as possible on modern computer architectures. In fact, it will inspect the computer it is running on and create an encryption thread for each processing core the computer has. This will maximize the performance without creating extra threads that will not further improve performance.

We will work with dynamic lists and the `Environment.ProcessorCount` property to create threads on the fly according to the number of cores on the machine. However, we need some technique to distribute the SMS messages that must be encrypted to the many encrypting threads. At the same time, we must provide feedback through many `BackgroundWorker` components. It sounds complex, and it is indeed complex.

To achieve this goal, we must pass specific parameters to the common procedure that the many threads will run. We want to reuse the procedure because we want it to be dynamically organized according to the number of available cores at runtime.

How to do it

Now, we are going to make some big changes to the application, modifying variables to be lists, or lists of lists, so they can be accessed by multiple threads created dynamically. In order to accomplish that, we must share data between the many threads:

1. Open the `SMSEncryption` project.

2. Add the following line in the `MainWindow` class definition to declare a new private variable that will tell us the number of cores on the machine:

   ```
   // The number of processors or cores available in the computer
   for this application
   private int priProcessorCount = Environment.ProcessorCount;
   ```

3. Change the definition for the following private variables in the `MainWindow` class definition to make them lists:

   ```
   // The string list with SMS messages encrypted (output)
   private List<List<string>> prlsEncryptedSMS;
   // The number of the last encrypted string
   private List<int> priLastEncryptedString;
   ```

4. Add the following line in the `MainWindow` class definition to declare a new private variable that will hold the list of the `Thread` class instances:

   ```
   // The threads list
   private List<Thread> prloThreadList;
   ```

5. The variables required to grow dynamically, according to the number of cores found in the computer, have been added to the application.

One potential problem of manually assigning a value greater than the number of available cores to the `priProcessorCount` variable is that the increasing context switches needed by the operating system scheduler will degrade performance. Therefore, you must be wary of wrong fine-tuning.

Now, let's change the different methods to allow multiple threads to encrypt the strings as fast as possible.

It is going to be easier rewriting these than making the changes, as we are replacing single variables by lists. In order to accomplish this, we must create a thread with a parameter indicating its number:

1. Open the `SMSEncryption` project.

2. Replace the definition for `ThreadEncryptProcedure` with the following (now it receives a parameter):

    ```
    private void ThreadEncryptProcedure(object poThreadParameter)
    ```

3. Change the text in the labels from `Encrypted Message` to `Encrypted Message(by thread 1)` and `Number of Messages Encrypted` to `Number of Messages Encrypted(by thread 1)`.

4. Replace the code in the `ThreadEncryptProcedure` procedure with the following:

    ```
    string lsEncryptedText;
    // Retrieve the thread number received in object
       poThreadParameter
    int liThreadNumber = (int) poThreadParameter;
    // ThreadNumber + 1
    int liStringNumber;

    // Create a new string list for the prlsSMSToEncrypt
       corresponding to the thread
    prlsEncryptedSMS[liThreadNumber] = new List<string>
     ((prlsSMSToEncrypt.Count / priProcessorCount));
    priLastEncryptedString[liThreadNumber] = 0;

    liStringNumber = 0;
    int i;
    // steps the thread number
    string lsText;
    // Iterate through each string in the prlsSMSToEncrypt string
       list stepping by priProcessorCount
    // To distribute the work among each concurrent thread
    ```

```
for (i = liThreadNumber; i < prlsSMSToEncrypt.Count; i +=
    priProcessorCount)
{

    lsText = prlsSMSToEncrypt[i];
    lsEncryptedText = Encrypt(lsText);
    // Append a string with the Encrypted text
    prlsEncryptedSMS[liThreadNumber].Add(lsEncryptedText);

    priLastEncryptedString[liThreadNumber]++;
    liStringNumber++;
}
```

5. Replace the code where the threads were initialized and started
   in the `Click` event handler in the `butRunInThread` button, after the
   line `prlsSMSToEncrypt.AddRange(txtOriginalSMS.Lines);`, with
   the following:

```
// Thread number
int liThreadNumber;
// Create the thread list and string lists
prloThreadList = new List<Thread>(priProcessorCount);
prlsEncryptedSMS = new List<List<string>>(priProcessorCount);
priLastEncryptedString = new List<int>(priProcessorCount);

// Initialize the threads
for (liThreadNumber = 0; liThreadNumber < priProcessorCount;
    liThreadNumber++)
{
    // Just to occupy the number
    prlsEncryptedSMS.Add(new List<string>());
    // Just to occupy the number
    priLastEncryptedString.Add(0);
    // Add the new thread, with a parameterized start (to
allow
        parameters)
    prloThreadList.Add(new Thread(new ParameterizedThreadStart
                    (ThreadEncryptProcedure)));
}

// Now, start the threads
for (liThreadNumber = 0; liThreadNumber < priProcessorCount;
    liThreadNumber++)
{

    prloThreadList[liThreadNumber].Start(liThreadNumber);
}

// Start the BackgroundWorker with an asynchronous execution
bakShowEncryptedStrings.RunWorkerAsync();
```

6. Open the `DoWork` event in the `BackgroundWorker` `bakShowEncryptedStrings` and make the following code replacements to the existing code:

   ° Replace `priLastEncryptedString` with `priLastEncryptedString[0]`

   ° Replace `proThreadEncryption` with `prloThreadList[0]`

7. Open the `ProgressChanged` event in the `BackgroundWorker` `bakShowEncryptedStrings` and make the following code replacements to the existing code:

   ° Replace `priLastEncryptedString` with `priLastEncryptedString[0]`

   ° Replace `prlsEncryptedSMS[i]` with `prlsEncryptedSMS[0][i]`

8. Build and run the application.

9. Enter or copy and paste a very long text (with more than 20,000 lines) in the textbox labeled **Original Messages** and click on the **Run in a Thread** button. You will see the strings representing the messages encrypted by thread 1 appearing in the textbox labeled **Encrypted Messages (by thread 1)**, while the number of messages encrypted by thread 1 increases. In this example, there were 119 lines in the text message with a `ProcessorCount` of 4:

How it works

The code has become more complex. However, running this application in a quad-core computer improves the performance by almost a factor of four. We do not realize the full 4x performance gain because of the overhead of multithreading that we discussed in *Chapter 1, Understanding Multiprocessing and Multiple Cores*.

Now, when the user clicks on the **Run in a Thread** button, the encryption runs in as many threads as there are available cores in the computer with an asynchronous execution. At the same time, the BackgroundWorker component starts running concurrently displaying the results just for the first thread.

The private string list that works as an input for the many threads is the same as in the previous examples (prlsSMSToEncrypt), but is accessed in a different way by each thread.

The private string list that works as an output (prlsEncryptedSMS) is now a list of string lists. Thus, each thread can work in its own output.

```
private List<List<string>> prlsEncryptedSMS;
```

There is a new thread list that will be aligned with the value in the priProcessorCount variable:

```
private List<Thread> prloThreadList;
```

This replaces the line that declared the proThreadEncryption variable with the Thread type.

When the user clicks on the **Run in a Thread** button, the following lines create an instance of the Thread class specifying the method it must execute in the new thread when started. In order to accomplish this, we use the ParameterizedThreadStart delegate because we need to send a parameter with the number of threads to identify each thread in the method it runs. This is an important change to note. Earlier, we just called the ThreadStart method. This new method allows us to start a thread that has a delegate method that takes a parameter:

```
for (liThreadNumber = 0; liThreadNumber < priProcessorCount;
    liThreadNumber++)
{
    prlsEncryptedSMS.Add(new List<string>());
    priLastEncryptedString.Add(0);
    prloThreadList.Add(new Thread(new ParameterizedThreadStart
                    (ThreadEncryptProcedure)));
}
```

Once each thread is created, it does not start running the code in the specified ThreadEncryptProcedure procedure until we call the Start method. But first we initialize the threads, and then we call the Start method for each one. We want to send a parameter (the thread number) to the method. Therefore, we use the Start method with one parameter. Take a moment to make sure you understand how these methods operate.

```
for (liThreadNumber = 0; liThreadNumber < priProcessorCount;
liThreadNumber++)
{
    prloThreadList[liThreadNumber].Start(liThreadNumber);
}
```

This method tells the scheduler to start running the code in the new threads (one per available core). Then, we want to run the BackgroundWorker thread concurrently to report the UI with feedback from the first created thread (thread number 0):

```
bakShowEncryptedStrings.RunWorkerAsync();
```

In a dual-core or dual-processor computer, we will have two encrypting threads and one BackgroundWorker thread. In a quad-core computer, we will have four encrypting threads and one BackgroundWorker thread.

It makes the new threads run the ThreadEncryptProcedure method code (with the thread number as a parameter), and when they finish their execution, it returns the control to the main thread and goes on with the next statement.

Separating the code into many concurrent threads using the Thread class and sending parameters to them is easy if we follow this simple code pattern and we have a good knowledge of working with lists or dynamic arrays.

We did not want to use many methods, one for each new thread. We wanted to share the same method and differentiate among the threads using a parameter with a number that identifies each.

There are many ways to distribute the work in many concurrent threads working on the same algorithm, taking the same input and producing almost the same output. We used one of them, and we will learn more in the following chapters using both the Thread and Task classes and the Parallel library.

The parameter that is sent when calling the Start method for the thread instance is received in the object parameter, poThreadParameter, as shown in the following declaration:

```
private void ThreadEncryptProcedure(object poThreadParameter)
```

Therefore, we must use typecasting to convert it to an integer:

```
int liThreadNumber = (int) poThreadParameter;
```

With the thread number and the total number of threads (the value in the priProcessorCount variable) that will be sharing the work to be done, we can easily distribute the work of a list to be processed (encrypted). A simple way to do this is to make each thread take the input it must process and leave the rest untouched.

This is done in the iteration, which goes through the string list from the thread number (hence, each thread will begin in a different number) to the total number of strings to encrypt, stepping up the value in the priProcessorCount variable (the total number of threads):

```
for (i = liThreadNumber; i < prlsSMSToEncrypt.Count;
        i += priProcessorCount)
```

For example, let's suppose that there are four threads. They will work on the following strings from the list:

- Thread #1: 0; 4; 8; 12; 16; 20; …
- Thread #2: 1; 5; 9; 13; 17; 21; …
- Thread #3: 2; 6; 10; 14; 18; 22; …
- Thread #4: 3; 7; 11; 15; 19; 23; …

Here, we will consider them running concurrently.

The string list capacity for prlsEncryptedSMS[liThreadNumber] is determined by the total number of strings to be encrypted divided by the total number of threads (the value in the priProcessorCount variable):

```
prlsEncryptedSMS[liThreadNumber] = new List<string>((
        prlsSMSToEncrypt.Count / priProcessorCount));
```

It can be wrong by 1, but it does not matter in this case (reserving capacity is better), because the thread increments a variable with the number of processed strings:

```
priLastEncryptedString[liThreadNumber]++;
```

The code in the BackgroundWorker component was modified to show only the progress of the first thread. This can be changed or additional BackgroundWorker components added to display the progress of all encryption threads.

Have a go hero – concurrent UI feedback

As mentioned earlier, there is still some work to be done. The FBI wants to see all the code being encrypted and not just the work done by the first thread. Remember, they have a computer with 16 quad-core microprocessors (64 cores).

Using everything we have learned, develop a new version of this application that shows the progress for each dynamically created thread. Show the progress in numbers, in a progress bar, and in textboxes (adding the encrypted SMS messages). For all these controls, as many concurrent threads as the number of available cores are running in the application.

Then, use the control procedures of the Thread class instances we learned in order to create a final collection procedure that takes the results of all the running threads and shows the complete list of encrypted messages.

Enhance the application changing the string lists with instances of a new class, using the following information:

- Caller ID
- Destination number
- SMS message

Encrypt all the fields and compute the total number of characters sent.

Show the incoming and outgoing SMS messages with their information in a grid with many columns, instead of using textboxes.

Switch off the webcam. The FBI is looking for you for a new mission!

Summary

We learned a lot in this chapter about working with threads and the Thread class. We learned how to create threads, coordinate them synchronously and asynchronously, and pass parameters to them.

In this chapter, we learned about the following:

- Developing applications that are able to provide greater control over multiple running threads, created using the Thread class
- Programming the code to be executed by the Thread class instance when started
- Creating independent and flexible threads using the powerful Thread class

- Starting, controlling, and coordinating multiple threads with great flexibility
- Sending parameters and retrieving data from independently running threads
- Sharing data between many threads
- Combining asynchronous and synchronous execution
- Matching the number of available cores with the number of concurrent threads to take full advantage of parallel processing capabilities in modern computers

In the next chapter, we will take an even deeper dive into the Thread class.

4

Advanced Thread Processing

In this chapter, we will continue to learn about the Thread class and thread processing. In the previous chapter, we began discussing the Thread class and how to create and use threads. Now that we have begun learning about the Thread class, in this chapter we will take the discussion to the next level. We'll study new ways to keep control over concurrent threads and will continue to improve our parallel programming capabilities working with more challenging problems to solve. After following the instructions in this chapter, we will be able to:

- Break down a problem into pieces that can be run concurrently
- Create highly independent blocks of code to run in multiple threads avoiding many concurrency problems
- Use flags in multiple threads for coordination
- Use techniques to have complete control over asynchronous and synchronous execution of threads
- Use techniques to use multithreading in non-thread-safe components
- Perform error handling in a multithreaded application

Pipelining

Pipelining is a common design pattern used in multithreaded applications. In *Chapter 9, Pipeline and Producer-consumer Design Patterns*, we will cover this in detail. But I wanted to briefly introduce it here, because we will use it in the examples in this chapter. Pipelining is a technique to solve a problem using concurrency. First, you divide the problem into parts that have to be executed in sequence with parts that can be executed in parallel. Then you implement the parallel parts using threads or tasks and run them concurrently to improve performance instead of running all of the functionality in sequence.

So far, we have worked with the BackgroundWorker component and the Thread class to create multithreaded applications. Parallel programming allowed us to achieve incredible performance enhancements and better UI feedback. How can we use threading and the Thread class to divide image-processing algorithms into many concurrent blocks of code? In this design pattern, we will take a problem, divide it into multiple pieces that we can tackle concurrently, and then assemble the pieces in the end to a final result.

In *Chapter 9, Pipeline and Producer-consumer Design Patterns*, we will learn different common design patterns for tackling common problems in a multithreaded approach. But without going into too much detail, in this chapter, we will perform a simple form of pipelining to accomplish our task:

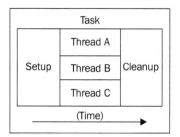

C# offers many techniques for working with images and bitmaps. However, many of them are not thread-safe. We cannot run many concurrent threads changing pixels in the same instance of the Bitmap (System.Drawing.Bitmap) class. Nevertheless, as we learned in the previous chapters, in order to apply parallel algorithms, we can avoid the problems instead of finding difficult solutions to them by using different design patterns such as **pipelining**. We can split the original bitmap into a number of completely independent bitmaps. Each thread can work with its independent bitmap instance safely. We can develop an algorithm that performs image manipulation of bitmap pixels and then, with great performance improvements over the single-threaded one, perform this algorithm in parallel on many bitmaps. Besides, we can also add code to pause and then restart the threads. The performance results will depend upon the number of cores or processors available in the computer (which we discussed in *Chapter 1, Understanding Multiprocessing and Multiple Cores*) in which we run the application.

By using the Thread class and the pipelining design pattern, we can achieve incredible performance improvements, an impressive user experience, and great scalability with reasonable programming efforts. The application we will build will be scalable to any size bitmap image and will be able to increase performance automatically as more core processors are added to the hardware without any coding changes!

Explaining pipelining using an image processing application

For our example in this chapter, we will use a Windows Forms application to perform image processing. We can do this in a **Windows Presentation Foundation (WPF)** application, but I find that doing bitmap and pixel-level manipulation is more straightforward in the GDI-based System.Drawing library than the WPF-based System, Windows Media library. This same application can be redone using the BitmapImage and CroppedBitmap classes using the same core logic.

Image processing on large image files is a good candidate for a multithreaded solution because you can break the image into pieces and process each piece concurrently and then reassemble the pieces. In this example, we will take a bitmap image from NASA, break it into smaller bitmap files, search each bitmap for "old star", and then reassemble the bitmaps back into one large bitmap image file.

You will use your parallel programming skills to develop an application that has to detect the older stars from huge infrared portraits obtained by NASA's Spitzer Space Telescope. In the following screenshot, you can see a wispy star-forming region, called **W5**:

Image by NASA/JPL-Caltech/Harvard-Smithsonian CfA

In this portrait, the oldest stars can be seen as blue dots, especially in the center of the two hollow cavities. The white knotty areas are where the youngest stars are forming.

This image contains some of the best evidence yet for the triggered star formation theory. Scientists analyzing the photo have been able to show that the ages of the stars become progressively and systematically younger with distance from the center of the cavities.

You have to work on a very fast and efficient algorithm for detection of old stars, capable of changing the pixel colors of the old stars in the huge image to make them more visible to the scientists. They want you to use a fine-tuned, multithreading application that is capable of working with as many threads as the number of cores available in the computer where the star detection algorithm is being executed.

How to do it

To do this, we are going to build a new C# application and put the program logic into methods to detect old stars in any bitmap and prepare the bitmap input for many threads:

1. Create a new C# project using the Windows Application template in Visual Studio. Use `OldStarsFinder` as the project's name.

2. Add the following lines of code at the beginning of the form class definition (as we are going to use the `System.Threading.Thread` and `System.Drawing.Imaging` classes):

   ```
   using System.Threading;
   using System.Drawing.Imaging;
   ```

3. Add the following lines in the form class definition to declare three new private variables:

   ```
   // The number of processors or cores available in the computer for
   this application
   private int priProcessorCount = Environment.ProcessorCount;
   // The bitmaps list
   private List<Bitmap> prloBitmapList;
   // The long list with the old stars count
   private List<long> prliOldStarsCount;
   ```

4. Add the following function, `CropBitmap`. It will crop the bitmap received as a parameter and return the portion of the original defined by the `Rectangle` instance, `proRectangle`. This will allow us to split up any large image into a set of smaller images. The number in the set will correspond to the number of cores in the machine the application is running. This way we can maximize performance by using every core simultaneously to process the large image:

```
private Bitmap CropBitmap(Bitmap proBitmap, Rectangle
                          proRectangle)

{
// Create a new bitmap copying the portion of the original
          defined by proRectangle and keeping its PixelFormat
Bitmap loCroppedBitmap = proBitmap.Clone(proRectangle,
                          proBitmap.PixelFormat);
// Return the cropped bitmap
return loCroppedBitmap;
}
```

5. Add the following function, `IsOldStar`. It will compare the pixel hue, saturation, and brightness to determine if their levels correspond to the typical color range offered by an old star in the infrared portraits:

```
public bool IsOldStar(Color poPixelColor)
{
// Hue between 150 and 258
// Saturation more than 0.10
// Brightness more than 0.90
return ((poPixelColor.GetHue() >= 150) &&
            (poPixelColor.GetHue() <= 258) &&
            (poPixelColor.GetSaturation() >= 0.10) &&
            (poPixelColor.GetBrightness() <= 0.90));

}
```

6. Add the following procedure, `ThreadOldStarsFinder`. It will iterate through each pixel in the corresponding bitmap for the thread that launches it and count the old stars:

```
private void ThreadOldStarsFinder(object poThreadParameter)
{
// Retrieve the thread number received in object
          poThreadParameter
int liThreadNumber = (int)poThreadParameter;
// The pixel matrix (bitmap) row number (Y)
int liRow;
// The pixel matrix (bitmap) col number (X)
int liCol;
// The pixel color
```

```
Color loPixelColor;
// Get my bitmap part from the bitmap list
Bitmap loBitmap = prloBitmapList[liThreadNumber];

// Reset my old stars counter
prliOldStarsCount[liThreadNumber] = 0;
// Iterate through each pixel matrix (bitmap) row
for (liRow = 0; liRow < loBitmap.Height; liRow++)
{
// Iterate through each pixel matrix (bitmap) cols
for (liCol = 0; liCol < loBitmap.Width; liCol++)
{
// Get the pixel color for liCol and liRow
loPixelColor = loBitmap.GetPixel(liCol, liRow);
if (IsOldStar(loPixelColor))
{
// The color range corresponds to an old star
// Change its color to a pure blue
loBitmap.SetPixel(liCol, liRow, Color.Blue);
// Increase the old stars counter
prliOldStarsCount[liThreadNumber]++;
}
}
}
}
```

How it works

The code required to find and count the potential old stars in any large bitmap portrait is now held in named functions and procedures, already prepared for dynamically created concurrent threads. We have laid the groundwork to implement this function in a Pipeline design pattern.

Why do we have to create a CropBitmap function? That is because we cannot access a single Bitmap instance pixel matrix from many different concurrent threads. If we do so, we will get an InvalidOperationException, as GDI+ is not prepared for multithreaded access.

We must split the original `Bitmap` into as many independent portions as the number of concurrent threads that will be working on it. The `CropBitmap` function will allow us to obtain a specific portion of a `Bitmap` instance and generate a list of new `Bitmap` instances (`prloBitmapList`).

As we have learned so far, there are many problems related to multithreaded applications and parallel algorithms. Since there are many threads running concurrently, we must be very careful when changing the values of variables in different threads. The best solution to such concurrency problems is *avoiding them* or preventing them via **synchronization mechanisms**. However, synchronization mechanisms have to be used very carefully, because they can decrease performance and generate too many context switches. Also, using them can introduce potential bugs that can be very difficult to debug.

How can we avoid the concurrency problems? It is very simple. As much as possible, we have to make each thread independent of the other concurrent threads working in the same global portion of resources. As we will see in later chapters, the Task Parallel Library is convenient for defining tasks and then running the tasks in parallel. In this case, the processing of each bitmap can be a task.

Splitting the original bitmap using the simple `CropBitmap` function avoids many conflicts related to concurrency that would have otherwise been very complex to troubleshoot. As each thread is going to work with its own bitmap, we are avoiding a potentially dangerous problem. This is one of the keys to developing multithreaded applications – properly segmenting work into pieces that can run in parallel. Dividing the bitmap image is a perfect example.

Another potential problem is counting the total number of old stars detected in the huge infrared bitmap portrait. If we used a shared member variable, we might have locking problems. If we have many threads concurrently changing the same variable value (at the same time), we will have to lock that variable each time its value is incremented. Locking a variable implies context switches and hence reduced performance. For this reason, we use the `long` list `prliOldStarsCount`. There is one counter for each thread, and we will obtain the total sum adding the n long values (`prliOldStarsCount`) to a new variable (where n is the number of star finder threads).

This way, we avoid locks as each thread has its own independent counter and we achieve a better performance compared to a solution that would use the confusing and complex locks.

In order to process an image in many concurrent threads, we must divide it into as many independent portions as the number of threads that will be running. As we have seen earlier, the CropBitmap function offers this utility.

This change in the image processing algorithm has its costs, and is not free. In this case, we will be counting stars on a per-pixel basis. However, when we must apply other more complex algorithms, we must consider many important additional changes to the basic code. We will continue with this topic later in this chapter.

Once each image part is processed, we must collect the results and recompose the original image with the changes made to its pixels.

Understanding the pixels' color compositions

The infrared bitmap portrait does not have an exact blue (red = 0, green = 0, and blue = 255) color for an old star. There is a complex technique used to determine a star's age according to color ranges. This is easy to understand for human beings, but difficult for computers.

However, it is simple to generate an algorithm obtaining the following three components of a Color (System.Drawing.Color) instance:

- **Hue**: This is obtained by the GetHue() method
- **Saturation**: This is obtained by the GetSaturation() method (from 0.01 to 1.00)
- **Brightness**: This is obtained by the GetBrightness() method (from 0.01 to 1.00)

Using these color components, we can apply the following rules to determine whether a pixel in the infrared bitmap portrait corresponds to a potential old star or not:

- Hue is between 150 and 258
- Saturation is more than 10% (0.10)
- Brightness is more than 90% (0.90)

It is easier to work with hue, saturation, and brightness values than with red, green, and blue values in order to determine an old star.

The `IsOldStar` function receives a `Color` instance as a parameter and returns the results of applying the aforementioned rules to its hue, saturation, and brightness, as shown in the following lines of code:

```
return ((poPixelColor.GetHue() >= 150)
    && (poPixelColor.GetHue() <= 258)
    && (poPixelColor.GetSaturation() >= 0.10)
    && (poPixelColor.GetBrightness() <= 0.90));
```

This function is called for each pixel in the infrared bitmap portrait, and it returns a `bool` value.

Pausing and restarting threads

It is important in a lot of cases to coordinate and wait on threads. Take, for example, a pipelining design. Once we start a group of concurrent threads, we then need to wait on them all to finish, collate their results, and move onto the nonconcurrent section. We need to know when threads finish and what their results are, so we can determine how to proceed.

There are several ways to coordinate and wait between threads. In the following example, we will show how you can check to see if a thread is still alive and processing and then wait on all of the threads to complete their bitmap processing work before we continue the rest of the application and reassemble the bitmap pieces.

In this example, we will use the `IsAlive` method to check the thread and then pause the main thread with the `Sleep` method for a period of time before checking again. This is a common design pattern to coordinate work between threads and monitor threads to know when they are finished.

How to do it

Now, we are going to create the UI and make some changes to create multiple threads dynamically to process each portion of a bitmap. In order to accomplish this, we must share data between the various threads, as we learned in the previous chapters. Perform the following steps:

1. Stay in the project, `OldStarsFinder`.

2. Open Windows Form, `Form1` (`frmStarsFinder`), in the form designer; add the following controls and align them as shown in the following screenshot:

The following are the controls:

- One picture box (`picStarsBitmap`) showing one of the infrared portraits obtained by NASA's Spitzer Space Telescope (you can find many of them at `www.nasa.gov` or `http://www.nasa.gov/multimedia/imagegallery/`), with its `SizeMode` property set to `StretchImage`.

○ One button showing a star and its `Text` property set to `Find old star` (`butFindOldStars`). This button will start multiple old stars finder threads.

3. Add the following lines in the form's class definition to declare two new private variables:

```
// The threads list
private List<Thread> prloThreadList;
// The original huge infrared bitmap portrait
Bitmap proOriginalBitmap;
```

4. Add the following procedure, `WaitForThreadsToDie`. It will make the main thread sleep in order to wait until the many concurrent threads finish their work:

```
private void WaitForThreadsToDie()
{
    // A bool flag
    bool lbContinue = true;
    int liDeadThreads = 0;
    int liThreadNumber;
    while (lbContinue)
    {
        for (liThreadNumber = 0; liThreadNumber
            < priProcessorCount; liThreadNumber++)
        {
            if (prloThreadList[liThreadNumber].IsAlive)
            {
                // One of the threads is still alive,
                // exit the for loop and sleep 100
                // milliseconds
                break;
            }
            else
            {
                // Increase the dead threads count
                liDeadThreads++;
            }
        }
        if (liDeadThreads == priProcessorCount)
        {
            // All the threads are dead, exit the while
            // loop
            break;
        }
```

```
            Thread.Sleep(100);
            liDeadThreads = 0;
        }
    }
```

5. Add the following procedure, ShowBitmapWithOldStars. It will rebuild the bitmap adding each previously separated portion:

```
private void ShowBitmapWithOldStars()
{
    int liThreadNumber;
    // Each bitmap portion
    Bitmap loBitmap;
    // The starting row in each iteration
    int liStartRow = 0;

    // Calculate each bitmap's height
    int liEachBitmapHeight = ((int)(proOriginalBitmap.Height /
priProcessorCount)) + 1;

    // Create a new bitmap with the whole width and
    // height
    loBitmap = new Bitmap(proOriginalBitmap.Width,
                          proOriginalBitmap.Height);
    Graphics g = Graphics.FromImage((Image)loBitmap);
    g.InterpolationMode = System.Drawing.Drawing2D.
                          InterpolationMode.
HighQualityBicubic;

    for (liThreadNumber = 0; liThreadNumber <
priProcessorCount; liThreadNumber++)
    {
        // Draw each portion in its corresponding
        // absolute starting row
        g.DrawImage(prloBitmapList[liThreadNumber], 0,
                    liStartRow);
        // Increase the starting row
        liStartRow += liEachBitmapHeight;
    }
    // Show the bitmap in the PictureBox picStarsBitmap
    picStarsBitmap.Image = loBitmap;

    g.Dispose();
}
```

6. Open the `Click` event in the button, `butFindOldStars`, and enter the
    following code:

```
proOriginalBitmap = new Bitmap(picStarsBitmap.Image);

// Thread number
int liThreadNumber;
// Create the thread list; the long list and the bitmap list
prloThreadList = new List<Thread>(priProcessorCount);
prliOldStarsCount = new List<long>(priProcessorCount);
prloBitmapList = new List<Bitmap>(priProcessorCount);

int liStartRow = 0;

int liEachBitmapHeight = ((int)(proOriginalBitmap.Height /
priProcessorCount)) + 1;

int liHeightToAdd = proOriginalBitmap.Height;
Bitmap loBitmap;

// Initialize the threads
for (liThreadNumber = 0; liThreadNumber < priProcessorCount;
liThreadNumber++)
    {
        // Just to occupy the number
        prliOldStarsCount.Add(0);

        if (liEachBitmapHeight > liHeightToAdd)
        {
            // The last bitmap height perhaps is less than the
other bitmaps height
            liEachBitmapHeight = liHeightToAdd;
        }

        loBitmap = CropBitmap(proOriginalBitmap, new Rectangle(0,
liStartRow, proOriginalBitmap.Width,
            liEachBitmapHeight));
        liHeightToAdd -= liEachBitmapHeight;
        liStartRow += liEachBitmapHeight;
        prloBitmapList.Add(loBitmap);

        // Add the new thread, with a parameterized start
        // (to allow parameters)
        prloThreadList.Add(new Thread(new ParameterizedThreadStart
(ThreadOldStarsFinder)));
```

```
    }

    // Now, start the threads
    for (liThreadNumber = 0; liThreadNumber < priProcessorCount;
liThreadNumber++)
    {
        prloThreadList[liThreadNumber].Start(liThreadNumber);
    }

    WaitForThreadsToDie();

    ShowBitmapWithOldStars();
```

7. Build and run the application.

8. Click on the **Old Star Finder** button. After a few seconds (depending on the parallel processing capabilities of the computer) in the W5 wispy star-forming region, a huge infrared portrait will be shown with its probable old stars in pure blue, as shown in the following screenshot:

How it works

When the user clicks on the **Old Star Finder** button, the process executes in the following manner:

1. The original image is divided into many independent bitmaps. Each portion will be assigned to a different thread.

2. Many threads are created and then started (executed asynchronously) with a parameter so that they know which bitmap belongs to them.

3. The main thread waits until all the star finder threads finish their work, sleeping 100 milliseconds in each query of the threads' state.

4. Once all the threads finish their work, the main thread (the only one capable of touching the UI) rebuilds the divided bitmap and shows it in the picture box control.

Each thread works in its independent block, without disturbing or interfering with the other threads.

The code used to divide the original bitmap dynamically into many smaller bitmaps is a bit complex. That is the price we have to pay for the performance enhancement and scalability of our application.

This line obtains a `Bitmap` instance from the `picStarsBitmap` picture box (we begin decoupling the UI, as we cannot touch it from independent threads):

```
proOriginalBitmap = new Bitmap(picStarsBitmap.Image);
```

These lines create the thread list, the `long` numbers list, and the bitmap list in order to let them grow dynamically at runtime depending on the number of available cores in the computer where the application runs:

```
prloThreadList = new List<Thread>(priProcessorCount);
prliOldStarsCount = new List<long>(priProcessorCount);
prloBitmapList = new List<Bitmap>(priProcessorCount);
```

We must create bitmaps corresponding to the the number of cores available. We use the rows to select a similar number of rows for each bitmap portion.

We define a variable `liStartRow` of type `int` as the starting row from where we will begin cropping the original bitmap:

```
int liStartRow = 0;
```

Then, we must determine the approximate number of rows for each bitmap:

```
int liEachBitmapHeight = ((int)(proOriginalBitmap.Height /
                         priProcessorCount)) + 1;
```

However, depending on the number of cores and the original bitmap height, the result of this division might not be exact. That is another problem. Therefore, we use another `int` variable to calculate the height to be added to each iteration to solve that problem:

```
int liHeightToAdd = proOriginalBitmap.Height;
```

Then, the algorithm is simple; for each iteration of `liThreadNumber` do the following:

```
if (liEachBitmapHeight > liHeightToAdd)
{
    liEachBitmapHeight = liHeightToAdd;
}
loBitmap = CropBitmap(proOriginalBitmap, new Rectangle(0, liStartRow,
proOriginalBitmap.Width, liEachBitmapHeight));
liHeightToAdd -= liEachBitmapHeight;
liStartRow += liEachBitmapHeight;
prloBitmapList.Add(loBitmap);
```

If the height calculated for each bitmap is greater than the height to be added (this could happen in the last bitmap portion to be cropped), we reduce this number from the height to be added, which is the result of this line in each iteration:

```
liHeightToAdd -= liEachBitmapHeight;
```

Besides, in each iteration, the starting row increases the height calculated for each bitmap.

The following screenshot shows the results of applying this algorithm to the infrared portraits obtained by NASA's Spitzer Space Telescope with four threads:

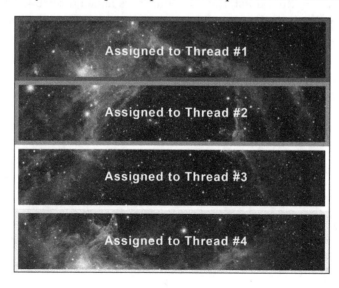

Using our classic C# programming skills, we can generate smart algorithms to split the work into many independent blocks of safe concurrent code. Again, mastering the lists is indeed necessary in parallel programming.

Signals between threads

To help in coordinating the activity between the multiple threads, we can create variables accessible to the whole class and hence each thread. Then the threads can write to and read from these variables to help them coordinate activity and to keep overall track of what is happening between all of the threads.

We use threads with parameters, as we learned in the previous chapters, and start them with an asynchronous execution using the following loop:

```
for (liThreadNumber = 0; liThreadNumber < priProcessorCount;
liThreadNumber++)
{
    prloThreadList[liThreadNumber].Start(liThreadNumber);
}
```

Nevertheless, we must wait until the concurrent star finder threads finish their work in order to show the final modified bitmap in the UI. We do not want to use the `BackgroundWorker` component.

For this reason, we created the `WaitForThreadsToDie` procedure, which is called synchronously by the main application's thread. When this method returns, we can safely show the resulting bitmap in the UI because all the threads have finished their work. Of course, to achieve the same goal, we can also use the `BackgroundWorker` component combined with the threads created as instances of the `Thread` class, as we learned in the previous chapters.

The code in the `WaitForThreadsToDie` procedure is complex because we have to check for each created thread and we know the number of threads at runtime, as they are dynamically aligned with the number of available cores. We use a `bool` flag to determine whether the `while` loop must go on running or not. However, in this case, we did not change the value of the flag, but there are other cases in which this code pattern could be useful to modify the value of this variable used as a flag.

Once in the `while` loop (`lbContinue`), we must check for each thread to finish its work. We use the well-known `IsAlive` property:

```
for (liThreadNumber = 0; liThreadNumber < priProcessorCount;
    liThreadNumber++)
{
    if (prloThreadList[liThreadNumber].IsAlive)
```

```
    {
        break;
    }
    else
    {
        liDeadThreads++;
    }
}
```

If one thread is alive, we will exit the `for` loop. If all the threads are not alive, `liDeadThreads` will equal the total number of created threads. Hence, we will exit the outer loop:

```
if (liDeadThreads == priProcessorCount)
{
    break;
}
```

The `break;` statement could be replaced by `lbContinue = false;` and we would achieve the same result.

If there is still a thread running, we call the `Sleep` method for the main thread and make it sleep for 100 milliseconds (0.1 seconds), and then reset the `liDeadThreads` variable:

```
Thread.Sleep(100);
liDeadThreads = 0;
```

The line with the call to the `Sleep` method is indispensable.

Using methods like these, and flags, we can have complete control over independent threads, without causing the classic problems related to concurrency and the loss of control over the independent threads.

As mentioned earlier, when the call to the `WaitForThreadsToDie` method returns, we can safely show the resulting bitmap in the UI because all the threads have finished their work. Hence, we call the `ShowBitmapWithOldStars` procedure.

This method reproduces the work done when dividing the original bitmap into several independent portions, but in the reverse order.

We repeat the height calculation process explained previously. Then, we must create a new bitmap with the whole width and height. This bitmap must hold the different portions aligned as they were extracted from the original bitmap:

```
loBitmap = new Bitmap(proOriginalBitmap.Width,
                      proOriginalBitmap.Height);
```

```
Graphics g = Graphics.FromImage((Image)loBitmap);
g.InterpolationMode = System.Drawing.Drawing2D.InterpolationMode.
                    HighQualityBicubic;
```

Therefore, we use the `Bitmap` constructor passing the original bitmap width and height as parameters to define its size. Then, we create a `Graphics` instance from the `Bitmap` typecast to an `Image` (the `Bitmap` class is a descendant of the `Image` class).

Once we have the `Graphics` instance, we must draw each bitmap image processed by each thread in its corresponding row (`liStartingRow`), which is calculated the same way we did when separating the bitmap portions:

```
for (liThreadNumber = 0; liThreadNumber < priProcessorCount;
    liThreadNumber++)
{
    g.DrawImage(prloBitmapList[liThreadNumber], 0, liStartRow);
    liStartRow += liEachBitmapHeight;
}
```

Besides, in each iteration, the starting row increases the height calculated for each bitmap. Then, we are ready to show the rebuilt bitmap in the picture box, `picStarsBitmap`:

```
picStarsBitmap.Image = loBitmap;
```

Decoupling the UI, we can generate impressive performance improvements changing basic linear programming algorithms.

The following screenshot shows the results of applying this algorithm to the infrared portraits obtained by NASA's Spitzer Space Telescope processed by four threads:

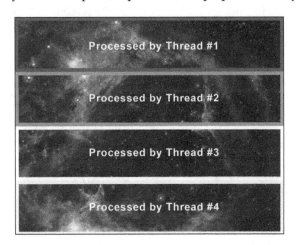

The screenshot shows a clear independency achieved by each thread.

Run the application changing the value of the `priProcessorCount` private variable from 1 to the number of available cores in your computer, and then compare the results.

How to do it

Now, we are going to make some changes to the code in order to use the event wait handles instead of using a loop to check for the threads that are alive:

1. Stay in the project, `OldStarsFinder`.

2. Open the code for `Program.cs`.

3. Replace the line `[STAThread]` with the following line (before the `Main` method declaration):

    ```
    [MTAThread]
    ```

4. Open the code for the Windows Form, `Form1` (`frmStarsFinder`).

5. Add the following private variable:

    ```
    // The AutoResetEvent instances array
    private AutoResetEvent[] praoAutoResetEventArray;
    ```

6. Replace the code in the `WaitForThreadsToDie` method with the following line:

    ```
    // Just wait for the threads to signal that every work
    // item has finished
    WaitHandle.WaitAll(praoAutoResetEventArray);
    ```

7. Add the following line of code in the local variables declaration of the `ShowBitmapWithOldStars` method, before the line `int liStartRow = 0;` (we must create the array according to the number of available cores):

    ```
    // Create the AutoResetEvent array with the number of
    // cores available
    praoAutoResetEventArray = new AutoResetEvent[priProcessorCount];
    ```

8. Add the following line of code in the thread creation loop in the `ShowBitmapWithOldStars` method, before the line `prloThreadList.Add(new Thread(new ParameterizedThreadStart(ThreadOldStarsFinder)));` (we must create an `AutoResetEvent` instance with a false initial state for each thread):

    ```
    // Create a new AutoResetEvent instance for that thread with
    its initial state set to false
    praoAutoResetEventArray[liThreadNumber] = new
        AutoResetEvent(false);
    ```

9. Add the following line of code at the end of the `ThreadOldStarsFinder` method (we must signal that the work item has finished):

```
// The thread finished its work. Signal that the work
// item has finished.
praoAutoResetEventArray[liThreadNumber].Set();
```

10. Build and run the application.

11. Click on the **Old Star Finder** button. After a few seconds (depending on the parallel processing capabilities of the computer), the W5 wispy star-forming region will be shown in the huge infrared portrait with the probable old stars shown in pure blue. You will not notice any changes in the application.

How it works

When the user clicks on the **Old Star Finder** button:

1. The original image is divided into many independent bitmaps. Each portion will be assigned to a different thread.

2. Many threads and their auto-reset event handlers are created to allow communication between the threads.

3. The threads are started (executed asynchronously) with a parameter so that they know which bitmap belongs to them.

4. Once each thread finishes its work, it signals that the work is done, setting the auto-reset event.

5. The main thread waits until all the star finder threads finish their work, waiting for all the necessary signals from the multiple auto-reset events.

6. Once all the threads finish their work, the main thread (the only one capable of touching the UI) rebuilds the divided bitmap and shows it in the picture box control.

The code used to wait for all the threads to finish their work is easier and more elegant.

Using the AutoResetEvent class to handle signals between threads

An `AutoResetEvent` instance allows us to notify a waiting thread that an event has occurred. It is a subclass of the `WaitHandle` and `EventWaitHandle` classes.

Event wait handles encapsulate operating-system-specific objects that wait for exclusive access to shared resources. Using them, it is easier to wait for the threads' signals to continue working when their jobs are done.

First, we have to create event wait handles corresponding to the number of threads. We do it in the following line, in the `FindOldStarsAndShowResult` method:

```
praoAutoResetEventArray = new AutoResetEvent [priProcessorCount];
```

We use an array because the `WaitAll` method receives an array of wait handles as a parameter.

Before creating each new instance of the `Thread` class, we create a new `AutoResetEvent` instance for each thread, with its initial state (a `bool` state) set to `false`:

```
praoAutoResetEventArray[liThreadNumber] = new AutoResetEvent (false);
```

Thus, each independent thread can access its own `AutoResetEvent` instance. Once the thread finishes its work, it signals that the job is done calling the `Set` method, as shown in the following line, at the end of the `ThreadOldStarsFinder` procedure:

```
praoAutoResetEventArray[liThreadNumber].Set();
```

The event wait handle's initial state was `false`; now it is `true`.

Using the WaitHandle class to check for signals

On the other side, the main UI thread has to wait until all the concurrent star finder threads finish their work in order to show the final modified bitmap in the UI. Thus, it must wait for all the event handles to have their state set to `true`, instead of the initial `false`.

This happens when all the threads have finished their work and have called the `Set` method for their corresponding `AutoResetEvent` instance.

We can check that using a single line of code in the `WaitForThreadsToDie` method:

```
WaitHandle.WaitAll(praoAutoResetEventArray);
```

The `WaitAll` method will monitor all the event handles, waiting for their signals to change (the threads' completion). It receives an array of event handles as a parameter.

We must change the application's threading model to a multithreaded apartment in order to be able to use the `WaitHandle.WaitAll` method. If we do not do so, the method call will fail and generate an exception. Therefore, we have to replace the line `[STAThread]`, before the `Main` method declaration, with `[MTAThread]`.

Joining threads

We have already examined *joining* a thread in the previous chapter. When you join a thread, you tell the current thread to wait on the thread, which you are joining, to complete. This allows you to coordinate work between two threads.

This was very handy in the example where we wanted to know when one piece is complete before we start the next piece.

For our application, let's say we want to examine how the performance changes if all of the bitmap processing threads run sequentially instead of concurrently.

How to do it

If we want all of our bitmap processing threads to run sequentially, then right after we start a thread, we will join the thread. This will halt execution of the main thread until the bitmap processing thread we just started has finished. To do this, change the bottom `for` loop in the `butFindOldStars_Click` event handler and add the following line:

```
prloThreadList[liThreadNumber].Join();
```

So, now the `for` loop looks like this:

```
            // Now, start the threads
            for (liThreadNumber = 0; liThreadNumber <
    priProcessorCount; liThreadNumber++)
                {
                    prloThreadList[liThreadNumber].Start(liThreadNumber);

                    //Wait here on the Thread you just created to
                    // complete.
                    prloThreadList[liThreadNumber].Join();

                }
```

How it works

Now, run the application and click on the **Old Star Finder** button. Comment the line out and rerun the application. What do you see?

You will notice that the time to process the image and complete the process is much slower with the extra line of code versus without the extra line of code. As we mentioned previously, this is because we are pausing the main thread each time we execute a new thread to process part of the bitmap image. So, we are not processing the image concurrently but sequentially.

For our application, this is not very practical, but for many problems there is a reason why you might want to do this. The main lesson here is that the `Thread` class has several ways to control processing, so you, the developer, can have complete control over how threads are created, executed, and coordinated. This is also why this is referred to as **heavyweight concurrency** because it takes extra effort and work by the developer to accomplish the exact behavior that you want.

Locking resources to ensure thread-safe data

So far we have chosen to design our application in a manner so that there is no need to lock resources to protect them from being "stomped" on by other threads, thereby causing race conditions and other unexpected behavior.

The lock syntax is as follows:

```
lock (objVariable)
{

}
```

The code between the brackets is executed in a thread-safe manner and will not let other threads operate on the object being locked until the lock execution is completed.

Other threads that try to perform an operation on an object that is locked will wait until the lock is freed before they continue their operation on the object. This is important to note because it can create "locking" issues where one thread is waiting on a resource locked by another thread. This can be self-defeating when trying to gain performance improvements with multithreading code if the multiple threads are constantly waiting on each other to let go of a resource. This is one of the reasons we have designed the code to use a separate list of long values to count old stars with one item in the list for each thread instead of one variable total that all of the threads update.

On a separate note, when using locks, you need to be careful not to create a deadlock situation. This occurs when one thread is waiting on an object locked by another thread and that thread is waiting on an object locked by the first thread. Hence, each thread is waiting on the other thread and neither can proceed.

It is also worthwhile noting that locks are handled differently in between C# 3.0 and C# 4.0. In 3.0, the following is how a lock is translated into code:

```
var temp = object1;

Monitor.Enter(temp);

try
{
    // body
}
finally
{
    Monitor.Exit(temp);
}
```

In C# 4.0, it is handled as follows:

```
bool locked = false;
var temp = object1;
try
{
    Monitor.Enter(temp, ref locked);
    // body
}
finally
{
    if (locked)
    {
        Monitor.Exit(temp);
    }
}
```

As you can see, in C# 4.0, if the lock is not taken on an object, nothing different happens to the object.

How to do it

Now, let's look at our code and make a simple change to use a single variable to hold our old star count. Let's do it with and without the lock and see the different behaviors.

1. First, let's add the following to the top of our class in the declaration statements:

```
//Old stars count using a lock to protect thread safety.
        private String prsOldStarsCount = "0";
```

2. Also, add a label control and set the Text property to Old Stars Count and add a textbox control and set the Name property to tbCount.

This variable will hold our old star count and all of the threads will update this one variable. You will notice that we are using a string instead of an integer. This is because an integer is a base type of the language and not an object. Because of this, it is thread-safe by default and does not need to be locked. So, to demonstrate our point, we will use a String object as a counter.

Now, in the ThreadOldStarsFinder method, add the following code to the end (and inside) of the nested for loop:

```
lock (prsOldStarsCount)
        {
            int i = Convert.ToInt32(prsOldStarsCount);
            i= i + 1;
            prsOldStarsCount = i.ToString();
        }
```

How it works

As you can see from this example, each time one of the processing threads updates the count, it will lock the resource, update prsOldStarsCount, and then unlock it. This protects its integrity but will slow down the overall processing because of the extra context switching that the lock will cause.

Error handling with threads

In this section, we will discuss various ways of using the try..catch block to perform error handling and coordination of multiple threads.

In this example, we are going to write a simple console application that demonstrates a typical producer-consumer model. We will also demonstrate using a try..catch to coordinate activities as well as the join and lock mechanism previously discussed. This exercise will cement everything we have learned in this chapter so far.

Also, as we will see in future chapters the producer-consumer design pattern is one of the most commonly used design patterns in multithreaded problem solving and is used a lot with the Task Parallel Library. It describes a design where one thread (or a group of threads) "produces" some output, and a second thread (or group of threads) "consumes" that output and performs some logic on it. Typically, you will multithread the "production" of some results into a queue, and then will multithread the "consumption" of the produced results from the queue.

How to do it

Perform the following steps:

1. Open up Visual Studio and create a new project called ProducerConsumer.

2. Let's create three classes, a Producer class, a Consumer class, and a Cell class. The Producer class will produce cells, and the consumer class will consume cells. In the Main method, we will start a producer and a consumer thread and then join them.

3. Add the following code in the Program.cs file so it looks like this:

```csharp
using System;
using System.Threading;

public class ProducerConsumer
{
    public static void Main(String[] args)
    {
        int result = 0;    // Results output
        Cell cell = new Cell();

        Producer producer = new Producer(cell, 5);
        Consumer consumer = new Consumer(cell, 5);

        Thread producerThread = new Thread(new
ThreadStart(producer.ThreadRun));
        Thread consumerThread = new Thread(new
ThreadStart(consumer.ThreadRun));

        try
        {
```

```
        producerThread.Start();
        consumerThread.Start();

        // Join both threads.
        producerThread.Join();
        consumerThread.Join();

    }
    catch (ThreadStateException e)
    {
        System.Diagnostics.Debug.WriteLine(e);  // Output text
of exception.
        result = 1;            // Set result to indicate an
error.
    }
    catch (ThreadInterruptedException e)
    {
        System.Diagnostics.Debug.WriteLine(e);  // Output text
noting an interruption.
        result = 1;            // Set result to indicate an
error.
    }

    Environment.ExitCode = result;
    }
}

public class Producer
{
    Cell cell;
    int quantity = 1;

    public Producer(Cell box, int request)
    {
        cell = box;
        quantity = request;
    }
    public void ThreadRun()
    {
        for (int looper = 1; looper <= quantity; looper++)
            cell.Write(looper);  // "producing"
    }
}

public class Consumer
```

```
{
    Cell cell;
    int quantity = 1;

    public Consumer(Cell box, int request)
    {
        cell = box;
        quantity = request;
    }
    public void ThreadRun()
    {
        int value;
        for (int looper = 1; looper <= quantity; looper++)
            value = cell.Read();    // Consume the result by
putting it in value
    }
}

public class Cell
{
    int cellContents;
    bool State = false;
    public int Read()
    {
        lock (this)    // Synchronizing block of code.
        {
            if (!State)
            {            // Wait until Cell.Write is done
producing
                try
                {
                    Monitor.Wait(this);    // Waits for the
Monitor.Pulse in Write
                }
                catch (SynchronizationLockException e)
                {
                    System.Diagnostics.Debug.WriteLine(e);
                }
                catch (ThreadInterruptedException e)
                {
                    System.Diagnostics.Debug.WriteLine(e);
                }
            }
            System.Diagnostics.Debug.WriteLine(String.
Format("Consumed cell item {0}", cellContents));
```

```
            State = false;    // Consumption is done.

            Monitor.Pulse(this);    // Pulse tells Cell.Write that
Cell.Read is finished.
        }

        return cellContents;
    }


    public void Write(int n)
    {
        lock (this)  // Synchronization block
        {
            if (State)
            {      // Wait until Cell.Read is done consumption.
                try
                {
                    Monitor.Wait(this);    // Wait for the Monitor.
Pulse in Read.
                }
                catch (SynchronizationLockException e)
                {
                    System.Diagnostics.Debug.WriteLine(e);
                }
                catch (ThreadInterruptedException e)
                {
                    System.Diagnostics.Debug.WriteLine(e);
                }
            }
            cellContents = n;
            System.Diagnostics.Debug.WriteLine(String.
Format("Produced cell item {0}", cellContents));
            State = true;    // Set State to indicate production
is done.

            Monitor.Pulse(this);  // Pulse tells Cell.Read that
Cell.Write is finished.

        }
    }
}
```

4. Let's run this console application. In Visual Studio, make sure that you are displaying the **Output** window. You can do this by going to the **View** menu and selecting **Output**. Once you run the application, you should see something like the following in your **Output** window:

```
127          catch (SynchronizationLockException e)
128          {
129              System.Diagnostics.Debug.WriteLine(e);
130          }
131          catch (ThreadInterruptedException e)
```
100 %   ▾

Output

Show output from: Debug   ▾

```
'ProducerConsumer.vshost.exe' (CLR v4.0.30319: ProducerConsumer.vshost.exe): Load
The thread 0x18e0 has exited with code 259 (0x103).
The thread 0x1134 has exited with code 0 (0x0).
The thread 0x1cfc has exited with code 259 (0x103).
'ProducerConsumer.vshost.exe' (CLR v4.0.30319: ProducerConsumer.vshost.exe): Load
'ProducerConsumer.vshost.exe' (CLR v4.0.30319: ProducerConsumer.vshost.exe): Load
Produced cell item 1
Consumed cell item 1
Produced cell item 2
Consumed cell item 2
Produced cell item 3
Consumed cell item 3
Produced cell item 4
Consumed cell item 4
Produced cell item 5
The thread 0x11bc has exited with code 259 (0x103).
Consumed cell item 5
The thread 0x5d8 has exited with code 259 (0x103).
The thread 0x1e0 has exited with code 259 (0x103).
The thread 0x10b0 has exited with code 259 (0x103).
The program '[5804] ProducerConsumer.vshost.exe' has exited with code 0 (0x0).
```

As you can see in our application, we coordinate between the producer and the consumer, and using the try..catch block and locks, we are able to produce one item and then consume that item.

How it works

Here, in this example, we show how synchronization is done using locks and a Monitor object. The Pulse method notifies a thread, which is in the waiting queue, of a change in the object's state.

In this example, we create a Cell object that has two methods, Read and Write. Two other objects are created from the Producer and Consumer classes. These objects have a method ThreadRun whose job is to call Cell.Read and Cell.Write. The synchronization is done by waiting for "pulses" from the Monitor object. These pulses will come in the order they are received.

So, first an item is produced (the consumer at this point is waiting for a pulse), then a pulse occurs, and then the consumer "consumes" what was produced. Meanwhile the producer is waiting for a pulse. This is then repeated until we reach the limit we set when we created the `Producer` and `Consumer` objects.

Summary

In this chapter, we took a deeper dive into working with the `Thread` class. Through our examples, we learned how to coordinate threads in a more advanced way. We learned how to use the `try..catch` block, the `Monitor` object, locks, `Join`, `IsAlive`, and `Sleep` methods to coordinate activities between threads.

We also introduced two common design patterns that we will explore in much more detail in the later chapters—the pipelining and the producer-consumer patterns. These are commonly used to solve problems in a parallel application. They are good ways to segment the work that can be done in parallel from the work that cannot be done in parallel.

As we have discussed, this type of parallel programming is called heavyweight concurrency because the heavy lifting is done by you, the programmer. You have to manage and control the different threads to achieve the behavior you intended. You have to track which threads run and when and which threads are waiting and why. This does create complexity and work for the programmer but it also allows for very tight control of the execution. There are times when this is the best way to ensure proper behavior of your application.

Next, in *Chapter 5, Lightweight Concurrency – Task Parallel Library (TPL)*, we will start to examine lightweight concurrency and the Task Parallel Library. This allows you to let .NET handle some of this coordination for you. It is important that you have full understanding of the `Thread` class before moving on to the Task library and lightweight concurrency.

5
Lightweight Concurrency – Task Parallel Library (TPL)

In .NET 4.0, Microsoft delivered what is called the **Task Parallel Library** (TPL) and answered users' concerns by developing multithreaded applications. TPL allows developers to focus on the functionality that they are trying to implement and not get bogged down with managing multiple threads, the threadpool, and the number of processing cores available to them.

So far, we have covered the BackgroundWorker component and the Thread class to show ways to accomplish multithreaded functionality in a C#/.NET application. These two ways to perform multithreaded functionality have been around since the very early stages of .NET. The Thread class was introduced in Version 1.1 of .NET and the BackgroundWorker in Version 2.0 of .NET. We classify these methods as heavyweight concurrency because they take quite a bit of work from the developer and add to the complexity of the code's design. The developer has to manage the different threads, and to achieve maximum performance, determine the number of processing cores in a machine.

After completing this chapter you will:

- Have a complete understanding of the Task Parallel Library and the different classes that make it up
- Understand how to create and use the Task class
- Understand how tasks are managed in .NET and the threadpool
- Understand the Parallel class and how to start tasks using it
- Know the evolution of multithreading from heavyweight to lightweight concurrency

- Learn when to use tasks instead of `Threads`
- Understand task parallelism versus data parallelism
- Understand concurrent data collection and concurrent data processing

Task Parallel Library

The Task Parallel Library was introduced as part of .NET with the release of Version 4.0. Originally, it was developed under the name Parallel Extensions, which was a joint effort by Microsoft Research and the CLR team. Parallel Extensions consisted of the TPL and **Parallel LINQ (PLINQ)**, which we will cover in a later chapter. TPL is now preferred over threads and `BackgroundWorker` components to develop multithreaded applications.

The idea was to create a managed concurrency library to take the multithreaded capabilities of .NET to the next level. TPL consists of a set of APIs and public types located in the `System.Threading` and `System.Threading.Tasks` namespaces.

One of the advantages of using TPL over threads is that .NET can dynamically scale an application to most effectively use the processing cores of the hardware it is running. .NET is smart enough to determine the number of processing cores in a machine and manage the `ThreadPool` appropriately. When programming with threads directly, the developer has to handle this work. No longer does the developer have to determine the number of cores and corresponding threads created to achieve maximum performance. If you remember our earlier examples with threads and `BackgroundWorker` components, we had to do this in code.

TPL also manages the `ThreadPool` for us. It handles scheduling of threads, cancelation of threads, and state management. This managed `ThreadPool` allows .NET to have a higher degree of intelligence in managing tasks versus threads. The `Task.Factory` class can be told if a task is a long running one that is not CPU-intensive versus a CPU-intensive task. With this information, it can be managed by the `ThreadPool` to create a single thread per core (CPU-intensive tasks) or multiple threads per core (long running tasks that wait on other resources). This is the logic that previously needed to be handled by the developer. Now .NET does it for you.

Next, we will examine the center of the TPL, the `Task` class.

Exploring tasks

The Task class represents some work that can be done atomically in an asynchronous manner. It is an item of work executed and managed on the ThreadPool by the TPL. It is very similar to a thread but with a higher level of abstraction and functionality built around it. It is the central control of the Task Parallel Library.

The Task class has a complete set of methods for status updates, cancelation, exception handling, scheduling, and waiting that allows it to be "lightweight" compared to the thread. It can also make more efficient use of system resources given the functionality that the TPL provides to manage the ThreadPool behind the scenes.

Let's start by creating and executing a task. First, we will create a couple of methods that will represent the work to be done. Then we will execute this work using tasks. There are two main ways to accomplish this: Parallel.Invoke and Task.Factory. StartNew. Let's take a look at each. We will start with tasks that do not return a value. The next section will look at ways to run tasks that return values.

How to do it

We will start by creating a new console application using Visual Studio 2013. We will name our application, TaskExample.

1. First, we will add two using statements to the Program.cs file to allow us to work with the TPL classes.

   ```
   using System.Threading;
   using System.Threading.Tasks;
   ```

2. Next, let's define three different static methods that will represent the work done by three tasks: WriteNumbers, WriteWords, and WriteColors. One will loop through the first 20 numbers and write each one to the console. The other will loop through a sentence and write each word to the console. The final one will loop through an array of colors and write each color to the console. Now, add the following three methods to your Program.cs file:

   ```
   static void WriteNumbers()
   {
       //Set thread name.
       Thread.CurrentThread.Name = "Thread 1";

       for (int i = 0; i < 20; i++)
       {
   Console.WriteLine("Thread name {0}, Number: {1}", Thread.
   CurrentThread.Name, i);
               Thread.Sleep(2000);
   ```

```
        }
    }

    static void WriteWords()
    {
        //Set thread name.
        Thread.CurrentThread.Name = "Thread 2";

        String localString = "This is an example for using
tasks";
        String[] localWords = localString.Split(' ');
        foreach (String s in localWords)
        {
Console.WriteLine("Thread name {0}, Word: {1}", Thread.
CurrentThread.Name, s);
            Thread.Sleep(2000);
        }
    }

    static void WriteColors()
    {
        //Set thread name.
        Thread.CurrentThread.Name = "Thread 3";

String[] localColors = {"red", "orange", "blue", "green",
"yellow", "white", "black"};
        foreach (String s in localColors)
        {
Console.WriteLine("Thread name {0}, Colors: {1}",Thread.
CurrentThread.Name, s);
            Thread.Sleep(2000);
        }
    }
```

3. Finally, we will add code to run each method as a task:

```
        //Create the 3 Tasks.
        Task t1 = new Task(() => WriteNumbers());
        Task t2 = new Task(() => WriteWords());
        Task t3 = new Task(() => WriteColors());

        //Run the 3 Tasks.
        t1.Start();
        t2.Start();
        t3.Start();

        Console.ReadLine();
```

4. Now, compile and run the application and you should see a console window that looks something like this:

This is a simple example, but allows you to see the three tasks run in separate threads with each executing a different method. You can see the thread name of each task and you will notice that the threads do not always run concurrently in sequence.

5. Now, let's replace the code in the Main method with the following code:

```
//Create the 3 Tasks.
//Task t1 = new Task(() => WriteNumbers());
//Task t2 = new Task(() => WriteWords());
//Task t3 = new Task(() => WriteColors());

//Run the 3 Tasks.
//t1.Start();
//t2.Start();
//t3.Start();
```

```
            Parallel.Invoke
            (
                new Action(WriteNumbers),
                new Action(WriteWords),
                new Action(WriteColors)
            );
        Console.ReadLine();
```

6. Now, rebuild and run the application again. You should see an identical or almost identical result.

 The reason the results may be different is because the three methods are being run in three separate threads on three separate cores. So, depending on performance and other items running on your computer, the three tasks can run with different timings, as a result of which the console output can be in a different order.

How it works

In the previous exercise, you learned two ways to use the `Task` class to implement functionality in a separate thread. These examples take methods that do not return a value and instantiate a `Task` class to execute the methods.

The `Task` constructor takes an `Action` delegate:

```
public delegate void Action<in T>(
    T obj
)
```

We use a lambda expression to define the `Action` delegate, which encapsulates a method to be performed. Later in this chapter, we will define delegates and lambdas in more detail.

First, we used the `Task.Start()` method to execute the task. This puts the task on the `ThreadPool` and lets .NET manage the execution of it. To instantiate the `Task` class, we used a lambda expression in the constructor.

In the second example, we used another class in the TPL and ran the tasks using the `Parallel.Invoke()` method. Here, we were able to put all three tasks on the `ThreadPool` at once by using this method and the `Action` class.

We use the `Console.ReadLine()` command to just hold the command window open after the execution of the threads has completed. This allows us to study the results and control the closing of the window. To close the window, simply press the *Enter* key; this will complete the `ReadLine` statement. The console is waiting to read a line of input.

Tasks with return values

Now, we will take a look at how to start a task that returns a value. In most cases, if we care about the result of a task or if a task does some work to be consumed by the rest of the program, then we will want the task to return some values for us to use. We will demonstrate this by developing a simple console application that starts three tasks and then prints the return values of these three tasks.

How to do it

We will start by creating a new console application using Visual Studio 2013. We will name our application, TaskExampleWithReturnValues.

Next, place the following code in the Program class of Program.cs:

```
class Program
    {
        static void Main(string[] args)
        {
            //Create the 3 Tasks.
            Task<String> t1 = new Task<String>(() => WriteNumbers());
            Task<String> t2 = new Task<String>(() => WriteWords());
            Task<String> t3 = new Task<String>(() => WriteColors());

            //Run the 3 Tasks.
            t1.Start();
            t2.Start();
            t3.Start();

            Console.WriteLine(t1.Result);
            Console.WriteLine(t2.Result);
            Console.WriteLine(t3.Result);

            Console.ReadLine();

        }

        static String WriteNumbers()
        {
            //Set thread name.
            Thread.CurrentThread.Name = "Task 1";

            for (int i = 0; i < 20; i++)
            {
```

```
Console.WriteLine("Thread name {0}, Number: {1}",Thread.CurrentThread.
Name, i);
                Thread.Sleep(2000);
        }

return String.Format("This Task has completed - {0}", Thread.
CurrentThread.Name);
        }


        static String WriteWords()
        {
            //Set thread name.
            Thread.CurrentThread.Name = "Task 2";

            String localString = "This is an example for using tasks";
            String[] localWords = localString.Split(' ');
            foreach (String s in localWords)
            {
Console.WriteLine("Thread name {0}, Word: {1}", Thread.CurrentThread.
Name, s);
                Thread.Sleep(2000);
        }

return String.Format("This Task has completed - {0}", Thread.
CurrentThread.Name);
        }


        static String WriteColors()
        {
            //Set thread name.
            Thread.CurrentThread.Name = "Task 3";

String[] localColors = { "red", "orange", "blue", "green", "yellow",
"white", "black" };
            foreach (String s in localColors)
            {
Console.WriteLine("Thread name {0}, Colors: {1}",Thread.CurrentThread.
Name, s);
                Thread.Sleep(2000);
        }

return String.Format("This Task has completed - {0}", Thread.
CurrentThread.Name);
        }
    }
```

Finally, let's build and run our application. Your console window should look like this:

How it works

In this example, we use the `Task<TResult>` version of the `Task` class, which allows us to specify a return object from the task when it has completed execution. The return value will be placed in the `Task.Result` property and will be of the type you define in the declaration. So, in the following line of code, we tell .NET to create an object of type `Task` that will execute the `WriteNumbers()` method and return a `String` value:

```
Task<String> t1 = new Task<String>(() => WriteNumbers());
```

This is very helpful because it allows us to return any object type.

By using the line `Console.WriteLine(t1.Result);`, we automatically tell .NET to block or halt the main thread and wait on the `t1` task to complete and return the value `t1.Result`. .NET is smart enough to know that we want to wait until a value is present before executing this statement. Otherwise, if it is executed immediately, the value may or may not be there. If it was not there, we would get a null reference error. This is another way to say that using TPL is easier than using threads. The TPL API handles these details for you, the developer, managing it in the code itself.

Also, in each method, we set the current thread name, so in our output, we can see that each of the three tasks operate in a different thread.

Next, we will examine the API in TPL that allows us to use concurrent collections.

Concurrent collections

Another namespace that was introduced in .NET 4.0 is `Systems.Collections.Concurrent`. This is not directly a part of TPL, but it is often used in conjunction with TPL to provide much of the common parallel design patterns such as producer-consumer that we will discuss in *Chapter 9, Pipeline and Producer-consumer Design Patterns*.

`System.Collections.Concurrent` provides a thread-safe version of collection classes in the `Systems.Collections` namespace. These work very well in conjunction with tasks. This namespace has `ConcurrentBag`, which is a collection of objects such as `ConcurrentDictionary`, `ConcurrentQueue`, `ConcurrentStack`, and `BlockingCollection` to name the most popular ones.

All of these concurrent collections implement interfaces for the underlying collection. This essentially wraps the collection and provides a thread-safety mechanism. This is handy for the multithreaded developer because you can use them and not have to design thread-safe logic around them.

In this section, we will look at the `ConcurrentQueue` class and show an example of how to use this with tasks to perform a simple multithreaded example. This will demonstrate the power and simplicity that TPL provides for multithreaded processing. We do not have to worry about locking resources to make them thread-safe. We do not have to worry about the number of processing cores on our hardware. We do not have to worry about race conditions between variables. And we do not have to worry about using global variables in a class to provide thread-safety. All of this is handled for us with the classes. We just have to worry about the logic.

Having a set of thread-safe collections to be used by many threads makes multithreaded design easy. Notice how fewer things we have to account for than our previous examples. Before we divided up work, we had to know the number of cores to create a thread for. This is handled by `Task` and `ThreadPool` now.

We had to divide our dataset into chunks and give each thread a known chunk of the data (that is, in the image-processing example, each thread got a distinct section of the image). Also, we had to come back in the end and reassemble the results from each thread. We no longer have to worry about these three concerns.

In this project, we will take a list of numbers from 0 to 5000 (that is, 0 + 1 + 2 + 3 + 4 and so on) and sum them up by three different threads. We will not give each thread a range to sum then add the results from the three, like before. We will just use a `ConcurrentQueue` collection with the 5000 numbers in queue and have each of the three threads remove items, sum them up, and add the sum to the overall total.

How to do it

Let's open Visual Studio and create a new console application project named `ConcurrentCollection`; then perform the following steps:

1. Place the following code in the `Program.cs` file:

```
using System;
using System.Collections.Concurrent;
using System.Threading;
using System.Threading.Tasks;

class ConcurrentCollection
{
    static void Main()
    {
        ConcurrentQueue<int> queue = new ConcurrentQueue<int>();

        //Sum of a single thread adding the numbers as we queue them.
        int SingleThreadSum = 0;

        // Populate the queue.
        for (int i = 0; i < 5000; i++)
        {
            SingleThreadSum += i;
            queue.Enqueue(i);
        }

        //Print the Sum of 0 to 5000.
        Console.WriteLine("Single Thread Sum = {0}", SingleThreadSum);

        //Sum of a multithread adding of the numbers.
```

```
            int MultiThreadSum = 0;

            //Create an Action delegate to dequeue items and sum them.
            Action localAction = () =>
            {
                int localSum = 0;
                int localValue;

                while (queue.TryDequeue(out localValue)) localSum +=
    localValue;

                Interlocked.Add(ref MultiThreadSum, localSum);
            };

            // Run 3 concurrent Tasks.
            Parallel.Invoke(localAction, localAction, localAction);

            //Print the Sum of 0 to 5000 done by 3 separate threads.
            Console.WriteLine("MultiThreaded  Sum = {0}",
    MultiThreadSum);

            Console.ReadLine();
        }
    }
```

2. Now, let's build and run the application. What do you think the results will be? They should look like the following output:

How it works

In this program, we declare a ConcurrentQueue object using the following statement:

```
ConcurrentQueue<int> queue = new ConcurrentQueue<int>();
```

Then we place into the queue the numbers from 1 to 5000 using the following loop:

```
for (int i = 0; i < 5000; i++)
    {
        SingleThreadSum += i;
        queue.Enqueue(i);
    }
```

Next, we start three parallel tasks that each dequeue items from the queue without having to lock the queue to protect thread-safety because it is a concurrent queue. They use the following command to take all the items out of the queue:

```
queue.TryDequeue(out localValue)) localSum += localValue;
```

By using this `ConcurrentQueue` object, .NET handles all of the thread-safety issues and allows all three tasks to just focus on the work to be performed. They all then add their local sums to the `MultiThreadSum` value. But notice that this value needs to be locked because it is not thread-safe by default, since three separate tasks are all trying to add to it in parallel.

So, in the end, no matter how the three independent tasks run, the `MultiThreadSum` will always be the same because each number between 1 and 5000 is taken from the queue only once and added to the overall sum.

Exploring the TaskFactory class

A key class of the TPL in the `System.Threading.Tasks` namespace is the `TaskFactory` class. `TaskFactory` is used in the creation and scheduling of tasks. The `TaskFactory` class has a number of methods that make scheduling and managing tasks very easy. These include starting and continuing methods as well as a series of methods that conform to the asynchronous programming model that we will cover in *Chapter 11, The Asynchronous Programming Model*. Essentially, this class wraps many of the common task design patterns into methods for ease of use and development. This is yet another way that TPL makes multithreaded development "lightweight".

Most of our work with `TaskFactory` will be covered in *Chapter 6, Task-based Parallelism*, and *Chapter 7, Data Parallelism*, and then again in *Chapter 11, The Asynchronous Programming Model*. But in this chapter, we will perform a simple example to demonstrate how they are used.

How to do it

Let's start by opening up Visual Studio and creating a new console application named `TaskFactoryExample`. Now, let's add the following code to our `Program.cs` file:

```
using System;
using System.Collections.Generic;
using System.Linq;
using System.Text;
using System.Threading;
using System.Threading.Tasks;

namespace TaskFactoryExample
{
    class TaskFactoryExample
    {

        static TaskFactory TF = new TaskFactory(TaskScheduler.
Default);

        static void Main(string[] args)
        {
            List<Task> tasklist = new List<Task>();

            tasklist.Add(TF.StartNew(() => Worker("Task 1"),
CancellationToken.None, TaskCreationOptions.PreferFairness,
TaskScheduler.Default));
            tasklist.Add(TF.StartNew(() => Worker("Task 2"),
CancellationToken.None, TaskCreationOptions.PreferFairness,
TaskScheduler.Default));
            tasklist.Add(TF.StartNew(() => Worker("Task 3"),
CancellationToken.None, TaskCreationOptions.PreferFairness,
TaskScheduler.Default));
            tasklist.Add(TF.StartNew(() => Worker("Task 4"),
CancellationToken.None, TaskCreationOptions.PreferFairness,
TaskScheduler.Default));
            tasklist.Add(TF.StartNew(() => Worker("Task 5"),
CancellationToken.None, TaskCreationOptions.PreferFairness,
TaskScheduler.Default));



            //wait for all tasks to complete.
            Task.WaitAll(tasklist.ToArray());

            //Wait for input before ending program.
```

```
            Console.ReadLine();
        }

        static void Worker(String taskName)
        {
            Console.WriteLine("This is Task - {0}", taskName);
        }
    }
}
```

Now, let's compile and run this application. You should see results as shown in the following screenshot:

How it works

Let's now examine what we just accomplished and why it worked. You can see from the output that we ran five tasks all in different threads and then waited on them to complete. First, we created a static `TaskFactory` class to use:

```
static TaskFactory TF = new TaskFactory(TaskScheduler.Default);
```

There are several overloads for the `TaskFactory` constructor. The one we used just takes a `TaskScheduler` object and we chose the default. In the next section of this chapter, we will examine the `TaskScheduler` class in more detail.

Next, we created and ran the five tasks using the `StartNew()` method of the `TaskFactory` class, as shown in the following line of code. There are many overloads for this method to allow you to create and start tasks according to your requirements and design pattern. In *Chapter 6, Task-based Parallelism*, and *Chapter 7, Data Parallelism*, we will examine more of these:

```
TF.StartNew(() => Worker("Task 1"), CancellationToken.None,
TaskCreationOptions.PreferFairness, TaskScheduler.Default)
```

Let's take a minute to look at the different parameters passed into the `StartNew()` method. We passed it a cancellation token, a task-creation option, and a scheduler. This allows a lot of the thread management of the task to be handled without having to manually do it.

The cancellation token allows us to tell .NET if the tasks can be canceled or not. It also allows us to set a wait handle that is signaled if the task is canceled. The task creation options allow for the following settings, which give us a lot more control over the task than we had with the thread (referenced from `http://msdn.microsoft.com/en-us/library/vstudio/system.threading.tasks.taskcreationoptions`):

	Member name	Description
	AttachedToParent	Specifies that a task is attached to a parent in the task hierarchy. For more information, see Attached and Detached Child Tasks.
	DenyChildAttach	Specifies that an InvalidOperationException will be thrown if an attempt is made to attach a child task to the created task.
	HideScheduler	Prevents the ambient scheduler from being seen as the current scheduler in the created task. This means that operations like StartNew or ContinueWith that are performed in the created task will see Default as the current scheduler.
	LongRunning	Specifies that a task will be a long-running, coarse-grained operation involving fewer, larger components than fine-grained systems. It provides a hint to the TaskScheduler that oversubscription may be warranted. Oversubscription lets you create more threads than the available number of hardware threads.
	None	Specifies that the default behavior should be used.
	PreferFairness	A hint to a TaskScheduler to schedule a task in as fair a manner as possible, meaning that tasks scheduled sooner will be more likely to be run sooner, and tasks scheduled later will be more likely to be run later.

We also passed the `TaskFactory` constructor a lambda expression for the `Action` object, which tells it what the task should execute:

```
() => Worker("Task 1")
```

Finally, we performed a `Task.WaitAll` on the list of tasks, so we had to wait for all of the tasks to complete. We will see in the next chapter how we can do this directly with the `TaskFactory` object:

```
Task.WaitAll(tasklist.ToArray());
```

This is a basic example of using `TaskFactory` but you can see the many benefits it provides and how much work is reduced for the developers as compared to using straight threads.

Task schedulers

One of the main benefits of the Task Parallel Library versus developing using the `Thread` class is the `TaskScheduler`. This class does a lot of the logic that you had to program into your multithreaded code to achieve maximum performance and efficiency. This is what truly makes using TPL "lightweight" concurrency programming. The main job of the `TaskScheduler` class is to handle the work of queuing tasks to threads, or more specifically, the `ThreadPool`, and managing the `ThreadPool` to best utilize the number of processing cores on the machine it is being executed on.

One of the best features of the `TaskScheduler` is that it is an `abstract` class that you can derive your own classes from. The `TaskScheduler` allows you to schedule tasks on the `ThreadPool` exactly how you need if the default `TaskScheduler` does not meet your needs. This gives you the ultimate in flexibility and control.

Let's talk for a minute about the `ThreadPool`. The `ThreadPool` consists of a queue (FIFO) of work items for threads in an application domain. Tasks are put on this queue until a thread is available to process them. In .NET 4.0, the `ThreadPool` was enhanced to improve performance by essentially making the work queue a `ConcurrentQueue` collection object, which eliminates the need for the locking logic to make the queue thread-safe.

Another point to note is that tasks that are not the children of other tasks are put in a **global** queue, while tasks that are children of other tasks are put in **local** queues of the parent task. So, when a thread is finished processing a work item, it first looks in the task's local queue for more work before going to the global queue. This is another way .NET 4.0 improved the performance of the `ThreadPool`.

The following are four ways that the `TaskScheduler` improves performance of the `ThreadPool` and removes work from the developer (referenced from `http://msdn.microsoft.com/en-us/library/dd997402(v=vs.110).aspx`):

◢ Work Stealing

The .NET Framework 4 ThreadPool also features a work-stealing algorithm to help make sure that no threads are sitting idle while others still have work in their queues. When a thread-pool thread is ready for more work, it first looks at the head of its local queue, then in the global queue, and then in the local queues of other threads. If it finds a work item in the local queue of another thread, it first applies heuristics to make sure that it can run the work efficiently. If it can, it de-queues the work item from the tail (in FIFO order). This reduces contention on each local queue and preserves data locality. This architecture helps the .NET Framework 4 ThreadPool load-balance work more efficiently than past versions did.

◢ Long-Running Tasks

You may want to explicitly prevent a task from being put on a local queue. For example, you may know that a particular work item will run for a relatively long time and is likely to block all other work items on the local queue. In this case, you can specify the LongRunning option, which provides a hint to the scheduler that an additional thread might be required for the task so that it does not block the forward progress of other threads or work items on the local queue. By using this option you avoid the ThreadPool completely, including the global and local queues.

◢ Task Inlining

In some cases, when a Task is waited on, it may be executed synchronously on the Thread that is performing the wait operation. This enhances performance, as it prevents the need for an additional Thread by utilizing the existing Thread which would have blocked, otherwise. To prevent errors due to re-entrancy, task inlining only occurs when the wait target is found in the relevant Thread's local queue.

◢ Specifying a Synchronization Context

You can use the TaskScheduler.FromCurrentSynchronizationContext method to specify that a task should be scheduled to run on a particular thread. This is useful in frameworks such as Windows Forms and Windows Presentation Foundation where access to user interface objects is often restricted to code that is running on the same thread on which the UI object was created. For more information, see How to: Schedule Work on the User Interface (UI) Thread.

Introducing the Parallel class

The last class we will touch on in this TPL primer is the `Parallel` class. This class will be covered in detail in *Chapter 7, Data Parallelism*, when we discuss data parallelism; but it is worth an introduction here. The `Parallel` class is part of the `System.Threading.Tasks` namespace and provides functionality for using parallel loops. The two most used methods are `Parallel.For` and `Parallel.ForEach`, which allow you to loop through a collection and perform logic on each item of the collection concurrently.

We briefly saw it earlier in this chapter when we used the `Parallel.Invoke` method to run a group of tasks in parallel. But its main use is for data parallelism.

We can call the `Parallel.For` method using a named method, an anonymous method, or a lambda expression.

The following are examples of the three ways:

```
// Named method.
Parallel.For(0, 5, Method);

//Anonymous method.
Parallel.For(0, 5, delegate(int i)
{
    // Do something
});

//Lambda expression.
Parallel.For(0, 5, i =>
{
    // Do something
});
```

In the named method version, you would need to write a method called `Method` that receives an integer parameter and does not return anything. Using `Parallel.For` causes .NET to run each iteration of the loop concurrently. Whether it does this or not depends on the number of processing cores and other work going on at the same time.

The `Parallel.ForEach` method takes an `IEnumerable` data source and an `Action` delegate and iterates through the data source and calls the `Action` delegate on each item. It also returns a `ParallelLoopResult` object with the results for the processing, if there are any. The basic syntax for this is as follows:

```
Parallel.ForEach(IEnumerable<TSource> source, Action<TSource> body)
```

How to do it

Let's see a simple example. Open Visual Studio, create a new console application named `ParallelForEach`, and perform the following steps:

1. Place the following code in the `Program.cs` file:

    ```
    using System;
    using System.IO;
    using System.Threading;
    using System.Threading.Tasks;
    ```

```
class SimpleForEach
{
    static void Main()
    {
        string[] localStrings = "I am doing a simple example of a
Parallel foreach loop".Split(' ');

        Parallel.ForEach(localStrings, currentString =>
            {

                Console.WriteLine("Current word is - {0}, and
the current thread is - {1}", currentString,
                                        Thread.CurrentThread.
ManagedThreadId);
            }
        );

        Console.ReadLine();
    }
}
```

2. Now, let's compile and run the application. Your results should look like this:

How it works

First, we create an `IEnumerable` collection by splitting a sentence into an array of strings for each word in the sentence. Then we perform a `Parallel.ForEach` looping on each word and simply print the word and current thread ID to the console.

Something to note here is that you see thread IDs 8, 9, 10, and 11. There is a separate thread for each iteration of the loop and the thread IDs are not starting with 0 or 1. Remember that the TPL uses `ThreadPool`. So, the `Action` delegate is queued as a separate task to the `ThreadPool` for each iteration of the list, which has 11 words. The `TaskScheduler` and .NET use the `ThreadPool` as efficiently as they can to process these queued tasks concurrently. On my particular machine, there are four processing cores. So, it does split the work out between four threads. But then, based on the rest of the work the computer is doing, thread 8 handles two of the tasks, thread 9 handles seven of the tasks, and thread 10 and 11 handle one task each.

But the thing to note here is that we did not have to manage any of this. Using threads directly, we would have had to interrogate the hardware and realize there are four processing cores. Then, break the array into four smaller arrays and hand each of the smaller arrays to a single thread to achieve maximum performance.

Delegates and lambda expressions

In this chapter, we have used delegates and lambda expressions. These two concepts are confusing for some new developers, so let's take a moment to discuss them in a little more detail.

Delegates are often used when creating event handlers. A **delegate** defines a reference type that encapsulates a method with a certain set of parameters and a return type. It functions a lot like a function pointer in C++. It allows us to pass a delegate object that can be used to call a method without having to know the method at compile time.

In our example, the `Task` constructor takes an `Action` delegate to define the *action* to be performed by the task. In our example, we set the method for the delegate in the constructor definition, but we do not have to. We can write it like this:

```
Action task1Method;
task1Method = new Action(WriteNumbers);
Task t1 = new Task(task1Method);
```

This way, we declare the `Action` delegate. Then we instantiate it with the method `WriteNumbers`, and finally, we instantiate a `Task` object with the delegate. Later in the code, we can always change the method the `Action` delegate uses, based on business logic. So, we are not bound for this task to have to execute the `WriteNumbers` method, every time the task is performed.

All we need to know at design time is that we want to execute a method with no parameters and no return type in this task. This gives us a lot of power and flexibility.

A lambda expression is an anonymous function that can be used to create delegates. In a lambda expression, there is the lambda operator, `=>`, and the left- and right-hand side of this operator. The left-hand side contains any input parameters and the right-hand side contains the expression of the code block. Empty parentheses represent zero parameters. Let's look at the following statement:

```
Task t1 = new Task(() => WriteNumbers());
```

In this statement, we are using a lambda expression to represent the delegate that the `Task` constructor takes as an input: `() => WriteNumbers()`

This lambda expression is telling us that the delegate has no input parameters(`()`) and that the code block for the method of the delegate is `WriteNumbers()`.

So, we can see that in the preceding examples, the `Task` constructor takes a delegate reference type and we use a lambda expression to define that delegate. By doing this, we have flexibility to change at runtime what method a task will execute when it is run. The only constraint at compile time is the parameters passed into the delegate and the return type of the delegate.

Summary

In this chapter, we started our journey into the Task Parallel Library and this will be the focus of the rest of the book. You learned about the `Task`, `Action`, `TaskFactory`, `Parallel`, and `TaskScheduler` classes.

You also learned what the meaning of lightweight concurrency versus heavyweight concurrency is, and started to see the many benefits for the developer.

The code examples in this chapter were very simple but designed to get you to start thinking from a TPL mindset and out of the `Thread` and `BackgroundWorker` mindset. Throughout the rest of this book, we will explore many more detailed features of the TPL classes and several common parallel design patterns and how they are implemented using TPL.

You should already be able to see just how powerful the TPL is and how much of the complexity to make an application designed for concurrency it handles. When building a multithreaded application, there are usually four considerations that need to be handled by the developer that are not part of a single-threaded application; they are listed as follows:

- What pieces of functionality in the application can we process concurrently?
- How do I manage achieving maximum performance without knowing ahead of time what machine it will be running on and how many processing cores it might have?
- How do I ensure thread-safety in the data and values that overlap between threads? Or split the data and values to not overlap?
- How do I manage and coordinate the different threads?

Even though we have only just begun discussing TPL, you can already see how the last three are handled for you unlike doing concurrent programming with threads directly.

The first one is a design decision and, as we discuss common parallel design patterns, you will see that TPL helps us there as well.

Now, let's move on to *Chapter 6, Task-based Parallelism*, and start to really become comfortable developing software using the TPL.

6
Task-based Parallelism

In this chapter we will cover the **Task Parallel Library** (**TPL**) and the details of using the Task class to write concurrent code.

In *Chapter 5, Lightweight Concurrency – Task Parallel Library (TPL)*, we started our exploration of lightweight concurrency and .NET's new most preferred way to accomplish multithreaded programming — the TPL. In this chapter, we will explore task-based parallelism further and show how to wait on tasks or multiple tasks, custom scheduling of a task, error handling, and canceling a task.

The TPL gives us an easy way to schedule, run, and coordinate tasks at a higher level of abstraction than working directly with threads. As mentioned earlier, a task is a set of instructions to carry out an objective, a unit of work if you wish. We can define a task in a method called by a delegate or in a lambda expression defined directly in the task-creation command.

When running more than one task concurrently, there will be times when we need to wait on one or more tasks to complete before performing a function, or be able to cancel one or more tasks if a certain condition arises, or coordinate exception handling if one or more tasks throws an error when running in parallel. We will discuss all of these scenarios in this chapter and work through examples. By the end of this chapter, you will be very comfortable with all the aspects of using tasks in parallel in your applications.

In this chapter, you will learn how to:

- Wait on a particular task when multiple tasks are running concurrently
- Wait on all or many tasks that are running concurrently
- Cancel one or more tasks when certain conditions occur
- Handle exceptions thrown by one or more tasks
- Fully coordinate the execution and completion of concurrently running tasks

Waiting for a task to complete

The first thing we need to do when we execute a task is to know when it has completed, and if it returns results, what the results are. Let's see a simple example by creating a task, waiting for it to complete, and then checking the results.

We will do this using a task that doesn't return a result and one that does, and see the difference between Task and Task<TResult>. When a task returns a result value, the wait is implicit, and when it doesn't, we need to explicitly wait for it.

How to do it

First, let's open up Visual Studio and create a new console application called WaitonTask. Once we have the new project created, we will add the following code to the Program.cs file:

```
using System;
using System.Threading;
using System.Threading.Tasks;

class Program
{
static Random ran = new Random();
static void Main(string[] args)
    {
        // Wait on a single task with no timeout.
        Task taskA = Task.Factory.StartNew(() => Worker(10000));
taskA.Wait();
Console.WriteLine("Task A Finished.");


        // Wait on a single task with a timeout.
        Task taskB = Task.Factory.StartNew(() => Worker(2000000));
taskB.Wait(2000); //Wait for 2 seconds.

if (taskB.IsCompleted)
Console.WriteLine("Task B Finished.");
else
Console.WriteLine("Timed out without Task B finishing.");


Console.ReadLine();
    }
```

```
static void Worker(intwaitTime)
    {
Thread.Sleep(waitTime);
    }
}
```

As you can see from this code, we are creating a task to run for 10 seconds and we will wait on the task to finish. This task calls a method named `Worker` and is instantiated using a `Task.Factory` and a lambda expression. The task does not return a value.

Now, let's compile and run our new application. The following is an example of the output you should see:

As you can see, we first start a task with the `Worker` method and wait on it to complete and then we start a task with the `Worker` method and perform a wait with a time-out value. Did you notice a difference between the two executions?

The first time we run the task, we will wait the full 10 seconds for the task to complete. The second time we run the task, we set a timeout and continue on before the task completes. Since the task runs for longer than 2 seconds, the wait command times out and the program moves on, while the task is still running.

In both of these examples, we have a task that does not return a value. Now, let's change our worker task to return a value and see what happens. Let's add a new method to our program called `Worker1`. Add the following code to the `Worker1` method:

```
static double Worker1()
    {
int i = ran.Next(1000000);
Thread.SpinWait(i);
return i;
    }
```

Now, in the `Main` method of the `Program.cs` file, add the following two lines of code towards the end right before the `Console.ReadLine` command:

```
Task<double> taskC = Task<double>.Factory.StartNew(() => Worker1());

Console.WriteLine("TaskC finished = result is {0}.", taskC.Result);
```

Now, let's compile and run our program again. The following is the output that you should see when you run the program:

Did you notice that the program ran and waited for `TaskC` to complete? Shortly, we will get to the `SpinWait` method of the `Thread` class, but for now, why did the program wait on `TaskC` to finish running when we did not put a wait command in the code for it?

How it works

In the previous exercise, we saw three ways to wait for a task to complete. The first two examples used the `Task.Wait` method to tell our program to wait on the task. Since the task is running on a different thread, we have to wait for it to complete before we continue the execution of the program in our main thread. In these two examples, our task does not return a value. In this case, we need to explicitly wait on the task to complete if we do not want our main thread to continue after starting the task (or at least scheduling it in the threadpool). We do this using the `Task.Wait` method in the `Task` class.

The first time, we told our program to wait on the task to complete and then move on. The second time, we set a timeout value in the `Wait` method. This tells our main thread to wait for the amount of time in the timeout parameter and then move on. Then we checked the `Task.IsComplete` property to see whether our task has completed or not.

Since the task was set to run for longer than the timeout value, the task was still running when our main thread continued execution. That is why the `IsComplete` property is `false` and the `else` portion of our `if` statement gets executed:

```
Console.WriteLine("Timed out without Task B finishing.");
```

You can play around with this code and make the task run for less time than the timeout value and see what happens.

Next, we ran a task using the `Worker1` method that returns a `double` value. What did we see here? We did not place a `Task.Wait` command but our main program still waited on the task to complete before continuing on with its execution. Why is that?

We know it waited until the task was completed because when we wrote the `Task.Result` value to the console, it had a value and was not `null`. In this case, we do not need to use the `Task.Wait` method explicitly because the main thread will wait on the task to complete; it needs to wait until the `Task.Result` property is set. By defining a task with a return value, we are telling our main thread implicitly to wait on the task to complete.

So, as we have seen, if we do not return a value in our task, then we need to explicitly tell our program to wait. However, if we return a value, we are implicitly telling our program to wait on the task to complete.

Next, we will see how to control the execution of our main thread when we start many concurrent tasks at once. In this case, if our tasks return values, we might not implicitly want to wait on every task to complete. Maybe we just want to wait on one task to complete.

In our current program, we used the `Thread.SpinWait` method. This method is different from the `Thread.Sleep` method. The `Thread.Sleep` method waits for a specified time whereas the `SpinWait` method starts a loop for the specified iterations passed to the method. So, in this case, the speed of the processor will dictate the duration because the clock speed will determine how fast it can complete the number of iterations. By using this instead of a `Sleep` method, it also allows the scheduler to perform context switching if thread priorities dictate.

Waiting for multiple tasks to complete

In the previous section, we examined how to explicitly and implicitly wait on a task to complete. Now, let's see how we can control execution and waiting when we start many tasks instead of just one.

Sometimes, we may want to wait on one task out of a group to finish. Sometimes, we might want to wait on all of the tasks to finish, and other times we might want to wait on a certain condition of tasks to finish before proceeding.

The following screenshot shows all of the `Wait` and `When` methods provided with the `Task` class. The `Wait` methods are as shown:

Wait()	Waits for the Task to complete execution.
Wait(CancellationToken)	Waits for the cancellable Task to complete execution.
Wait(Int32)	Waits for the Task to complete execution within a specified number of milliseconds.
Wait(TimeSpan)	Waits for the Task to complete execution within a specified time interval.
Wait(Int32, CancellationToken)	Waits for the cancellable Task to complete execution.
WaitAll(Task[])	Waits for all of the provided Task objects to complete execution.
WaitAll(Task[], Int32)	Waits for all of the provided Task objects to complete execution within a specified number of milliseconds.
WaitAll(Task[], CancellationToken)	Waits for all of the provided cancellable Task objects to complete execution.
WaitAll(Task[], TimeSpan)	Waits for all of the provided cancellable Task objects to complete execution within a specified time interval.
WaitAll(Task[], Int32, CancellationToken)	Waits for all of the provided cancellable Task objects to complete execution within a specified number of milliseconds.
WaitAny(Task[])	Waits for any of the provided Task objects to complete execution.
WaitAny(Task[], Int32)	Waits for any of the provided Task objects to complete execution within a specified number of milliseconds.
WaitAny(Task[], CancellationToken)	Waits for any of the provided cancellable Task objects to complete execution.
WaitAny(Task[], TimeSpan)	Waits for any of the provided Task objects to complete execution within a specified time interval.
WaitAny(Task[], Int32, CancellationToken)	Waits for any of the provided cancellable Task objects to complete execution within a specified number of milliseconds.

The `When` methods are as shown:

WhenAll(IEnumerable<Task>)	Creates a task that will complete when all of the supplied tasks have completed.
WhenAll(Task[])	Creates a task that will complete when all of the supplied tasks have completed.
WhenAll<TResult>(IEnumerable<Task<TResult>>)	Creates a task that will complete when all of the supplied tasks have completed.
WhenAll<TResult>(Task<TResult>[])	Creates a task that will complete when all of the supplied tasks have completed.
WhenAny(IEnumerable<Task>)	Creates a task that will complete when any of the supplied tasks have completed.
WhenAny(Task[])	Creates a task that will complete when any of the supplied tasks have completed.
WhenAny<TResult>(IEnumerable<Task<TResult>>)	Creates a task that will complete when any of the supplied tasks have completed.
WhenAny<TResult>(Task<TResult>[])	Creates a task that will complete when any of the supplied tasks have completed.

Both images are references from http://msdn.microsoft.com/en-us/library/system.threading.tasks.task_methods(v=vs.110).aspx.

We will demonstrate how to perform different Wait and When techniques in this chapter, but this is to give you further ideas on what is possible.

Let's start by creating a simple program to demonstrate how the WaitAll method works by populating three circles with random numbers once three tasks complete.

How to do it

To get started, we need to create a WPF application using Visual Studio. Open Visual Studio and create a new WPF project called RandomCircles. Once we have created this project, proceed by performing the following steps:

1. Go into the design mode in Visual Studio and add the following controls to the MainWindow.xaml file:

    ° Add three Ellipse controls and name them Circle1, Circle2, and Circle3.

    ° Set their height and width properties to 120 for all three circles. This is done in the MainWindow.xaml file using the **Design** mode in Visual Studio.

    ° Next, add three textboxes and place them inside the circles. Name them text1, text2, and text3. Set the Text property on all three to an empty string and make their Background property the same color as the Fill property on the Ellipse controls.

    ° Next, add a button control and name it btnRandomAll. Set the Content property on this control to Random All.

Now, your `MainWindow.xaml` file should look like the following screenshot:

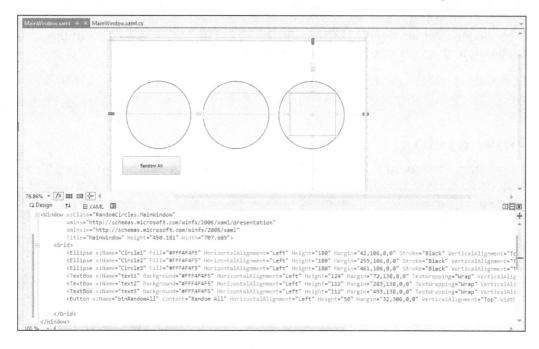

2. Next, let's go to the `MainWindow.xaml.cs` code behind this file. We need to add a `using` statement for the `Threading` namespace.

```
using System.Threading;
```

 The `System.Threading.Tasks` namespace should already be included when you created the WPF project, but check to make sure whether it is there.

3. Now, let's add a worker method to provide work for the tasks to perform, which we are about to create. Create a `Worker1` method that is `private` and returns a string value. Add the following code to it:

```
private String Worker1()
        {
int result = ran.Next(10000000);
Thread.SpinWait(result);
return String.Format("Random Number is {0} and Time is
{1}.",result, DateTime.Now.Millisecond);
        }
```

SpinWait is used here to demonstrate how processor speed can affect the speed of a function. SpinWait is very inefficient and does consume CPU resources more than Sleep().

4. Next, let's create an event handler for btnRandomAll—a click event called btnRandomAll_Click. Inside this method, add the following code:

```
private void btnRandomAll_Click(object sender, RoutedEventArgs e)
        {
// Wait for all tasks to finish.
Task<String>[] tasks = newTask<String>[3];
for (int i = 0; i< 3; i++)
        {
tasks[i] = Task<String>.Factory.StartNew(() => Worker1());
        }
Task.WaitAll(tasks);

            text1.Text = tasks[0].Result.ToString();
            text2.Text = tasks[1].Result.ToString();
            text3.Text = tasks[2].Result.ToString();
        }
```

That should be all you need to have a program that runs three tasks in separate threads. Each of these tasks will spin for a random time. The main thread will wait on all of these tasks to complete and then return a string that has the random number used by the task and the current time in milliseconds.

Finally, let's compile and run our new program. The following is what random circles should look like when it is first started:

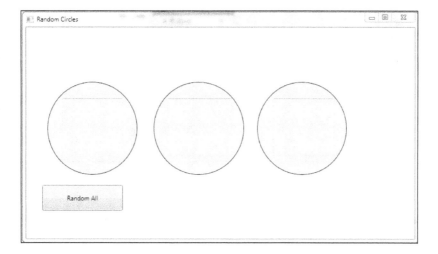

Now, click on the **Random All** button once and see what the output looks like. The following is what we got when we ran it:

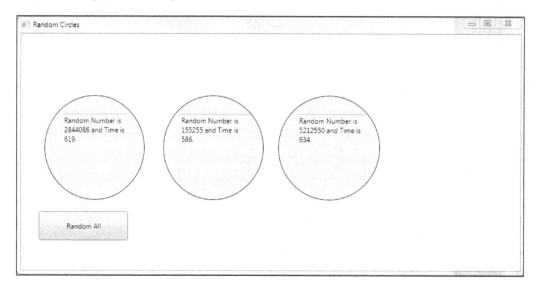

Now, click on the **Random All** button a second time and see what the program looks like. The following screenshot is what we got:

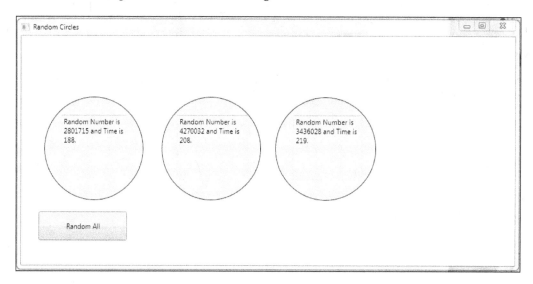

Now, let's make some changes to our program and try running it again. Make the following changes:

1. Add a new Ellipse control and name it `Circle4`.

2. Add a new textbox control and name it `text4` and set the `Text` property to an empty string.

3. Add another button control and name it `btnRandomFirst` and set the `Content` property to `RandomFirst`.

4. Add an event handler to the button, `btnRandomFirst`, and name it `btnRandomFirst_Click`. Add the following code to the event handler:

```
private void btnRandomFirst_Click(object sender, RoutedEventArgs
e)
        {
Task<String>[] tasks = newTask<String>[3];
for (int i = 0; i< 3; i++)
        {
tasks[i] = Task<String>.Factory.StartNew(() => Worker1());
        }
//Task.WaitAll(tasks);
int index = Task.WaitAny(tasks);

        text4.Text = "Task " + index.ToString() + " finished
first.";
        }
```

Now, let's compile and run our program. The following is the output before an action is taken:

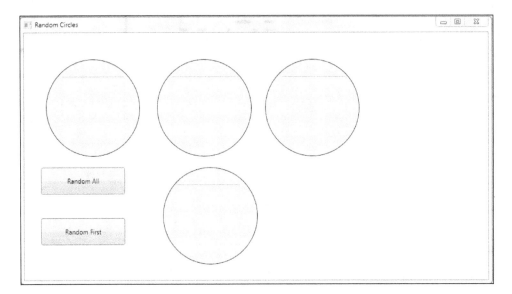

Now, click on the **Random First** button once and the output should look like the following screenshot:

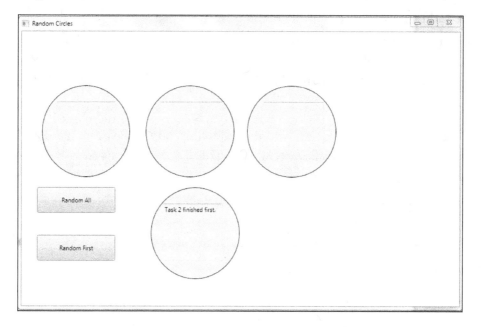

Finally, let's click on the **Random First** button a second time and look at the results. They should look like the following screenshot:

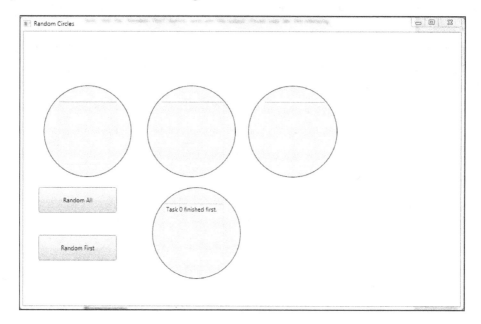

How it works

Let's take a minute to go through what we just did with this program.

First, our `Worker1` method that performs our *tasks* is a simple worker bee. It generates a random number and then does a `Thread.SpinWait` for that number of iterations. Then it returns the current time in milliseconds. So, every time this method is run as a task in a separate thread, it will run for a random amount of time. If multiple copies of this method are running in different threads, then they will each finish at a different time because `SpinWait` will run for a different randomly generated number of iterations.

1. When you click on the **Random All** button, the event handler is fired. The event handler starts three separate tasks each running the `Worker1` method using the following command:

   ```
   Task<String>.Factory.StartNew(() => Worker1());
   ```

2. We created a `Task` array with a string value `TResult` using this command:

   ```
   Task<String>[] tasks = newTask<String>[3];
   ```

3. Then, we wait on all of the tasks in the tasks array using this command:

   ```
   Task.WaitAll(tasks);
   ```

4. Then, we display the results of each task and see that they each have a different random number and finish at a different time even though each task is executing the same method.

5. Next, we created a second button that does much of the same work except for this time instead of the `Task.WaitAll` command, we use this command:

   ```
   int index = Task.WaitAny(tasks);
   ```

So, in this case, we only wait for any of the three tasks to complete before continuing execution in our main thread. You can verify this by clicking on the **Random First** button many times. Each time it can be either task 0, 1, or 2 that finishes first.

Take some time to play with these two commands and make sure you have a full understanding of how each works.

We will not spend time on this book playing with the `Continue`, `ContinueAll`, `When`, and `WhenAll` methods of the `Task` class, but take some time to experiment with these functionalities. These methods allow you to execute a task when other tasks have completed. So, you can chain task executions together. The alternative to these is to wait on tasks to complete and then start new tasks. The `Continue` and `When` methods allow you to combine this into one statement.

In the next section, we will explore canceling tasks. Depending on your requirements, you might want to cancel a task that you have started, before it ends.

Canceling a task

Let's explore canceling a task. Now that we know how to start one or more tasks and how to coordinate waiting on one or more of these tasks, what if something happens after we have started a group of tasks and we need to stop them?

Task cancellation is accomplished in the .NET framework by using **cancellation tokens**. The delegate used when running a task needs to have code to support cancelation and then any other code that needs to cancel a task can request cancelation of the task.

 The `CancellationToken` structure in .NET manages notification that an operation should be canceled. It has a property, `IsCancellationRequested`, that you can use to see if a cancellation request has been issued. This structure is a member of the `System.Threading` namespace and is used by threads and tasks to manage cancellation requests in a multithreaded environment.

Merely requesting to cancel a task will not cancel the task. The task delegate must support cancellation tokens. There are two ways that a delegate can choose to cancel. The delegate can simply return from execution, or it can throw an `OperationCanceledException` using the `ThrowIfCancellationRequested` method.

There are two main differences to these two methods of cancelation. If the delegate just returns from execution, then the following happens:

1. The task is put in a state of `TaskStatus.RanToCompletion` instead of `TaskStatus.Canceled`.

2. The code requesting to cancel the task does not know if the task simply finished or was canceled before finishing.

If the task delegate implements the latter method for canceling (throwing an `OperationCanceledException`), then the following happens:

1. The task is put in a state of `TaskStatus.Canceled`.

2. The requesting code can check this status and determine if the task was canceled or just finished.

So, now we will create a WPF application to allow the user to cancel tasks. We will demonstrate how to create cancellation tokens, monitor the task state to see if it is canceled, and then do some processing when it is canceled. This will also use the `Task.ContinueWith` method. This method allows us to execute a task when another task has completed.

In our application, we will start 10 tasks. Each task will take an integer parameter as input and will multiply it by the numbers from 1 to 10 million and take a sum of the results. It will then return a `double` value that is the result. While this may not be the world's most exciting computation, it will take a little time depending on your processor speed.

We will start each task with a task cancelation token pass to it and create `ContinueWith` tasks for it. One will *continue with* if the task runs to completion, and the other will *continue with* if the task is canceled. We will also have a **Cancel** button that allows you to cancel at any time and stop the tasks in progress.

Let's get started.

How to do it

Open up Visual Studio and create a new WPF application called `TaskCancel`. In the designer window in the `MainWindow.xaml` file, let's add the following items.

1. Add two button controls: one named `btnStart` and other named `btnCancel`.

2. Next, add a click event handler for each button: `btnStart_Click` and `btnCancel_Click` respectively.

3. Add a text block control named `textBlock1`.

Your `MainWindow.xaml` file should look like the following screenshot:

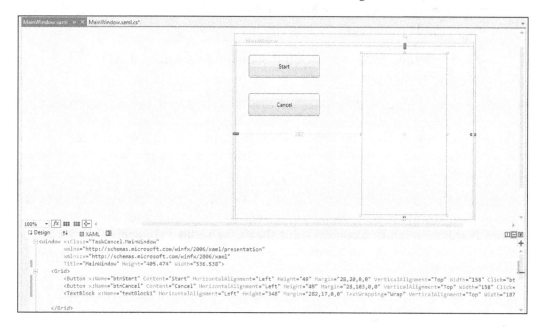

Now, move to the `MainWindow.xaml.cs` code behind the file. Let's add the following items:

1. Add a `using` statement for the `System.Threading` namespace:

   ```
   using System.Threading;
   ```

2. Then, inside the class definition at the top, let's add our cancelation token:

   ```
   CancellationTokenSourcets;
   ```

3. Next, let's add a method that will execute inside our 10 tasks. We will call this method `AddMultiple`. It takes an integer parameter and returns a value that is the datatype `double`. Add the following code to it:

   ```
   public double AddMultiple(int number)
           {
   double result = 1;
   for (int i = 1; i< 100000000; i++)
             {
   ts.Token.ThrowIfCancellationRequested();
   result = result + (number * i);
             }
   return result;
    }
   ```

4. Then, let's add the code to the click event handler of `btnStart` that will start the 10 tasks:

```
private void btnStart_Click(object sender, RoutedEventArgs e)
        {
ts = new CancellationTokenSource();

        textBlock1.Text = "";

List<Task> tasks = new List<Task>();

for (int i = 2; i<= 10; i++)
            {
int tmp = i;

Task<double> adder = Task.Factory.StartNew(() =>AddMultiple(tmp),
ts.Token);

tasks.Add(adder);

var show = adder.ContinueWith(resultTask =>
                                    textBlock1.Text += tmp.
ToString() + " - " + adder.Result.ToString() + Environment.
NewLine,
CancellationToken.None,
TaskContinuationOptions.OnlyOnRanToCompletion,
TaskScheduler.FromCurrentSynchronizationContext());

var showCancel = adder.ContinueWith(resultTask =>
                                    textBlock1.Text +=
tmp.ToString() + " canceled" + Environment.NewLine,
CancellationToken.None,
TaskContinuationOptions.OnlyOnCanceled, TaskScheduler.
FromCurrentSynchronizationContext());
            }
        }
```

5. Finally, let's add the code to the click event handler of `btnCancel`:

```
private void btnCancel_Click(object sender, RoutedEventArgs e)
        {
ts.Cancel();
        }
```

That is all we have to do. Now, let's compile and run our application. But this time, let's not run it through Visual Studio. We will run the application directly. Go to the `bin\Release` folder in our project directory and double-click on the `TaskCancel.exe` application. We will explain shortly why we are doing this and what happens when we run it in Visual Studio.

When you run the application, it should look like the following screenshot:

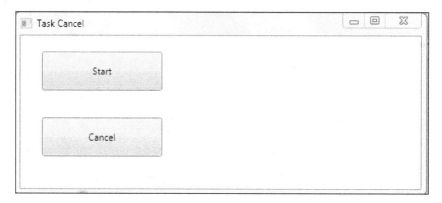

Now, click on the **Start** button. Then click on the **Cancel** button. You can decide how fast to click on the **Cancel** button but you should see an output like the following screenshot:

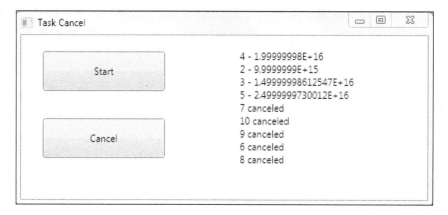

If you try running it in Visual Studio directly, you will notice that when you click on the **Cancel** button, an unhandled exception occurs. You can press *F5* a couple of times and it will continue on. But why does this happen?

The `ThrowIfCancellationRequested` method has *cooperative cancellation*. This throws an exception to indicate that it has accepted the cancellation requested and will stop. This exception is handled by .NET in the TPL and shouldn't be handled by your code. Since Visual Studio looks for all unhandled exceptions and shows them in debug mode, you will see it when running the application in debug mode through Visual Studio. There is a way to turn this off through the **Options-Debugging** settings under **Tools**, but we do not recommend it because it can mask other exceptions that you want to see. Nevertheless, the exception we encounter here is a nuisance when debugging.

How it works

Now that we've successfully canceled running tasks, let's see how we did it. First, we defined a cancellation token using `CancellationTokenSourcets`. Then we instantiated it using `ts = new CancellationTokenSource()`. This gives us a cancellation token that we can work with.

Let's skip, briefly, to the end. To cancel tasks, we just call the token's `Cancel` method, `ts.Cancel()`, in the **Cancel** button's click event handler. This will indicate to any task, which is using this cancelation token, that they need to cancel. Now it is up to the tasks to monitor the token and perform the cancelation.

So, let's take a look at the **Start** button's click method. Here, we create and start 10 tasks using the following code:

```
Task<double> adder = Task.Factory.StartNew(() =>AddMultiple(tmp),
ts.Token);
```

Here, we call the `Task.Factory.StartNew` command and pass it the delegate for the task to execute and the cancellation token.

Then, we also call the `ContinueWith` command to tell the task what to do after it finishes. We set up two of these depending on how the task finishes:

```
var show = adder.ContinueWith(resultTask =>
                                textBlock1.Text += tmp.ToString()
+ " - " + adder.Result.ToString() + Environment.NewLine,
CancellationToken.None,
TaskContinuationOptions.OnlyOnRanToCompletion,
TaskScheduler.FromCurrentSynchronizationContext());
```

```
var showCancel = adder.ContinueWith(resultTask =>
                                      textBlock1.Text += tmp.
ToString() + " canceled" + Environment.NewLine,
CancellationToken.None,

TaskContinuationOptions.OnlyOnCanceled, TaskScheduler.
FromCurrentSynchronizationContext());
```

For the first one, we pass the parameter, `TaskContinuationOptions.OnlyOnCanceled`, and for the second one, we pass the parameter, `TaskContinuationOptions.OnlyOnRanToCompletion`.

So, if the task is canceled, the second `ContinueWith` command is executed and, if the task runs to completion, the first `ContinueWith` command is executed. In each of these `ContinueWith` commands, we pass a lambda expression to execute, which prints the results of the task. This is how we update the UI with the status of each task, once it has completed.

From the output you can see which tasks run to completion and which tasks are canceled. Also, note that the output is not in sequential order. Since the 10 tasks are scheduled with the threadpool and the different cores on the machine we run have different workloads, the tasks finish in different orders.

Next, we will take a look at error handling with tasks.

Task exception handling

Well, we have learned how to start, coordinate, and cancel tasks. Now, let's talk about error handling with tasks. In C#, when we discuss error handling, we are really talking about the `try..catch..finally` structure. In this book, we assume you are familiar with the operation of a `try..catch` block.

A task has a lifecycle of states that it can be in. A task can be idle (scheduled), running, pending, cancelled, faulted, or completed. Each task has a `status` property that defines the current state of the task. We saw this in the last section and used `OnlyOnCanceled` and `OnlyOnRanToCompletion` as the options for `TaskContinuationOptions` for our `ContinueWith` methods.

So, when we talk about exception handling with TPL, we are referring to faulted tasks. There are several ways a task can reach a faulted status, for example, when the task delegate fails and throws an exception. A **faulted task** is basically a task that resulted in an error and carries the exception with it.

Your code will incur an exception if you perform one of the following on a faulted task:

- Waiting on a task
- Using the task's result value
- Performing an `Await` on the task

So, when you use the `Wait, WaitAll, Await,` or `Result` methods of a task, you should surround these statements with a `try..catch` block. The first two will always throw an exception of the `AggregateException` type, which is a container for multiple exceptions. The `Await` will throw the actual exception occurred by the task's delegate.

These are the basics of task exception handling. We want to do a `try..catch` around the `Result, Wait,` or `Await` of a task.

But what if we start a task and do not care about waiting on it or its results, but we want to know if it incurs an exception? How do we know if a start-and-forget task has a problem? In this case, we can use a simple technique with the help of the `ContinueWith` command. Look at the following command:

```
task.ContinueWith(resultTask =>DoSomething(), TaskContinuationOptions.
OnlyOnFaulted);
```

In this case, we create a task to execute on a `ContinueWith` command if the task is in an `OnlyOnFaulted` state.

So, you can perform exception handling with a `try..catch` on the result while waiting on a task or, if you are not waiting on the task or result, you can create a `ContinueWith` task to handle the exception.

Summary

In this chapter, we have looked at ways to wait on a task, cancel, chain, and perform exception handling with tasks. We have now covered all of the aspects that need to work with tasks in the TPL and the techniques needed to handle all of the scenarios your design might encounter.

We encourage you to further explore the techniques presented in this chapter and explore the world of task-based parallelism. The days of working directly with threads and the `BackgroundWorker` component will soon become a distant memory.

These last two chapters have been an overview of TPL and task-based parallelism. In the next chapter, we will cover data-based parallelism and working with data collections in a concurrent manner.

7
Data Parallelism

Concurrently performing a task or a set of operations on a collection of data is referred to as data parallelism. For example, if we have a list of files in a folder and we want to rename them all, we can create a `For` loop that goes through the collection and, during each iteration, the loop performs a rename command. We can also iterate through a collection datatype such as a `List` or `DataView` using a `foreach` statement. These are specialized `For` and `ForEach` statements that are part of the **Task Parallel Library (TPL)** in the `System.Threading.Tasks.Parallel` namespace.

The TPL provides the `Parallel` library to make it easy to perform concurrent operations on a dataset or data collection using the different overloads of the `Parallel.For` and `Parallel.ForEach` methods.

In this chapter, we will learn how to process items of a data source in parallel using the `Parallel.For` and `Parallel.ForEach` methods. We will also examine the `ParallelLoopState` class, which allows us to examine the results of a concurrent loop and perform actions with the results. Finally, we will learn how to cancel a concurrent loop before it has completed. In this chapter, we will cover:

- Parallel data processing with `Parallel.For`
- Parallel data processing of `IEnumerable` collections
- Using the results of concurrent data loops
- Canceling a parallel loop operation

Parallel loop processing

In this first section, we will examine the `Parallel.For` method and several variations of it. The most basic overload to this method takes a starting index, an ending index, and an `Action` delegate. In the `Parallel` method, the `Action` delegate can be implemented with a named method, anonymous method, or a lambda expression. The following is the basic syntax for each method:

```
// Named method.
Parallel.For(0, i, DoWork);

// Anonymous method
Parallel.For(0, i, delegate(int j)
{
    // Do Work.
});

// Lambda expression.
Parallel.For(0, i, j =>
{
    // Do Work
});
```

In each example, the method or lambda expression takes a single parameter that is the iteration value. If you need more control over the execution of the concurrent loop, there are overload methods that take a `ParallelLoopState` parameter that is internally generated by .NET. We will talk about this later in the chapter, but it allows us to do things such as canceling a parallel loop or performing an action for each iteration of the loop once it is completed.

Here is a list of all of the overloads of the `Parallel.For` method:

		Name	Description
⊘	S	For(Int32, Int32, Action<Int32>)	Executes a **for** (**For** in Visual Basic) loop in which iterations may run in parallel.
⊘	S	For(Int32, Int32, Action<Int32, ParallelLoopState>)	Executes a **for** (**For** in Visual Basic) loop in which iterations may run in parallel and the state of the loop can be monitored and manipulated.
⊘	S	For(Int64, Int64, Action<Int64>)	Executes a **for** (**For** in Visual Basic) loop with 64-bit indexes in which iterations may run in parallel.
⊘	S	For(Int64, Int64, Action<Int64, ParallelLoopState>)	Executes a **for** (**For** in Visual Basic) loop with 64-bit indexes in which iterations may run in parallel and the state of the loop can be monitored and manipulated.
⊘	S	For(Int32, Int32, ParallelOptions, Action<Int32>)	Executes a **for** (**For** in Visual Basic) loop in which iterations may run in parallel and loop options can be configured.
⊘	S	For(Int32, Int32, ParallelOptions, Action<Int32, ParallelLoopState>)	Executes a **for** (**For** in Visual Basic) loop in which iterations may run in parallel, loop options can be configured, and the state of the loop can be monitored and manipulated.
⊘	S	For(Int64, Int64, ParallelOptions, Action<Int64>)	Executes a **for** (**For** in Visual Basic) loop with 64-bit indexes in which iterations may run in parallel and loop options can be configured.
⊘	S	For(Int64, Int64, ParallelOptions, Action<Int64, ParallelLoopState>)	Executes a **for** (**For** in Visual Basic) loop with 64-bit indexes in which iterations may run in parallel, loop options can be configured, and the state of the loop can be monitored and manipulated.
⊘	S	For<TLocal>(Int32, Int32, Func<TLocal>, Func<Int32, ParallelLoopState, TLocal, TLocal>, Action<TLocal>)	Executes a **for** (**For** in Visual Basic) loop with thread-local data in which iterations may run in parallel, and the state of the loop can be monitored and manipulated.
⊘	S	For<TLocal>(Int64, Int64, Func<TLocal>, Func<Int64, ParallelLoopState, TLocal, TLocal>, Action<TLocal>)	Executes a **for** (**For** in Visual Basic) loop with 64-bit indexes and thread-local data in which iterations may run in parallel, and the state of the loop can be monitored and manipulated.
⊘	S	For<TLocal>(Int32, Int32, ParallelOptions, Func<TLocal>, Func<Int32, ParallelLoopState, TLocal, TLocal>, Action<TLocal>)	Executes a **for** (**For** in Visual Basic) loop with thread-local data in which iterations may run in parallel, loop options can be configured, and the state of the loop can be monitored and manipulated.
⊘	S	For<TLocal>(Int64, Int64, ParallelOptions, Func<TLocal>, Func<Int64, ParallelLoopState, TLocal, TLocal>, Action<TLocal>)	Executes a **for** (**For** in Visual Basic) loop with 64-bit indexes and thread-local data in which iterations may run in parallel, loop options can be configured, and the state of the loop can be monitored and manipulated.

MSDN reference—http://msdn.microsoft.com/en-us/library/system.threading.tasks.parallel.for(v=vs.110).aspx

Also, as well as a `ParallelLoopState` parameter, some overloads allow the method to return a thread-safe local variable.

Now, let's take a look at an example. We will build a simple **Windows Presentation Foundation (WPF)** application that takes an array of integer numbers, performs a calculation on them, and then updates the item in the array. This will be done concurrently instead of sequentially.

How to do it

For this example, we will create a WPF application that allows the user to enter numbers in 10 boxes and click on a button. Once the button is clicked, it will concurrently take each number and multiply it by the numbers 1 through 10 and sum the results. The result of each calculation will be placed back in each box. Perform the following steps to do so:

1. Open Visual Studio and create a WPF application named `ParallelMath1`.

2. In the `MainWindow.xaml` design view, change the page title to `ParallelMath`:

   ```
   Title="ParallelMath" Height="350" Width="525">
   ```

3. Now, create 10 textbox controls and place them in the `MainWindow.xaml` file with the names, `tb1`, `tb2`, `tb3`, `tb4`, `tb5`, `tb6`, `tb7`, `tb8`, `tb9`, and `tb10` respectively. Also, set their `Text` properties to `0`.

4. Now, place a button control on the `MainWindow.xaml` file and set the `Content` property to `Calculate` and the `Name` property to `btnCalculate`.

5. Next, create an event handler for the button's click event named `btnCalculate_Click`.

6. Inside the class definition, place a line of code to create an array of 10 integers:

```
int[] numbers = new int[10];
```

7. Now, put the following code inside the `btnCalculate_Click` event handler:

```
int[] numbers = new int[10];
numbers[0] = Convert.ToInt32(tb1.Text);
numbers[1] = Convert.ToInt32(tb2.Text);
numbers[2] = Convert.ToInt32(tb3.Text);
numbers[3] = Convert.ToInt32(tb4.Text);
numbers[4] = Convert.ToInt32(tb5.Text);
numbers[5] = Convert.ToInt32(tb6.Text);
numbers[6] = Convert.ToInt32(tb7.Text);
numbers[7] = Convert.ToInt32(tb8.Text);
numbers[8] = Convert.ToInt32(tb9.Text);
numbers[9] = Convert.ToInt32(tb10.Text);

Parallel.For(0, 9, CalculateNumbers);

tb1.Text = numbers[0].ToString();
tb2.Text = numbers[1].ToString();
tb3.Text = numbers[2].ToString();
tb4.Text = numbers[3].ToString();
tb5.Text = numbers[4].ToString();
tb6.Text = numbers[5].ToString();
tb7.Text = numbers[6].ToString();
tb8.Text = numbers[7].ToString();
tb9.Text = numbers[8].ToString();
tb10.Text = numbers[9].ToString();
```

8. Finally, create a method named `CalculateNumbers` and put the following code into it:

```
private void CalculateNumbers(int i)
{
    int j = numbers[i];
```

```
for (int k = 1; k <= 10; k++)
{
    j *= k;
}

numbers[i] = j;
```

```
}
```

That should be all. Now, let's run our application and see what happens. Remember we have not put in any error handling. The application expects a number and only a number in each textbox when the **Calculate** button is clicked. If it is not there, the application will throw an argument out of range exception.

You should see results similar to this before you click on the button:

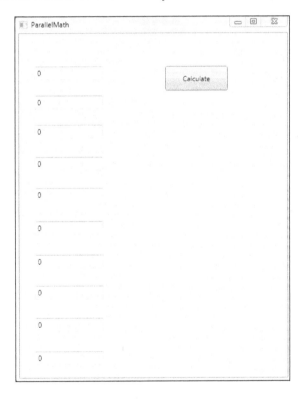

Now, let's enter 10 numbers into our textboxes so that the application looks something like the following:

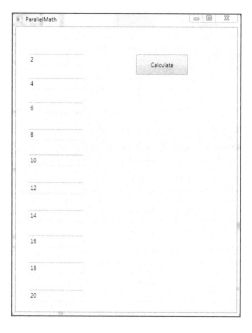

Now, click on the **Calculate** button and you should see the following results very quickly since we are doing these calculations concurrently:

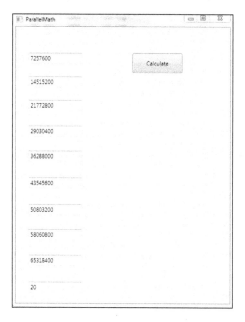

How it works

In the preceding exercise, we entered 10 numbers into 10 textboxes and then clicked on **Calculate**. The program then took each number, multiplied it by the numbers 1 through 10, and summed them together. It then placed the result back in the textbox it came from.

This was all done concurrently. Each textbox was processed in parallel. This may have been on 10 separate threads or fewer, depending on the hardware we run the program on. Unlike using threads directly by using the `Parallel` class and TPL, .NET manages the threadpool and maximizes how many threads to perform the concurrent operation on, using the processing cores available on the machine.

Let's look at how the concurrent loop is executed. It is the single command `Parallel.For(0, 9, CalculateNumbers);`. This command queues 10 tasks to the threadpool and each task will execute the `CalculateNumbers` method with an integer parameter.

Now, let's look at the `Parallel.ForEach` command.

Data parallelism on collections using Parallel.ForEach

The form of data parallelism that I find most helpful is performing concurrent operations on collections of data. This allows us to take data collections such as lists, dataviews, dictionaries, and so on and perform a task on each item in the collection in parallel with a single line of code! This makes using data parallelism simpler; you have to do nothing more than normal data processing. This is one of the reasons why the TPL is such a wonderful enhancement to .NET.

Much like the `Parallel.For` method, the structure of `Parallel.ForEach` looks like the following:

```
Parallel.ForEach(dataCollection, item => DoWork(item));
```

There are two parameters in the most basic version of this method. There is a data collection and an `Action` delegate to perform a task on an item of the `dataCollection`. The `Action` delegate takes a single parameter that is an item in the collection.

The following are all of the different overloads of the `ForEach` method:

	Name	Description
⬦ S	ForEach<TSource>(IEnumerable<TSource>, Action<TSource>)	Executes a **foreach** (**For Each** in Visual Basic) operation on an IEnumerable in which iterations may run in parallel.
⬦ S	ForEach<TSource>(IEnumerable<TSource>, Action<TSource, ParallelLoopState>)	Executes a **foreach** (**For Each** in Visual Basic) operation on an IEnumerable in which iterations may run in parallel, and the state of the loop can be monitored and manipulated.
⬦ S	ForEach<TSource>(IEnumerable<TSource>, Action<TSource, ParallelLoopState, Int64>)	Executes a **foreach** (**For Each** in Visual Basic) operation with 64-bit indexes on an IEnumerable in which iterations may run in parallel, and the state of the loop can be monitored and manipulated.
⬦ S	ForEach<TSource>(OrderablePartitioner<TSource>, Action<TSource, ParallelLoopState, Int64>)	Executes a **foreach** (**For Each** in Visual Basic) operation on a OrderablePartitioner<TSource> in which iterations may run in parallel and the state of the loop can be monitored and manipulated.
⬦ S	ForEach<TSource>(Partitioner<TSource>, Action<TSource>)	Executes a **foreach** (**For Each** in Visual Basic) operation on a Partitioner in which iterations may run in parallel.
⬦ S	ForEach<TSource>(Partitioner<TSource>, Action<TSource, ParallelLoopState>)	Executes a **foreach** (**For Each** in Visual Basic) operation on a System.Collections.Concurrent.Partitioner in which iterations may run in parallel, and the state of the loop can be monitored and manipulated.
⬦ S	ForEach<TSource>(IEnumerable<TSource>, ParallelOptions, Action<TSource>)	Executes a **foreach** (**For Each** in Visual Basic) operation on an IEnumerable in which iterations may run in parallel and loop options can be configured.
⬦ S	ForEach<TSource>(IEnumerable<TSource>, ParallelOptions, Action<TSource, ParallelLoopState>)	Executes a **foreach** (**For Each** in Visual Basic) operation on an IEnumerable in which iterations may run in parallel, loop options can be configured, and the state of the loop can be monitored and manipulated.
⬦ S	ForEach<TSource>(IEnumerable<TSource>, ParallelOptions, Action<TSource, ParallelLoopState, Int64>)	Executes a **foreach** (**For Each** in Visual Basic) operation with 64-bit indexes on an IEnumerable in which iterations may run in parallel, loop options can be configured, and the state of the loop can be monitored and manipulated.
⬦ S	ForEach<TSource>(OrderablePartitioner<TSource>, ParallelOptions, Action<TSource, ParallelLoopState, Int64>)	Executes a **foreach** (**For Each** in Visual Basic) operation on a OrderablePartitioner<TSource> in which iterations may run in parallel, loop options can be configured, and the state of the loop can be monitored and manipulated.
⬦ S	ForEach<TSource>(Partitioner<TSource>, ParallelOptions, Action<TSource>)	Executes a **foreach** (**For Each** in Visual Basic) operation on a Partitioner in which iterations may run in parallel and loop options can be configured.
⬦ S	ForEach<TSource>(Partitioner<TSource>, ParallelOptions, Action<TSource, ParallelLoopState>)	Executes a **foreach** (**For Each** in Visual Basic) operation on a Partitioner in which iterations may run in parallel, loop options can be configured, and the state of the loop can be monitored and manipulated.
⬦ S	ForEach<TSource, TLocal>(IEnumerable<TSource>, Func<TLocal>, Func<TSource, ParallelLoopState, TLocal, TLocal>, Action<TLocal>)	Executes a **foreach** (**For Each** in Visual Basic) operation with thread-local data on an IEnumerable in which iterations may run in parallel, and the state of the loop can be monitored and manipulated.

⬦ S	ForEach<TSource, TLocal>(IEnumerable<TSource>, Func<TLocal>, Func<TSource, ParallelLoopState, Int64, TLocal, TLocal>, Action<TLocal>)	Executes a **foreach** (**For Each** in Visual Basic) operation with thread-local data on an IEnumerable in which iterations may run in parallel and the state of the loop can be monitored and manipulated.
⬦ S	ForEach<TSource, TLocal>(OrderablePartitioner<TSource>, Func<TLocal>, Func<TSource, ParallelLoopState, Int64, TLocal, TLocal>, Action<TLocal>)	Executes a **foreach** (**For Each** in Visual Basic) operation with thread-local data on a OrderablePartitioner<TSource> in which iterations may run in parallel, loop options can be configured, and the state of the loop can be monitored and manipulated.
⬦ S	ForEach<TSource, TLocal>(Partitioner<TSource>, Func<TLocal>, Func<TSource, ParallelLoopState, TLocal, TLocal>, Action<TLocal>)	Executes a **foreach** (**For Each** in Visual Basic) operation with thread-local data on a Partitioner in which iterations may run in parallel and the state of the loop can be monitored and manipulated.
⬦ S	ForEach<TSource, TLocal>(IEnumerable<TSource>, ParallelOptions, Func<TLocal>, Func<TSource, ParallelLoopState, TLocal, TLocal>, Action<TLocal>)	Executes a **foreach** (**For Each** in Visual Basic) operation with thread-local data on an IEnumerable in which iterations may run in parallel, loop options can be configured, and the state of the loop can be monitored and manipulated..
⬦ S	ForEach<TSource, TLocal>(IEnumerable<TSource>, ParallelOptions, Func<TLocal>, Func<TSource, ParallelLoopState, Int64, TLocal, TLocal>, Action<TLocal>)	Executes a **foreach** (**For Each** in Visual Basic) operation with thread-local data and 64-bit indexes on an IEnumerable in which iterations may run in parallel, loop options can be configured, and the state of the loop can be monitored and manipulated.
⬦ S	ForEach<TSource, TLocal>(OrderablePartitioner<TSource>, ParallelOptions, Func<TLocal>, Func<TSource, ParallelLoopState, Int64, TLocal, TLocal>, Action<TLocal>)	Executes a **foreach** (**For Each** in Visual Basic) operation with 64-bit indexes and with thread-local data on a OrderablePartitioner<TSource> in which iterations may run in parallel, loop options can be configured, and the state of the loop can be monitored and manipulated.
⬦ S	ForEach<TSource, TLocal>(Partitioner<TSource>, ParallelOptions, Func<TLocal>, Func<TSource, ParallelLoopState, TLocal, TLocal>, Action<TLocal>)	Executes a **foreach** (**For Each** in Visual Basic) operation with thread-local data on a Partitioner in which iterations may run in parallel, loop options can be configured, and the state of the loop can be monitored and manipulated.

Reference—http://msdn.microsoft.com/en-us/library/system.threading.tasks.parallel.foreach(v=vs.110).aspx

As you can see, there are many different overloads to this method. They allow us to use a `ParallelLoopState` object or a thread-safe local variable.

We will focus on the simple form of just performing concurrent processing on a data collection. To further reiterate this point, let's revisit a project we worked on earlier in the book. In *Chapter 4*, *Advanced Thread Processing*, we wrote an application that took a JPG image, divided it into separate bitmaps, and then performed parallel functions on each bitmap to find old stars. It then reassembled the individual bitmaps back into a single image.

We will rewrite this application using data parallelism and the TPL instead of threads directly. This will demonstrate how TPL can simplify multithreaded code development

No longer do we have to manage threads (start them, wait on them to complete, or track them). We no longer have to manage the number of processing cores our machine has to maximize performance without starting too many individual threads. All we have to do is separate our large image into a collection of smaller bitmaps and use a `Parallel.ForEach` concurrent loop to process each bitmap. That's it. Let's get started.

How to do it

We will take our original `OldStarsFinder` Windows Form application and change it. To do this let's perform the following steps:

1. First, let's open our `OldStarsFinder` application in Visual Studio.

2. Let's add a new `using` statement so we can access the `Parallel` library:

    ```
    using System.Threading.Tasks;
    ```

3. At the beginning of the class definition, remove all of the old variable declarations and replace them with just these:

    ```
    private int Count = 0;
    // Number of bitmaps to break the original into and add to
    // the list of bitmaps.
    private List<Bitmap> BitmapList;
            //List of bitmaps to use the ParallelForEach on.
            Bitmap OriginalBitmap;
    private String prsOldStarsCount = "0";

    //Old stars count using a lock to protect thread safety.
    ```

4. Replace the `CropBitmap` method with this method definition:

```
        private Bitmap CropBitmap(Bitmap proBitmap, Rectangle
proRectangle)
        {
            // Create a new bitmap copying the portion of the
            // original defined by proRectangle
            // and keeping its PixelFormat
            Bitmap loCroppedBitmap = proBitmap.Clone(proRectangle,
proBitmap.PixelFormat);

            return loCroppedBitmap;
        }
```

5. You can leave the `IsOldStar` method as is.

6. Change the `ThreadOldStarsFinder` method to look like this:

```
        private void ThreadOldStarsFinder(Bitmap loBitmap)
        {
            int liRow;                      // The pixel matrix
(bitmap) row number (Y)
            int liCol;                      // The pixel matrix
(bitmap) col number (X)
            Color loPixelColor;             // The pixel color

            // Iterate through each pixel matrix (bitmap) rows
            for (liRow = 0; liRow < loBitmap.Height; liRow++)
            {
                // Iterate through each pixel matrix (bitmap) cols
                for (liCol = 0; liCol < loBitmap.Width; liCol++)
                {
                    // Get the pixel Color for liCol and liRow
                    loPixelColor = loBitmap.GetPixel(liCol,
liRow);

                    if (IsOldStar(loPixelColor))
                    {
                        // The color range corresponds to an old
star

                        // Change its color to a pure blue
                        loBitmap.SetPixel(liCol, liRow, Color.
Blue);

                        lock (prsOldStarsCount)
                        {
                            int i = Convert.
ToInt32(prsOldStarsCount);
```

```
                                            i = i + 1;
                                            prsOldStarsCount = i.ToString();
                                       }

                                  }
                              }
                          }
    }
```

7. Then change the `ShowBitmapWithOldStars` method to look like this:

```
private void ShowBitmapWithOldStars()
        {
                int liThreadNumber;
                // Each bitmap portion
                Bitmap loBitmap;
                // The starting row in each iteration
                int liStartRow = 0;


                // Calculate each bitmap's height
                int liEachBitmapHeight = ((int)(OriginalBitmap.Height
/ Count)) + 1;

                // Create a new bitmap with the whole width and height
                loBitmap = new Bitmap(OriginalBitmap.Width,
OriginalBitmap.Height);
                Graphics g = Graphics.FromImage((Image)loBitmap);
                g.InterpolationMode = System.Drawing.Drawing2D.
InterpolationMode.HighQualityBicubic;

                for (liThreadNumber = 0; liThreadNumber < Count;
liThreadNumber++)
                {
                        // Draw each portion in its corresponding absolute
starting row
                        g.DrawImage(BitmapList[liThreadNumber], 0,
liStartRow);
                        // Increase the starting row
                        liStartRow += liEachBitmapHeight;
                }
                // Show the bitmap in the PictureBox picStarsBitmap
                picStarsBitmap.Image = loBitmap;
                //picStarsBitmap.Image.Save("c:\\packt\\resulting_
image.png", ImageFormat.Png);

                tbCount.Text = prsOldStarsCount;
```

```
                    g.Dispose();
        }
```

8. Now, change the butFindOldStars_Click event handler to have the
    following code:

```csharp
private void butFindOldStars_Click(object sender, EventArgs e)
        {
                Count = Convert.ToInt32(tbTasks.Text);
                OriginalBitmap = new Bitmap(picStarsBitmap.Image);
                BitmapList = new List<Bitmap>(Count);

                int StartRow = 0;
                int EachBitmapHeight = ((int)(OriginalBitmap.Height /
Count)) + 1;

                int HeightToAdd = OriginalBitmap.Height;
                Bitmap loBitmap;

                // Breakup the bitmap into a list of bitmaps.
                for (int i = 0; i < Count; i++)
                {

                        if (EachBitmapHeight > HeightToAdd)
                        {
                                // The last bitmap height perhaps is less than
the other bitmaps height
                                EachBitmapHeight = HeightToAdd;
                        }

                        loBitmap = CropBitmap(OriginalBitmap, new
Rectangle(0, StartRow, OriginalBitmap.Width, EachBitmapHeight));
                        HeightToAdd -= EachBitmapHeight;
                        StartRow += EachBitmapHeight;
                        BitmapList.Add(loBitmap);
                }

                //Iterate through the list of bitmaps with the
Parallel.ForEach command.
                Parallel.ForEach(BitmapList, item =>
ThreadOldStarsFinder(item));

                ShowBitmapWithOldStars();
        }
```

9. Then add a label control with the text, `Number of bitmaps to divide into for processing:`.

10. Also, add a textbox control and set its `Name` property to `tbTasks`. This will be used to allow you to designate the number of sections you want the bitmap divided into.

11. Finally, we remove the `butFindOldStarsBatch` button because we do not need it in this application.

That should be all you need to do to run this application using data parallelism with the Task Parallel Library.

Let's compile and run our application. You should get something like this:

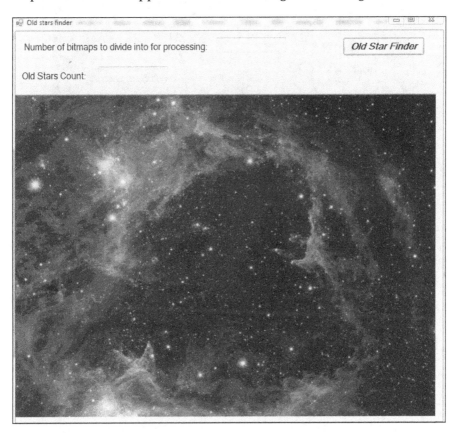

Now, enter the number of bitmaps to divide the image into and click on the **Old Star Finder** button. The application will now look like this:

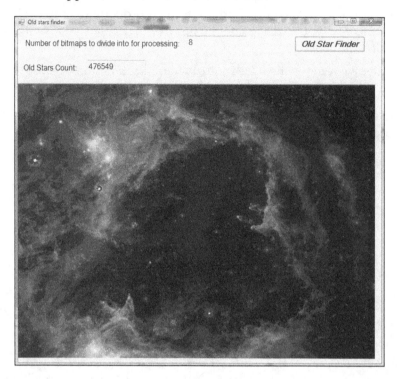

What just happened? We entered 8 for the number of bitmaps to divide into. The application splits the JPG image into 8 equal-sized bitmaps and then into a list collection of bitmaps. Then it concurrently processes each bitmap looking for old stars. Finally, it reassembles the bitmaps into one image and redisplays it.

Let's take a closer look at what just happened.

How it works

If you compare the two versions of the program, you will see that the second version is much simpler with less code. If we examine the `butOldStarsFinder_Click` event handler method, we will see most of the work. First, we divide our image up into a `List` collection of smaller bitmaps based on the number we entered. Here is the code that does this:

```
// Breakup the bitmap into a list of bitmaps.
for (int i = 0; i < Count; i++)
{
```

```
        if (EachBitmapHeight > HeightToAdd)
        {
            // The last bitmap height perhaps is less than
            // the other bitmaps height
            EachBitmapHeight = HeightToAdd;
        }


        loBitmap = CropBitmap(OriginalBitmap, new Rectangle(0,
StartRow, OriginalBitmap.Width, EachBitmapHeight));
        HeightToAdd -= EachBitmapHeight;
        StartRow += EachBitmapHeight;
        BitmapList.Add(loBitmap);
    }
```

Next, we take our list collection, `BitmapList`, and use it in a parallel `ForEach` command in this line of code:

```
Parallel.ForEach(BitmapList, item => ThreadOldStarsFinder(item));
```

Finally, when this loop has completed, we display the image with the old stars with this method:

```
ShowBitmapWithOldStars();
```

That is it. We no longer have to find out how many cores the processor has and create that many threads. No matter how many items there are in our collection, .NET maximizes the threads in the threadpool to achieve optimal performance. It will create threads if needed or reuse existing threads if possible. This saves on the overhead of starting more threads than can be effectively used by the number of cores in the machine.

You can now see why writing multithreaded code using TPL is called lightweight concurrency. This version of the Old Stars Finder is definitely "lighter" on the code and logic than the previous version written directly with threads or heavyweight concurrency.

Canceling a parallel loop

Now that we have learned how to execute a parallel loop using a `Parallel` class library, let's take a look at how we can stop or break a loop if needed. With a normal `For` or `ForEach` loop we can use a `Continue` command to break from a loop.

If we break from a parallel loop, then we complete all iterations on the threads that are currently executing and then stop. If we Stop a parallel loop, then we stop all currently running iterations of the loop as soon as possible, but we do not run them to completion. In either case, we will not schedule tasks on the threadpool for the rest of the iterations of the parallel loop that we are yet to get started with.

To perform a break or a stop of a parallel loop, we need to use the ParallelLoopState object. This means that we have to use one of the overloads or the Parallel.For or Parallel.ForEach method that takes a ParallelLoopState parameter.

 What is the ParallelLoopState class? This class cannot be instantiated in your user code. It is provided by the TPL and .NET and hence is a special class. This object provides your parallel loop with a mechanism to interact with other iterations in the loop.

The break and stop methods are the methods you will use most often, as well as the IsStopped and IsExceptional properties. These properties allow you to check whether any iteration of the loop has called Stop or thrown an exception.

Now, we will take our ParallelMath1 example and change it to stop the loop after seven iterations. This is arbitrary, for example purposes. But in a real example, there are many conditions where you will want to break or stop from a parallel loop.

How to do it

We just need to make a few adjustments to our previous program. Let's start by opening the ParallelMath1 WPF application in Visual Studio and making the following changes:

1. Create a new method called CalculateNumbers2 and place the following code into it:

```
private void CalculateNumbers2 (int i, ParallelLoopState pls)
{
    int j = numbers[i];

    if (i < 7)
    {
        for (int k = 1; k <= 10; k++)
        {
            j *= k;
        }

        numbers[i] = j;
    }
```

```
        else
        {
            pls.Stop();
            return;
        }
    }
}
```

2. Then change our `Parallel.For` command to call this new method:

   ```
   Parallel.For(0, 9, CalculateNumbers2);
   ```

That's it. Now, let's run our application and put numbers in each of the boxes so that it looks like the following screenshot:

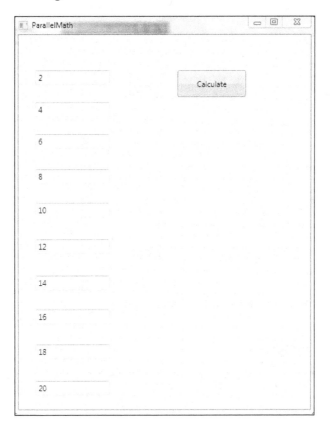

Now, click on the **Calculate** button and your results should look like the following screenshot:

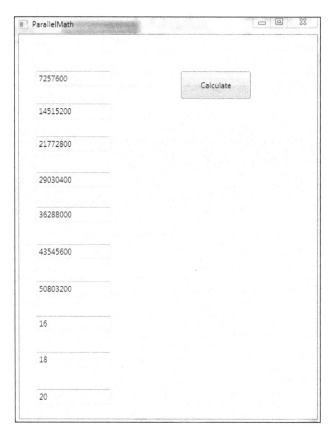

What do you see? Yes, after seven iterations of the parallel loop, the loop is stopped and the last three iterations are not finished. Let's examine why.

How it works

By adding the ParallelLoopState parameter to the method called by the parallel For method, we actually change the overload of the method that is called. We are now calling this overload:

✦ S	For(Int32, Int32, Action<Int32, ParallelLoopState>)	Executes a **for** (**For** in Visual Basic) loop in which iterations may run in parallel and the state of the loop can be monitored and manipulated.

You will notice that we do not create this `ParallelLoopState` variable and pass it into the `CalculateNumbers2` method. It is done by .NET and we can just use it. Pretty handy!

Now, in our `Action` delegate, `CalculateNumbers2`, we call the `Stop` method of this object using the following command:

```
pls.Stop();
```

Once this method is called, the rest of the iterations of the loop are not performed and the loop completes with the iterations it has already completed.

This is not a very practical example — why execute the loop for 10 iterations and just stop after seven? Why not execute the parallel for seven iterations in the first place? This is just an example for demonstration purposes. In your applications, you will find many conditions by which you will want to exit a parallel loop before completing all iterations, just like with a normal `For` loop.

Handling exceptions in parallel loops

Well, no matter how hard we try to write error-free code, the real world intervenes and inevitably there are exceptions that our code will encounter, for example, file not found, argument out or range, and so on. When we are processing a parallel loop command, since all of the iterations are running on potentially different threads, we need a way to gather all of the exceptions that any of the iterations of the loop may produce.

.NET provides the `AggregateException` class for just this purpose. This allows us to collect all of the exceptions into the `AggregateException` object and then "catch" it once the loop has completed.

Think of this like you would a normal error-handling situation. Typically, you put a `try` block around a section of the code and then a `catch` block after it to process any exceptions that occurred in the `try` block of the code. This will behave the same way. We will put a `try` block around our parallel loop command and then catch the exceptions that occur in all of the iterations of the loop. Only in this case, our `catch` block will catch the `AggregateException`, which is just a collection of exceptions.

Also, in our `Action` delegate, we will catch any exceptions that occur and add them to the `AggregateException` object.

That is all there is to it! Let's try this for ourselves by modifying our `ParallelMath1` project to generate an exception if any of the iterations produce a sum of over 5 million.

How to do it

To start, let's open the `ParallelMath1` project in Visual Studio and make the following changes:

1. We will be using a `Concurrent` queue to collect the exceptions, so add this `using` statement:

    ```
    using System.Collections.Concurrent;
    ```

2. Then, we need to declare our `ConcurrentQueue` instance where it is visible to the entire class. Add the following line right after the declaration on the number's integer array:

    ```
    ConcurrentQueue<Exception> exceptions = new
    ConcurrentQueue<Exception>();
    ```

3. Next, we will add a new method to be called by the `Action` delegate of our parallel loop command. We will call this method `CalculateNumbers3`. Add the following code to this method:

    ```
    private void CalculateNumbers3(int i, ParallelLoopState
    pls)
    {
        int j = numbers[i];

        try
        {
            for (int k = 1; k <= 10; k++)
            {
                j *= k;

                if (j > 5000000) throw new
    ArgumentException(String.Format("The value of text box {0} is {1}.
    ", i, j));
            }
        }
        catch(Exception e)
        {
            exceptions.Enqueue(e);
        }

        numbers[i] = j;

    }
    ```

4. Then, let's alter our `btnCalculate_Click` event handler. Change the code between the population of the numbers array and the population of the textboxes to include the following lines of code:

```
try
{
    Parallel.For(0, 10, CalculateNumbers3);

    if (exceptions.Count > 0) throw new
AggregateException(exceptions);
}

catch (AggregateException ae)
{
    // This is where you can choose which exceptions
to handle.
    foreach (var ex in ae.InnerExceptions)
    {
        if (ex is ArgumentException)
        {
            tbMessages.Text += ex.Message;
            tbMessages.Text += "\r\n";
        }
        else
            throw ex;
    }
}
```

5. Finally, in the `MainWindow.xaml` designer view, add a textblock control; set its `Name` property to `tbMessages` and its `Text` property to an empty string.

Now our changes are complete. When any of the iterations of the parallel loop reach above 5 million, we will throw an exception. All of the exceptions will be collected into a `ConcurrentQueue` and added to the `AggregateException` object. Once the parallel loop execution has completed, we will process the `AggregateException`, if there are any, and write their exception messages to the `Messages` textblock.

Build and run your application. Now, enter numbers in each of the boxes. You should have a screen that looks like the following screenshot:

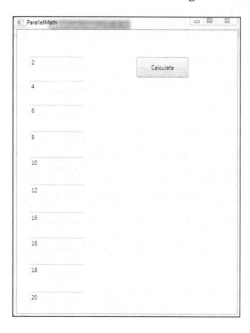

Now, click on the **Calculate** button and you should see results that look like the following screenshot:

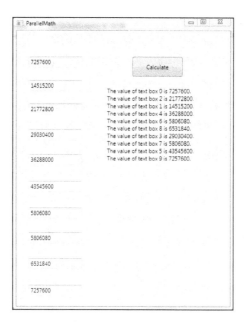

As you can see from the output, every box that has a total that goes over 5 million has a line printed in our **Messages** textblock. In this example, any number that goes over 5 million throws an exception. Once all of the iterations of the parallel loop have completed, we process these exceptions and print their messages to the `tbMessages` textblock.

How it works

The first thing we changed was adding an object that is in a concurrent queue, to hold all of our exceptions. This is done with this command:

```
ConcurrentQueue<Exception> exceptions = new
ConcurrentQueue<Exception>();
```

Next, in our `Action` delegate of the parallel `for` command, which in this version executes `CalculateNumbers3`, we check for numbers greater than 5 million through an exception using the following command:

```
if (j > 5000000) throw new ArgumentException(String.Format("The value
of text box {0} is {1}. ", i, j));
```

We then catch this exception within the delegate and add it to our concurrent queue of exception objects using these statements:

```
catch(Exception e)
{
    exceptions.Enqueue(e);
}
```

We do this because we do not want to interrupt other iterations of the parallel loop running on different threads. We want the loop to finish processing and then handle the exceptions. Since each iteration of the loop is running concurrently and is designed not to affect other iterations, we should not interrupt all of the iterations because one has an issue.

Once the loop has completed, we want to check for any exceptions and process them. Here is the code that handles this functionality:

```
try
{
    Parallel.For(0, 10, CalculateNumbers3);

    if (exceptions.Count > 0) throw new
AggregateException(exceptions);
}

catch (AggregateException ae)
```

```
        {
            // This is where you can choose which exceptions to
handle.

            foreach (var ex in ae.InnerExceptions)
            {
                if (ex is ArgumentException)
                {
                    tbMessages.Text += ex.Message;
                    tbMessages.Text += "\r\n";
                }
                else
                    throw ex;
            }
        }
}
```

If we see any exceptions in our ConcurrentQueue object, we throw an
AggregateException and give it the whole queue of exceptions. Then we
catch this AggregateException and process all of the exceptions it contains.

We could have also performed different actions based on the exception type
of each exception. You can play with your code and try this.

Using thread-local variables in parallel loops

Once you are comfortable using parallel loops, stopping them, and performing
exception handling with them, let's talk about how we can use thread-local variables
to better coordinate results. If we want to sum the results of all the iterations of a
parallel loop, how would we do that?

From what we have learned so far, we would create a class variable before the loop
and access it by each iteration of the loop using a lock statement so that it remains
thread-safe. This takes overhead and coordination time. To improve performance,
we can implement our parallel loop using a thread-local variable.

The Parallel.For and Parallel.ForEach loops both have overloads that
implement a thread-local variable. What do we mean by a thread-local variable?
This is a variable whose scope lasts the duration of the parallel loop, from just before
the first iteration starts to the completion of the last iteration. Each iteration of the
loop gets its own copy of the thread-local variable.

In these overloads of the parallel loop methods, there are three functions that get
passed to the loop as well as the iteration parameters. For a For loop, the iteration
parameters are the starting and ending values of the loop index, and for the ForEach
loop, it is the source collection.

The first function will initialize the thread-local variable. The second function is the `Action` delegate that the loop performs. The third function is the `Action` delegate that gets executed when all iterations of the loop have completed, and it receives the thread-local variable for each loop iteration. It can then process the results, which usually means combining the results.

Let's examine one of the `ForEach` overloads:

```
ForEach<TSource, TLocal>(IEnumerable<TSource>, Func<TLocal>,
Func<TSource, ParallelLoopState, TLocal, TLocal>, Action<TLocal>)
```

Let's dissect this for a minute. We will take each piece of the method definition and explain its role:

- `ForEach<TSource, TLocal>`: `TSource` is the datatype of the source collection, and `TLocal` is the datatype of the thread-local variable.

- `IEnumerable<TSource>`: This is the source collection. Since we are using a `ForEach` example, the source collection has to be `IEnumerable`.

- `Func<TLocal>`: This is the first function; it initializes the thread-local variable.

- `Func<TSource, ParallelLoopState, TLocal, TLocal>`: This is the second function; it is the `Action` delegate that is performed by each iteration of the loop.

- `Action<TLocal>`: This is the third function; it is the `Action` delegate that is performed on the local state of each iteration.

Even though this is a fairly straightforward concept, it leads itself to a method overload that looks very complicated. To make sure we understand, let's go to our `ParallelMath1` project and see how it works in the sample application we have been building.

How to do it

To use a thread-local variable to sum up our textboxes once we have performed our parallel loop on them, let's open our `ParallelMath1` project and make a few changes:

1. In the `MainWindow.xaml` file in the designer view, let's add a label control and set the `Content` property to `Sum:`.

2. Now, let's add a textbox control beside it and set the `Name` property to `tbSum` and make the `Text` property empty.

3. In the `MainWindow.xaml.cs` file, add the following `using` statement so that we can use the `Interlocked.Add` method:

```
using System.Threading;
```

4. Also, add a class variable below our `ConcurrentQueue` declaration for a sum variable we will call `total`:

```
long total = 0;
```

5. Then, comment out our current `Parallel.For` command because we are going to use the new overloaded version needed for thread-local variables:

```
//Parallel.For(0, 10, CalculateNumbers3);
```

6. It is easier for this version of a `Parallel.For` to use a lambda expression instead of the named methods for the `Action` delegates. So, use the following `Parallel.For` command:

```
Parallel.For<long>(0, 10,
            () => 0,
            (i, loop, subtotal) =>
            {
                int j = numbers[i];
                for (int k = 1; k <= 10; k++)
                {
                    j *= k;
                }

                numbers[i] = j;
                subtotal += j;
                return subtotal;
            },
            (finalResult) => Interlocked.Add(ref
total, finalResult)
        );
```

7. Finally, right after this statement, add the following statement so that we can see the total on the user interface:

```
tbSum.Text = total.ToString();
```

That is all the changes we need to make so that we can use our thread-local variable with the `Parallel.For` loop to calculate the sum of our textbox.

Once these changes have been made, build and run the application. Enter numbers in the textboxes and you should have a screen that looks like the following screenshot:

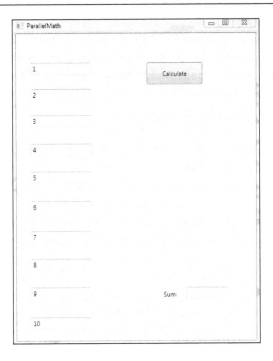

Now, click on the **Calculate** button and see what happens. The results should look like the following screenshot:

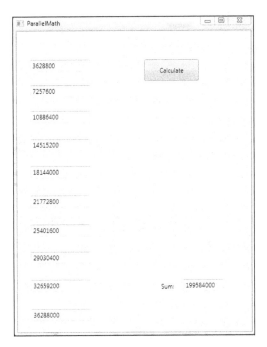

As you can see from the example, we now have a sum of all of the boxes once the parallel loop has processed them. We are able to do this without having to continually lock the class variable in each iteration when it wants to update the loop. We can do the summing once at the end of the parallel loop using the thread-local value from each iteration of the loop.

Now, let's examine what just happened

How it works

Just like in the previous versions of this project, we take the numbers in 10 different textboxes and multiply them by the numbers 1 through 10 and sum them. The result is then put back in the textbox. But this time, we take the new results in the 10 text boxes and sum them, and the final total is displayed in the tbSum textbox.

The only real difference in this version is the Parallel.For command. Let's take a deeper look at it:

```
Parallel.For<long>(0, 10,
        () => 0,
        (i, loop, subtotal) =>
        {
            int j = numbers[i];
            for (int k = 1; k <= 10; k++)
            {
                j *= k;
            }

            numbers[i] = j;
            subtotal += j;
            return subtotal;
        },
        (finalResult) => Interlocked.Add(ref
total, finalResult)
        );
```

First, we now have a TResult parameter that is a long Parallel.For<long>. This tells us that the Action delegate that each iteration of the loop executes will return a value with the datatype long. This Action delegate is implemented as a lambda expression this time and is the fourth parameter of our Parallel.For method:

```
(i, loop, subtotal) =>
        {
            int j = numbers[i];
            for (int k = 1; k <= 10; k++)
```

```
        {
            j *= k;
        }

        numbers[i] = j;
        subtotal += j;
        return subtotal;
    }
```

Let's create a back up; the first two parameters are the starting and ending indices of our iteration, 0 and 10. The third parameter is our `Action` delegate that initializes the thread-local variable. It is implemented with a lambda expression:

```
() => 0
```

Then, our final parameter to the `Parallel.For` method is the `Action` delegate that is executed on each iteration's thread-local variable:

```
(finalResult) => Interlocked.Add(ref total, finalResult)
```

We chose to use lambda expression for the three `Action` delegates in this example instead of named or anonymous methods because it is easier for us to see what is going on and what is being passed to what. However, we can use named methods to achieve the same results.

Summary

In this chapter, we covered all aspects of imperative data parallelism. In *Chapter 10, Parallel LINQ – PLINQ*, we will cover declarative data parallelism with PLINQ discussion. Data parallelism using TPL in .NET really comes down to performing parallel loops using the `Parallel.For` and `Parallel.ForEach` methods. These parallel loops allow us to iterate through a set or collection of data and perform the same function on each member of the set concurrently.

We learned how to perform a parallel loop on a set of data using `Parallel.For` and a collection of data using `Parallel.ForEach`. We then saw how to stop or break from a loop when a particular condition was reached; for this we used the `ParallelLoopState` object that .NET can generate.

Next, we explored error handling with parallel loops and the `AggregateException` object. We learned how to process all of the exceptions that might occur during the different iterations of the loop without affecting the other iterations.

In the last section, we saw how to use thread-local variables in our loops to have a thread-safe local copy of a variable and then use the results from all of these local copies at the end of the loop processing.

In the next chapter, we will take some time and explore the Visual Studio Debugger and the features it provides for debugging a parallel application that has multiple threads running at once.

8
Debugging Multithreaded Applications with Visual Studio

Multithreaded applications present their own set of challenges to develop as we have seen so far in this book, but they also have a unique set of challenges to debug. Visual Studio, starting with Visual Studio 2010, has developed additions to the debugger to assist with debugging tasks and the `Parallel` library.

Visual Studio has had the **Threads** window in their debugger since 2003 to assist with debugging threads. However, starting with Visual Studio 2010, they have added the **Parallel Stacks** window, **Parallel Watch** window, and the **Tasks** window to aid in debugging applications using the **Task Parallel Library** (TPL). In this chapter, we will examine all of these windows and demonstrate how to step through a multithreaded and multitask application to find program flow issues and race/lock conditions.

A **race condition** is a type of error that occurs when multiple threads interfere with each other and is based on the timing and execution of the different threads. Because of this, the condition does not happen every time the application executes. It takes a certain timing of the execution of the different threads.

A race condition happens when two or more threads access a data variable and try to modify it at approximately the same time. Since the OS scheduler can switch between threads at any time, you cannot predict the order in which the threads will access the data. The result of the change in data is dependent on the OS scheduling algorithm. Both the threads are "racing" to access the data.

Problems can happen when one thread examines the contents of a variable and performs an action but another thread changes the contents of the same variable during the time the first thread examines it and then acts on it.

A **lock condition** occurs when two or more threads are waiting on a resource that is locked by another thread. So, if thread 1 is waiting on a resource locked by thread 2 and thread 2 is waiting on a resource locked by thread 1, then both threads will remain "hung" forever waiting on each other to free up a resource. This is a type of a lock condition called a **deadlock**.

In this chapter, you will learn the following:

- Using the **Threads** window in the debugger
- Using the **Tasks** window in the debugger
- Accessing the **Parallel Stacks** and **Parallel Watch** windows
- Stepping through an application with more than one thread and more than one task
- Detecting a deadlock condition

Considerations for debugging multithreaded applications

There are several things to consider when debugging a parallel application. The first thing is probably the most obvious—there are multiple things happening at once. If you have an application with five threads, then all five threads can be executing at the same time depending on how many cores your machine has. If you step through a particular thread, the other threads are not just waiting on you unless there are breakpoints or they are waiting on a resource locked by the thread you are stepping through. You need to understand how your parallel application is designed and how it executes so you know what is happening in parallel—especially what is happening in threads other than the one you may by stepping through.

Secondly, debugging a concurrent application takes a lot of information. When using the debugger on a TPL application, you can have the **Local**, **Immediate**, **Threads**, **Task**, **Parallel Stack**, **Parallel Task**, **Process Explorer**, **Source Code**, and **Object Explorer** windows all open at the same time. This either takes a lot of screen real estate or requires constantly moving windows around to see the information that you need. I highly recommend doing this on a dual monitor setup. You can never have too much screen room when debugging a parallel application. There are few things more frustrating than not being able to easily see all the information you need as you step through an application.

Using the Threads window

The **Threads** window in the Visual Studio debugger allows you to view details of all of the threads in an application and work with them. You can view the stack of each thread. You can freeze or thaw a thread, and view all of the details concerning a thread.

If you start the debugger in an application and then go to **Debug** | **Windows**, you can select the **Threads** window. If you do this, you should see something like the following; this is the **Threads** window for the thread's version of the `OldStarFinder` program we did in *Chapter 7, Data Parallelism*:

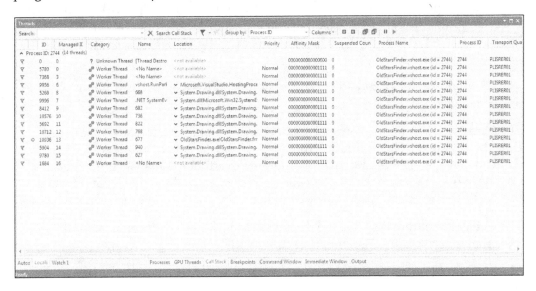

Let's take a look at this window and examine it in detail. It contains the following columns:

- **Flag**

- **Active**

- **ID**

- **Managed ID**

- **Category**

- **Name**

- **Location**

- **Priority**

- **Affinity Mask**

- **Suspended Count**
- **Process Name**
- **Process ID**
- **Transport Qualifier**

The **Flag** column allows you to designate a thread as one that you want to watch. If you right-click on a thread in this window, you can mark or unmark it as a flagged thread.

The **Active** column indicates which thread is the currently active thread. A yellow arrow designates the active thread in the debugger. It is also important to note that when stepping through a thread, other threads continue their operation unless a breakpoint is set. All of the threads do not block while you are stepping through a particular thread.

The **ID** column shows a thread's ID number in Windows, which is different from the .NET Managed ID.

The **Managed ID** column shows the managed ID number of a thread. A **managed thread** is different from a Windows thread. A managed thread, in this context, is a thread managed in .NET by the CLR and the threadpool. A managed thread can execute in one or more Windows threads. A .NET managed thread is created using the .NET Threads class. Also, remember when using Tasks that a task is not a thread.

The **Category** column displays the thread's classification as either the main thread, a user interface thread, a remote procedure handler thread, or a worker thread.

The **Name** column displays the thread's **Name** property if it is set, or otherwise displays **<No Name>**.

The **Location** column shows what method the thread is currently executing. By double-clicking on a row in this column, you can see the thread's full stack.

The **Priority** column shows the Windows priority for the thread.

The **Affinity Mask** column shows this mask for each thread. The affinity is a bitwise mask indicating which processors a thread is eligible to execute on. In our example, we have a four-processor system and all but one of the threads has a mask that ends with 1111. These are the four bits representing our four processors. This indicates that these threads can execute on any of the processors. There are methods in the Threads class that allow you to programmatically set which processors a thread can run on if you wish.

The **Suspended Count** column is a count manipulated by freezing and thawing threads. If you freeze a thread in managed code, then the thread will not run even if it is able to, and the suspended count will be 1.

The **Process Name** column displays the Windows process that the thread is associated with. Since we are running our application through the Visual Studio debugger, you will see that our threads have **OldStarsFinder.vshost.exe** as the process. You can also run the Task Manager in Windows and see this process.

Now that we have gone through all of the information the **Threads** window supplies, what are some of the functions you can do with it? You can show or hide columns in the display by clicking on the **Columns** dropdown in the header of this window; you can also do a Group By operation of the threads to group them for better management. We already saw how you can double-click on a row in the **Location** column and see a thread's call stack. You can also make any thread the **Active** thread by right-clicking on it and selecting **Switch To Thread**.

Next, let's examine the **Tasks** window.

Using the Tasks window

The **Tasks** window was added to the Visual Studio debugger in the 2010 version when the TPL was added to .NET in Version 4.0. It is similar to the **Threads** window and shows information about each task in your application. Tasks are created using the `System.Threading.Tasks.Task` class or by using the `async` and `await` keywords. The `async` and `await` keywords were introduced in Version 4.5 of .NET and will be covered in *Chapter 11, The Asynchronous Programming Model*. Like the **Threads** window, it can be accessed from the debugger in Visual Studio by navigating to **Debug | Windows**:

	ID	Status	Location	Task	AsyncState	Parent	Thread Assignment	AppDomain	Process
▽	4	⊘ Blocked	OldStarsFinder.frmStarsFinder.ThreadOldStarsFinder	butFindOldStars_Click.AnonymousMethod_1		1	7424 (163)	1 (OldStarsFinder.vshost.exe)	8632
▽	1	▶ Active	OldStarsFinder.frmStarsFinder.ThreadOldStarsFinder	butFindOldStars_Click.AnonymousMethod_1			5036 (272)	1 (OldStarsFinder.vshost.exe)	8632
▽	2	▶ Active	OldStarsFinder.frmStarsFinder.ThreadOldStarsFinder	butFindOldStars_Click.AnonymousMethod_1		1	8888 (810)	1 (OldStarsFinder.vshost.exe)	8632
▽	3	▶ Active	OldStarsFinder.frmStarsFinder.ThreadOldStarsFinder	butFindOldStars_Click.AnonymousMethod_1		1	8024 (130)	1 (OldStarsFinder.vshost.exe)	8632
▽	5	▶ Active	OldStarsFinder.frmStarsFinder.ThreadOldStarsFinder	butFindOldStars_Click.AnonymousMethod_1		1	3144 (304)	1 (OldStarsFinder.vshost.exe)	8632
▽ ⇨	6	▶ Active	OldStarsFinder.frmStarsFinder.ThreadOldStarsFinder	butFindOldStars_Click.AnonymousMethod_1		1	10052 (878)	1 (OldStarsFinder.vshost.exe)	8632
▽	7	▶ Active	OldStarsFinder.frmStarsFinder.ThreadOldStarsFinder	butFindOldStars_Click.AnonymousMethod_1		1	11144 (267)	1 (OldStarsFinder.vshost.exe)	8632
▽	8	▶ Active	OldStarsFinder.frmStarsFinder.ThreadOldStarsFinder	butFindOldStars_Click.AnonymousMethod_1		1	9592 (891)	1 (OldStarsFinder.vshost.exe)	8632

Tasks | Threads

Let's examine the information and functions you can use the **Tasks** window for:

- **Flags**: This column shows the tasks that you have flagged or unflagged. By clicking on this column for a task, you can flag the threads in this task. You can flag several tasks and then sort or use the Group By function to show the flagged tasks at the top. You can also filter the **Parallel Stacks** window by flagged tasks so you only see the parallel stacks of the tasks you are interested in.

- **Icons**: This column shows which is the current task present on the current thread. This is shown by a yellow arrow. A white arrow indicates that the current task is at a breakpoint in the debugger. A pause symbol indicates that a task has been frozen.

- **ID**: This column is a Windows-generated identification number for a task. In our example, I have entered 8 into the **Number of bitmaps to divide into for processing** textbox and then set a breakpoint after the `Parallel.ForEach` loop. You can see that we have created eight tasks that are all running an anonymous method, and that it is initiated from the **Find Old Stars** button's click event handler. Their IDs are numbers 1 through 8.

- **Status**: This column shows the task's state, which can be any of the following:
  - ° **Active**: The task is currently active on the stack
  - ° **Deadlocked**: The task is currently deadlocked waiting on a resource
  - ° **Waiting**: The task is currently waiting on CPU allocation
  - ° **Scheduled**: The task is scheduled to start executing when a thread in the threadpool is available
  - ° **Completed**: The task has completed its execution

  A task is considered in a deadlock state if its thread is in a lock condition with another thread in the application. A task is considered waiting if it is waiting on a lock to be freed or another task to complete.

- **Location**: This column displays the call stack for that particular task. Unlike the **Threads** window, to see the whole call stack, you need to hover over this column instead of double-clicking on it. Also, if a task has not started but is scheduled, then this column will not be populated yet.

- **Parent**: This column displays the ID of the task that created it.

- **Thread Assignment**: This column displays the thread ID and thread name of the thread the task is executing on. In our example, you can see we used a number to name the thread of our tasks in this line of code:

```
Parallel.ForEach(BitmapList, item =>
ThreadOldStarsFinder(item,ran.Next(1000).ToString()));
```

We pass in a random number between 1 and 1,000 as the second parameter of the `ThreadOldStarsFinder` method and then use the following line to set the thread name for the corresponding task:

```
Thread.CurrentThread.Name = ThreadName;
```

- **APPDomain**: This column shows the application domain the task is running inside. The **Process** column displays the Windows ID of the Windows process the task is executing inside.
- **AsyncState**: This column, if using the `async` or `await` keywords to run a task from a method call, shows the async state of the task.

When debugging TPL applications, this window is very helpful in getting an overview of all of the tasks your code has generated, which are active, and the call stack and thread information of each of them. Combining this with the **Threads** window will give you a good look at all of the entities running in your application and where they are in their execution.

The **Tasks** window is really only useful in debugging multithreaded applications if you are using the TPL. If you are using threads or the `BackgroundWorker` component, this window will not be helpful.

Using the Parallel Stacks window

The **Parallel Stacks** window is very helpful in debugging parallel applications because it shows you task and thread information in a graphical view almost like a flowchart. It shows a lot of the same information as the **Threads** and **Tasks** windows but in a different format and it shows relationships between the threads and tasks, which is very helpful.

The **Threads** and **Tasks** windows are a good tabular way to view all of the entities of your multithreaded application but they do not do a real good job of showing relationship and program flow information.

The **Parallel Stacks** information has a **Threads** view and a **Tasks** view. Each of these views can also be toggled to a **Method** view.

The following is the **Threads** view of our `OldStarsFinder` application after the `Parallel.ForEach` command executes and the bitmap is divided into eight sections:

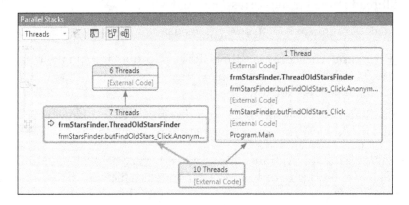

The following is the **Tasks** view of our `OldStarsFinder` application after the `Parallel.ForEach` command executes and the bitmap is divided into eight sections:

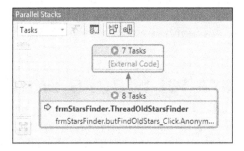

The following is the **Threads** view toggled to the **Method** view of our `OldStarsFinder` application after the `Parallel.ForEach` command executes and the bitmap is divided into eight sections:

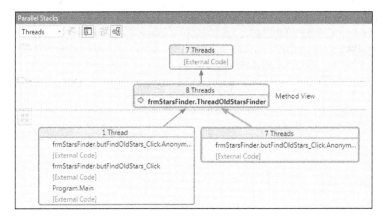

The following screenshot shows the **Tasks** view toggled to **Method** view of our `OldStarsFinder` application after the `Parallel.ForEach` command executes and the bitmap is divided into eight sections:

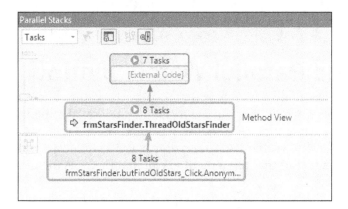

There are several items to note about this window. First is the toolbar. It allows you to select either **Threads** or **Tasks** from the drop-down menu. It also allows you to show only flagged threads in the window. Next, it allows you to toggle to the **Method** view, and also to zoom in on an area.

In the **Threads** and **Tasks** views, the call path of the current thread is highlighted in blue. That is why you can see more than one box highlighted. The arrows connected to the boxes show the call path of the task or thread, and each box in the diagram represents a call stack. Also, if you hover over a box's (also known as a node) header or a row in a node, you get a tooltip. The tooltip of the node header shows the thread ID and name of all the threads in the call path leading to this node. In the row or method tooltip, you'll see the stack of the method.

The yellow arrow in a node indicates the active frame of the currently active thread. Also, the method name in all the nodes of the active thread's current stack frame are styled in bold. If you right-click on a method row in a stack frame, you will get a menu that allows you to go to that task or thread, or to the source code.

The **Method** view we showed earlier shows all methods that either call or are called by the current method. The current method is shown in the middle with the methods that call it below and the methods it calls above. This is a nice way to get a current runtime view of the Visual Studio function, **Find All References**. It is not exactly the same but is similar.

The **Parallel Stacks** window is probably where you will spend most of your time in the debug mode except for actually stepping through the code. Typically, you will have the **Threads** and **Tasks** windows up for a tabular reference, the code up to set breakpoints and step through lines, and the **Parallel Stacks** window to follow all of the threads, tasks, and their relations.

Using the Parallel Watch window

The **Parallel Watch** window allows you to display the values of an expression that is held on multiple threads. You can see it running a parallel application and select **Parallel Watch** by navigating to **Window | Debug**. As you see in the following screenshot, the **Parallel Watch** window is empty until you add a watch statement. Each row shows a thread that has a method call that matches the method on the current stack frame.

If you click on the **<Add Watch>** bar, you can type in an expression to watch. This allows you to see the value of the same expression in multiple threads. You can show up to four **Parallel Watch** windows just like the regular **Watch** window if you would like to watch more than one expression. You can also filter the watch list by using the **Filter by Boolean Expression** box in the top-right corner of the window. If you type in an expression there, it will only show the threads in which that expression is true:

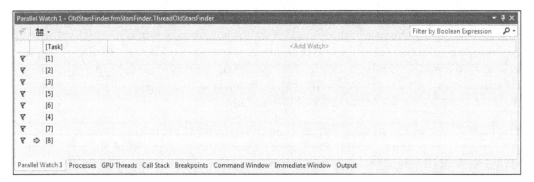

The **Parallel Watch** window is really just the **Watch** window but it allows you to watch the same expression on all the threads in your application. Any C# expression is valid in this window.

In the following example, we took the previously used example and added a watch on a variable. We are watching the `Thread.Name` value of the thread each task is assigned. Here is the same window after we have completed the `Parallel.ForEach` command. You can see only one of the tasks has executed but the others are scheduled. The one that has started has executed the first line of its delegate, which is to set the thread name:

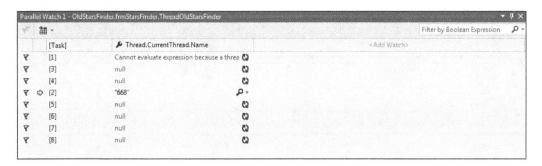

This window is a very good way in a `Parallel.For` or `Parallel.ForEach` loop that is executing the same delegate multiple times in multiple tasks to view the value of an expression in the delegate. It allows you to see the current value each task has at that moment of execution.

Debugging an entire application

Now that we have examined all of the windows that the Visual Studio debugger provides for debugging multithreaded applications let's go through a real example. We will use the `OldStarsFinder` application that uses tasks and the TPL that we finished in *Chapter 7, Data Parallelism*. Remember that this application takes a user-entered number and then divides a large bitmap file by that number into an equal number of smaller bitmap files. Then, using a parallel `ForEach` loop, it processes each bitmap to try and find old stars in the image. It keeps a track of how many old stars are found. When it finishes, it reassembles the pieces and displays the large bitmap with each old star colored blue. It also displays the final number of old stars it found. Let's get started.

How to do it

First, let's open our `OldStarsFinder` application in Visual Studio and set some breakpoints to help us get started. Then perform the following steps:

1. Put a breakpoint on the line of code that contains the `Parallel.ForEach` command as shown here:

2. Now let's place a second break in the `ThreadOldStarsFinder` method that each of the parallel tasks are executing. We will place it early in the method where we set the thread name using the random number that we pass in from the `Parallel.ForEach` command:

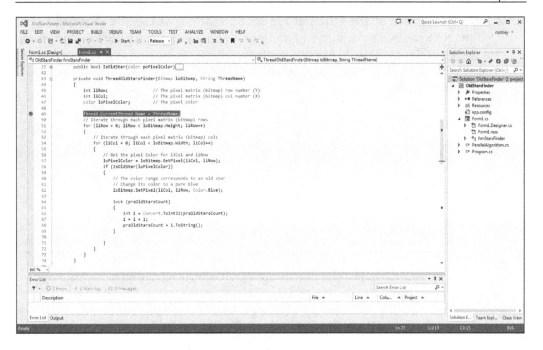

3. Now, let's start the application in the debugger and enter 6 in the textbox for how many bitmaps to divide the large image into:

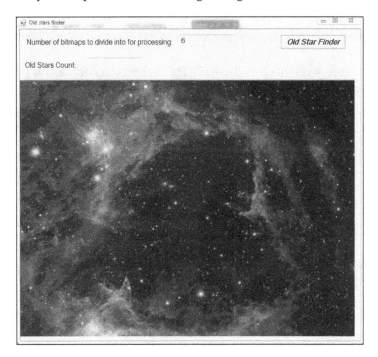

4. Next, let's click on the **Old Star Finder** button. We will see that the code enters the button's click event handler and comes to the first breakpoint that we set at the `Parallel.ForEach` command. The following screenshot shows how the debugger looks along with the **Thread**, **Tasks**, **Parallel Stacks**, and **Parallel Watch** windows:

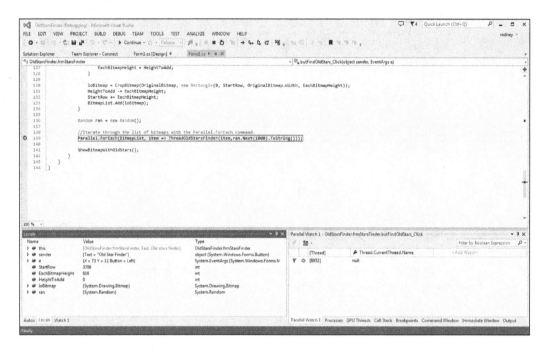

Right before we step over the `Parallel.ForEach` command, you can see that there are no tasks yet:

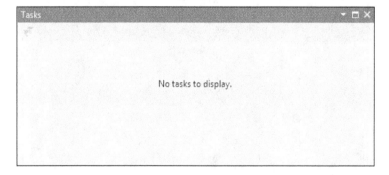

You will also see that there are no extra threads for these tasks because we have not executed the parallel data loop yet:

And looking at the **Parallel Stacks** window you only see the main thread of the application:

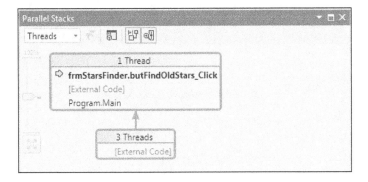

5. Now, let's step over the `Parallel.ForEach` command and look at these same windows while we are at a breakpoint in the delegate:

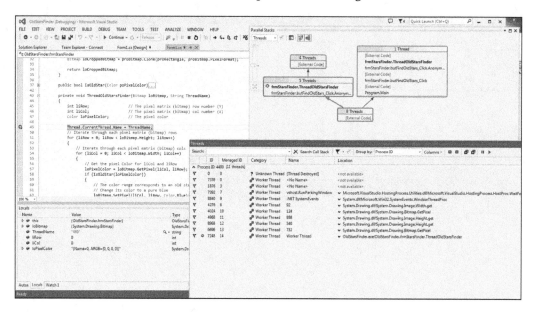

6. Now, if you hover over the line in the **Parallel Stacks** window with the yellow arrow, you will see the line of code each thread is executing. This is using the **Threads** view of the **Parallel Stacks** window:

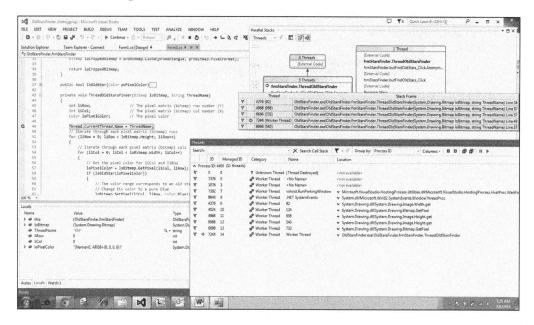

7. Now, let's examine the same thing using the **Tasks** view of the **Parallel Stacks** window:

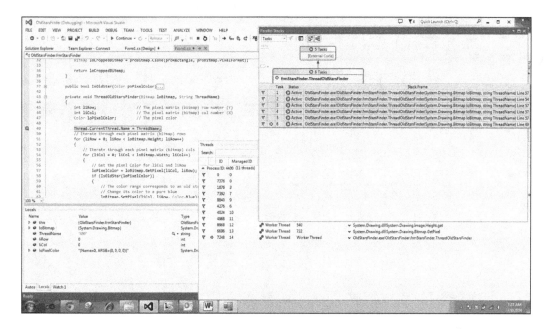

8. Also, at the same time, let's examine our **Parallel Watch** window:

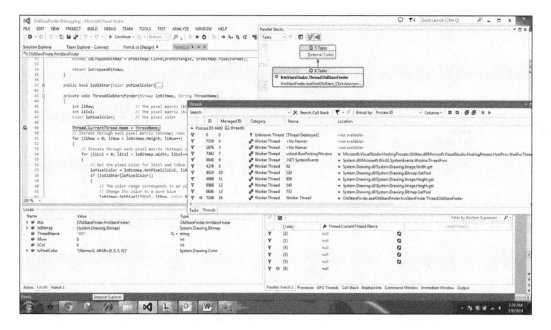

9. Next, let's step over the current line in the `ThreadOldStarsFinder` delegate method and take another look at our windows:

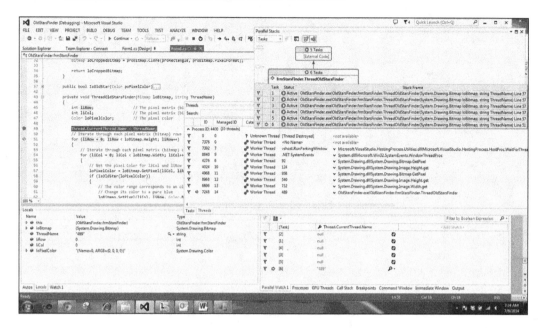

10. Then start stepping through the delegate and notice what happens. Here is a view from our example:

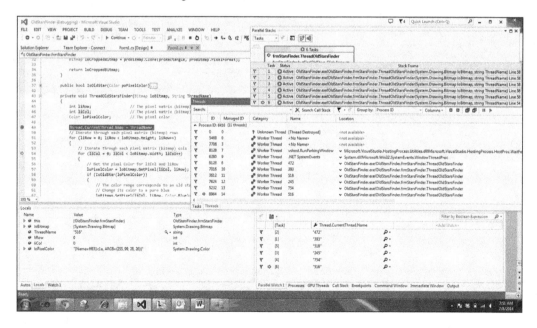

11. Notice how the information changes in the windows as you start to step through the delegate of one task on one thread. You will notice all of the tasks are, or can be, on different lines after you step over one line in this one thread. Also, the **Parallel Watch** window will show different values of the expression as you step through.

12. Now, let the program run until it has completed the parallel loop and it is ready to reassemble the pieces.

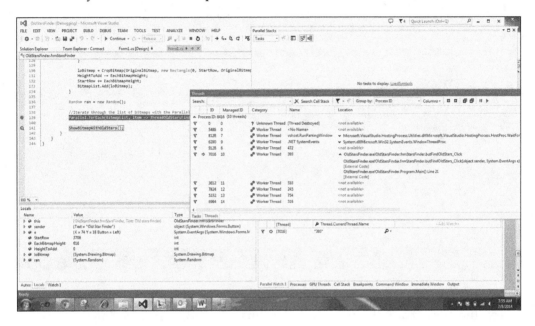

13. As you can see, we still have multiple threads running in our application but no tasks. This indicates that all of the tasks we created in the `Parallel.ForEach` loop have completed their delegate functions and the tasks are no longer on the threadpool. But the application still has threads it is using and some it needs to clean up.

Now we have seen how to open all of the various windows in the debugger for parallel debugging and stepped through our multithreaded TPL-based application. Let's talk about what just happened and what we saw.

How it works

You can see from our previous example that before we enter the `Parallel.ForEach` command, there are no tasks shown in our **Tasks** window or **Parallel Stacks** window in the **Tasks** view; this is shown in the following screenshot:

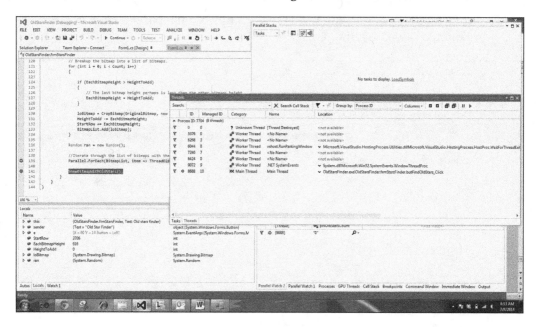

There are no tasks yet because we have not created any. But the application has several threads already. There is one for the main thread and it is the one we have a breakpoint on, one to handle .NET system events, and one for the visual studio debugger our application is running inside.

Let's switch our **Parallel Stacks** window to **Threads** view:

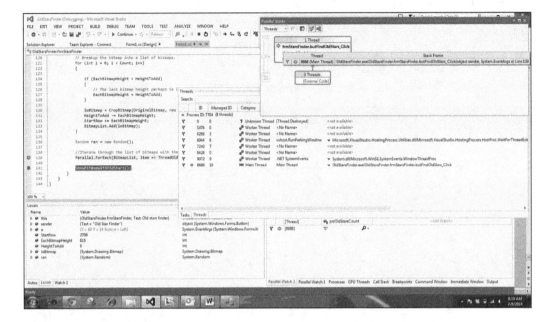

Now, you can see that the yellow arrow is in the **Old Stars Finder** button's click event handler on line **139** right where our breakpoint is. The prsOldStarsCount variable is set to 0 because that is how we initialized it, and none of the versions of the delegate have run yet to update it.

Now, I have stepped through the delegate line twice to let two of the parallel tasks get started. Let's look at the results so far:

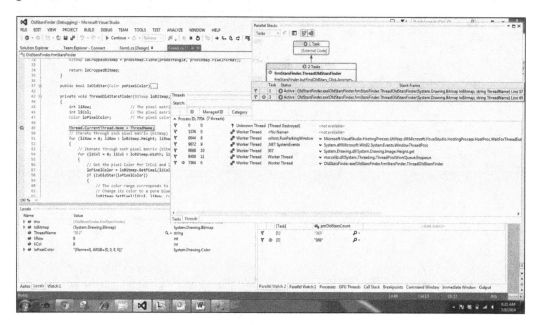

Remember that when we step over a line in one thread, the other threads continue to operate until the thread we step over completes and the control is returned back to the debugger. So, a lot of other things can happen while we execute one line in one thread. As we see here, we are currently in a task numbered **3** at line **49**. We can also see that task **1** is currently waiting on line **57**. We also notice in the **Parallel Watch** window that both tasks show the value of **369** in the variable, `prsOldStarsCount`. What does this tell us?

This tells us that while we are still on one of the first lines in the delegate method in task **3** and it has not begun any real processing yet, other tasks have already found **369** old stars. You'll also notice that both tasks in the **Parallel Watch** window show the same value for `prsOldStarsCount`. This is because this is a global variable and all tasks are looking at and updating the same copy. Now, let's step over one line of code in the task **3** delegate and see what happens:

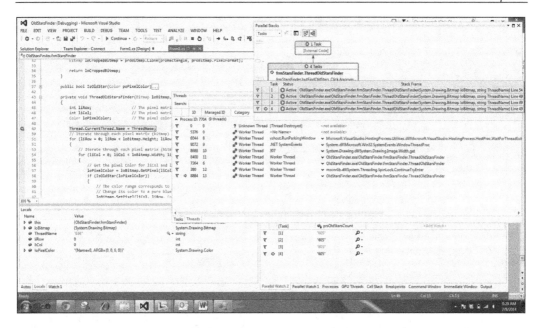

Now, we are on line **49** in the task numbered **4** and the value of `prsOldStarsCount` is **605**. What just happened? We stepped over one line in task **3** and ended up in task **4** on the same line.

Remember we have a breakpoint set in the delegate method of each of the six tasks that our `Parallel.ForEach` loop created. When you step over a line or continue in the debugger, it stops at the next break point that is encountered. Also, remember that when we step over a line, all of our threads and tasks can run during that time. So, when we stepped over the line in task **3**, the next breakpoint the debugger came to was that same line in task **4**. You can see several things from our window. Tasks **2**, **3**, and **4** are all on line **49** and haven't gotten to line **51** (the next executable line). This tells us that when we stepped over line **49** in task **3** the debugger encountered a break at line **49** in task **4** before the execution of line **49** in task **3** got completed. We also see that in the time it took to reach this next break point, our tasks have now counted **605** old stars, up from **369**. Since task **1** is the only task we see past line **49**, we can surmise that it is the one that has counted all of these stars.

Now, let's step over this line and see what happens next:

This time we moved to line **49** of task **2** and no more old stars have been counted. Let's step over one more line and examine:

Now we have stopped on line **49** of task **5**. You can also see that both tasks **1** and **3** are now past line **49** and we have now counted **869** old stars. Let's step over one more line:

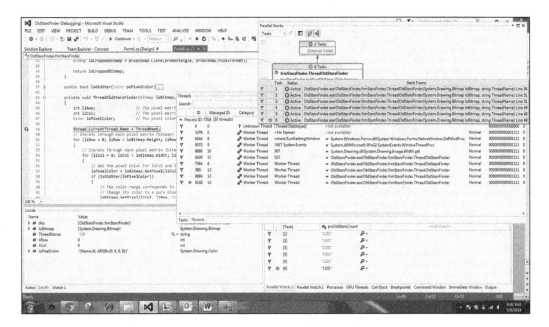

Now you can see we have started all six tasks that we asked for in our `Parallel.ForEach` loop and are already up to **1331** old stars. But even with **1331** old stars already found, we have not moved past line **49** in three of our six tasks. Let's step over one more line. Since we have reached this breakpoint line in all six tasks, we should now step through the current task we are on, which is task **6**.

But as we do so, the other tasks can all run. That being said, the machine we are running on has four processing cores, so not all of them can get CPU time at once, as shown:

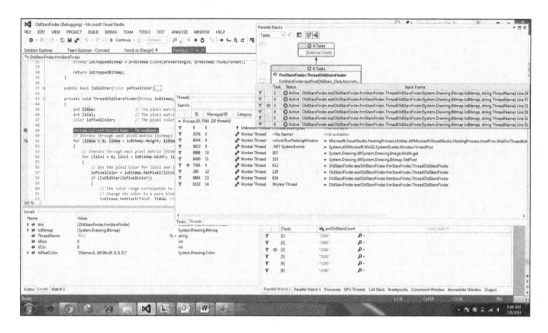

As you can see, we now can start to step through the current task without stopping because the delegate that all of the tasks are running has no more breakpoints that can interfere. You can also see that in the time it took to execute this one line in task **6**, we have now counted **1686** old stars and moved a couple of lines in a few other tasks.

Also note that when you see **[External code]** in the stack frame, this is referring to .NET code and not your own source code. You can set your debugger to show the stack of external code, but usually this provides you with too much information when you are mostly concerned with the flow and debugging of your own source code.

At this point, keep stepping through and see what happens; then stop your application and redo the exercise. Each time you run the application in the debugger, you should see slightly different results because we have multiple threads running and competing for processing time. Each time you step through the code, different threads will get different amounts of CPU time depending on availability and other competing processes running on your machine. Remember your application and debugging is not the only thing running in your Windows machine.

Summary

In this chapter, we have examined all of the functionality that Visual Studio provides multithreaded and parallel application developers to help them troubleshoot and debug their source code. We have examined the **Threads** window, **Tasks** window, **Parallel Tasks** window in **Threads** mode, the **Parallel Stacks** window in **Tasks** mode, and the **Parallel Stacks** window. We have also examined our `OldStarsFinder` application using these windows and then stepped through its execution.

You have learned how to:

- Examine all threads of your application as it runs
- Examine all tasks your application creates using the TPL
- Step through an application with multiple tasks and threads running
- View the stack of any thread or task in your application
- Set watch expressions and view them across all the threads

In the next chapter, we will discuss some popular design patterns for parallel applications.

9

Pipeline and Producer-consumer Design Patterns

In this chapter, we will explore two popular design patterns to solve concurrent problems — Pipeline and producer-consumer, which are used in developing parallel applications using the TPL. A **Pipeline** design is one where an application is designed with multiple tasks or stages of functionality with queues of work items between them. So, for each stage, the application will read from a queue of work to be performed, execute the work on that item, and then queue the results for the next stage. By designing the application this way, all of the stages can execute in parallel. Each stage just reads from its work queue, performs the work, and puts the results of the work into the queue for the next stage.

Each stage is a task and can run independently of the other stages or tasks. They continue executing until their queue is empty and marked completed. They also block and wait for more work items if the queue is empty but not completed.

The **producer-consumer** design pattern is a similar concept but different. In this design, we have a set of functionality that produces data that is then consumed by another set of functionality. Each set of functionality is a TPL task. So, we have a producer task and a consumer task, with a buffer between them. Each of these tasks can run independently of each other. We can also have multiple producer tasks and multiple consumer tasks. The producers run independently and produce queue results to the buffer. The consumers run independently and dequeue from the buffer and perform work on the item. The producer can block if the buffer is full and wait for room to become available before producing more results. Also, the consumer can block if the buffer is empty, waiting on more results to be available to consume.

In this chapter, you will learn the following:

- Designing an application with a Pipeline design
- Designing an application with a producer-consumer design
- Learning how to use `BlockingCollection`
- Learning how to use `BufferedBlocks`
- Understanding the classes of the `System.Threading.Tasks.Dataflow` library

Pipeline design pattern

The Pipeline design is very useful in parallel design when you can divide an application up into series of tasks to be performed in such a way that each task can run concurrently with other tasks. It is important that the output of each task is in the same order as the input. If the order does not matter, then a parallel loop can be performed. When the order matters and we don't want to wait until all items have completed task A before the items start executing task B, then a Pipeline implementation is perfect.

Some applications that lend themselves to pipelining are video streaming, compression, and encryption. In each of these examples, we need to perform a set of tasks on the data and preserve the data's order, but we do not want to wait for each item of data to perform a task before any of the data can perform the next task.

The key class that .NET has provided for implementing this design pattern is `BlockingCollection` of the `System.Collections.Concurrent` namespace. The `BlockingCollection` class was introduced with .NET 4.5. It is a thread-safe collection specifically designed for producer-consumer and Pipeline design patterns. It supports concurrently adding and removing items by multiple threads to and from the collection. It also has methods to add and remove that block when the collection is full or empty. You can specify a maximum collection size to ensure a producing task that outpaces a consuming task does not make the queue too large. It supports cancellation tokens. Finally, it supports enumerations so that you can use the `foreach` loop when processing items of the collection.

A producer of items to the collection can call the CompleteAdding method when the last item of data has been added to the collection. Until this method is called if a consumer is consuming items from the collection with a foreach loop and the collection is empty, it will block until an item is put into the collection instead of ending the loop.

Next, we will see a simple example of a Pipeline design implementation using an encryption program. This program will implement three stages in our pipeline. The first stage will read a text file character-by-character and place each character into a buffer (BlockingCollection). The next stage will read each character out of the buffer and encrypt it by adding 1 to its ASCII number. It will then place the new character into our second buffer and write it to an encryption file. Our final stage will read the character out of the second buffer, decrypt it to its original character, and write it out to a new file and to the screen. As you will see, stages 2 and 3 will start processing characters before stage 1 has finished reading all the characters from the input file. And all of this will be done while maintaining the order of the characters so that the final output file is identical to the input file:

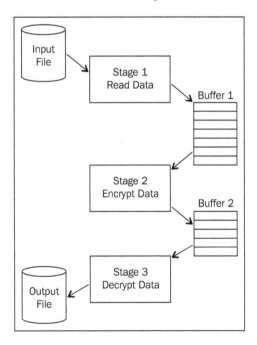

Let's get started.

How to do it

First, let's open up Visual Studio and create a new **Windows Presentation Foundation (WPF)** application named `PipeLineApplication` and perform the following steps:

1. Create a new class called `Stages.cs`. Next, make sure it has the following `using` statements.

```
using System;
using System.Collections.Concurrent;
using System.Collections.Generic;
using System.IO;
using System.Linq;
using System.Text;
using System.Threading.Tasks;
using System.Threading;
```

2. In the `MainWindow.xaml.cs` file, make sure the following `using` statements are present:

```
using System;
using System.Collections.Concurrent;
using System.Collections.Generic;
using System.IO;
using System.Linq;
using System.Text;
using System.Threading.Tasks;
using System.Threading;
```

3. Next, we will add a method for each of the three stages in our pipeline. First, we will create a method called `FirstStage`. It will take two parameters: one will be a `BlockingCollection` object that will be the output buffer of this stage, and the second will be a string pointing to the input data file. This will be a text file containing a couple of paragraphs of text to be encrypted. We will place this text file in the `projects` folder on `C:`. The `FirstStage` method will have the following code:

```
public void FirstStage(BlockingCollection<char> output, String
PipelineInputFile)
        {
            String DisplayData = "";
            try
            {
                foreach (char C in GetData(PipelineInputFile))
                {
    //Displayed characters read in from the file.
```

```
                    DisplayData = DisplayData + C.ToString();

    // Add each character to the buffer for the next stage.
                    output.Add(C);


            }
        }
        finally
        {
            output.CompleteAdding();
        }
    }
```

4. Next, we will add a method for the second stage called `StageWorker`.
    This method will not return any values and will take three parameters.
    One will be a `BlockingCollection` value that will be its input buffer,
    the second one will be the output buffer of the stage, and the final one
    will be a file path to store the encrypted text in a data file. The code for
    this method will look like this:

```
public void StageWorker(BlockingCollection<char> input,
BlockingCollection<char> output, String PipelineEncryptFile)
        {
            String DisplayData = "";

            try
            {
                foreach (char C in input.GetConsumingEnumerable())
                {
                    //Encrypt each character.
                    char encrypted = Encrypt(C);

                    DisplayData = DisplayData + encrypted.
ToString();

    //Add characters to the buffer for the next stage.
                    output.Add(encrypted);


                }

    //write the encrypted string to the output file.
                using (StreamWriter outfile =
                        new StreamWriter(PipelineEncryptFile))
                {
                    outfile.Write(DisplayData);
```

```
            }

        }
        finally
        {
            output.CompleteAdding();
        }
    }
```

5. Now, we will add a method for the third and final stage of the Pipeline design. This method will be named `FinalStage`. It will not return any values and will take two parameters. One will be a `BlockingCollection` object that is the input buffer and the other will be a string pointing to an output data file. It will have the following code in it:

```
public void FinalStage(BlockingCollection<char> input, String
PipelineResultsFile)
    {
        String OutputString = "";
        String DisplayData = "";

        //Read the encrypted characters from the buffer,
decrypt them, and display them.
        foreach (char C in input.GetConsumingEnumerable())
        {
            //Decrypt the data.
            char decrypted = Decrypt(C);

            //Display the decrypted data.
            DisplayData = DisplayData + decrypted.ToString();

            //Add to the output string.
            OutputString += decrypted.ToString();

        }

        //write the decrypted string to the output file.
        using (StreamWriter outfile =
                new StreamWriter(PipelineResultsFile))
        {
            outfile.Write(OutputString);
        }
    }
```

6. Now that we have methods for the three stages of our pipeline, let's add a few utility methods. The first of these methods will be one that reads in the input data file and places each character in the data file in a `List` object. This method will take a string parameter that has a filename and will return a `List` object of characters. It will have the following code:

```
public List<char> GetData(String PipelineInputFile)
        {
                List<char> Data = new List<char>();

                //Get the Source data.
                using (StreamReader inputfile = new StreamReader(Pipel
ineInputFile))
                {
                    while (inputfile.Peek() >= 0)
                    {
                        Data.Add((char)inputfile.Read());
                    }

                }

                return Data;
        }
```

7. Now we will need a method to encrypt the characters. This will be a simple encryption method. The encryption method is not really important to this exercise. This exercise is designed to demonstrate the Pipeline design, not implement the world's toughest encryption. This encryption will simply take each character and add one to its ASCII numerical value. The method will take a character type as an input parameter and return a character. The code for it will be as follows:

```
public char Encrypt(char C)
        {
                //Take the character, convert to an int, add 1, then
convert back to a character.
                int i = (int)C;
                i = i + 1;
                C = Convert.ToChar(i);

                return C;
        }
```

8. Now we will add one final method to the `Stages` class to decrypt a character value. It will simply do the reverse of the `encrypt` method. It will take the ASCII numerical value and subtract 1. The code for this method will look like this:

```
public char Decrypt(char C)
        {
                int i = (int)C;
                i = i - 1;
                C = Convert.ToChar(i);

                return C;
        }
```

9. Now that we are done with the `Stages` class, let's switch our focus back to the `MainWindow.xaml.cs` file. First, you will need to add three `using` statements. They are for the `StreamReader`, `StreamWriter`, `Threads`, and `BlockingCollection` classes:

```
using System.Collections.Concurrent;
using System.IO;
using System.Threading;
```

10. At the top of the `MainWindow` class, we need four variables available for the whole class. We need three strings that point to our three data files — the input data, encrypted data, and output data. Then we will need a `Stages` object. These declarations will look like this:

```
private static String PipelineResultsFile = @"c:\projects\
OutputData.txt";
        private static String PipelineEncryptFile = @"c:\projects\
EncryptData.txt";
        private static String PipelineInputFile = @"c:\projects\
InputData.txt";
        private Stages Stage;
```

11. Then, in the `MainWindow` constructor method, right after the `InitializeComponent` call, add a line to instantiate our `Stages` object:

```
//Create the Stage object and register the event listeners to
update the UI as the stages work.
Stage = new Stages();
```

12. Next, add a button to the `MainWindow.xaml` file that will initiate the pipeline and encryption. Name this button control `butEncrypt`, and set its `Content` property to `Encrypt File`. Next, add a click event handler for this button in the `MainWindow.xaml.cs` file. Its event handler method will be `butEncrypt_Click` and will contain the main code for this application. It will instantiate

two `BlockingCollection` objects for two queues. One queue between stages 1 and 2, and one queue between stages 2 and 3. This method will then create a task for each stage that executes the corresponding methods from the `Stages` classes. It will then start these three tasks and wait for them to complete. Finally, it will write the output of each stage to the input, encrypted, and results data files and text blocks for viewing. The code for it will look like the following code:

```
private void butEncrpt_Click(object sender, RoutedEventArgs e)
        {
            //PipeLine Design Pattern

            //Create queues for input and output to stages.
            int size = 20;
            BlockingCollection<char> Buffer1 = new
BlockingCollection<char>(size);
            BlockingCollection<char> Buffer2 = new
BlockingCollection<char>(size);

            TaskFactory tasks = new
TaskFactory(TaskCreationOptions.LongRunning,
TaskContinuationOptions.None);

            Task Stage1 = tasks.StartNew(() => Stage.
FirstStage(Buffer1, PipelineInputFile));
            Task Stage2 = tasks.StartNew(() => Stage.
StageWorker(Buffer1, Buffer2, PipelineEncryptFile));
            Task Stage3 = tasks.StartNew(() => Stage.
FinalStage(Buffer2, PipelineResultsFile));

            Task.WaitAll(Stage1, Stage2, Stage3);

            //Display the 3 files.
            using (StreamReader inputfile = new StreamReader(Pipel
ineInputFile))
            {
                while (inputfile.Peek() >= 0)
                {
                    tbStage1.Text = tbStage1.Text + (char)
inputfile.Read();
                }

            }
            using (StreamReader inputfile = new StreamReader(Pipel
ineEncryptFile))
            {
```

```
                    while (inputfile.Peek() >= 0)
                    {
                            tbStage2.Text = tbStage2.Text + (char)
            inputfile.Read();
                    }


            }
            using (StreamReader inputfile = new StreamReader(Pipel
    ineResultsFile))
                    {
                    while (inputfile.Peek() >= 0)
                    {
                            tbStage3.Text = tbStage3.Text + (char)
            inputfile.Read();
                    }


            }
        }
```

13. One last thing. Let's add three textblocks to display the outputs. We will call these `tbStage1`, `tbStage2`, and `tbStage3`. We will also add three label controls with the text `Input File`, `Encrypted File`, and `Output File`. These will be placed by the corresponding textblocks. Now, the `MainWindow.xaml` file should look like the following screenshot:

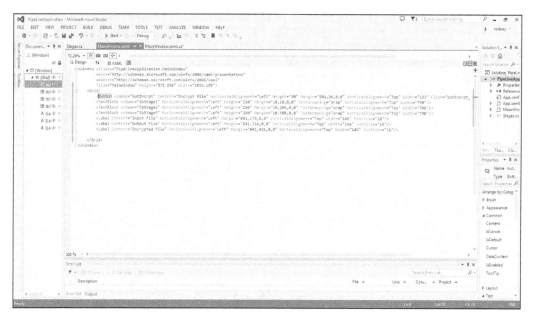

14. Now we will need an input data file to encrypt. We will call this file `InputData.txt` and put it in the `C:\projects` folder on our computer. For our example, we have added the following text to it:

```
In this chapter we will explore two popular design patterns used in
developing parallel applications using the TPL. Pipline and Producer-
Consumer are two methods to solve typical concurrent problems.
A Pipeline design is one where an application is designed with multiple
tasks or stages of functionality with queues of work items between them.
So, for each stage the application will read from a queue of work to be
performed, execute the work on that item, and then queue the results for
the next stage. By designing the application this way, all of the stages
can execute in parallel. Each stage just reads from its work queue,
performs the work, and puts the results of the work into the queue for
the next stage.

Each stage is a task and can run independently of the other stages or
tasks. They continue executing until their queue is empty and marked
completed. They also block and wait for more work items if the queue is
empty but not completed.

The producer-Consumer design pattern is a similar concept but different.
In this design we have a set of functionality that "produces" result data
that is "consumed" by another set of functionality. Each set of
functionality is a TPL task. So, we have a producer task and a consumer
task. Then there is a buffer between them. Each of these tasks can run
independently of each other. We can also have multiple producer tasks and
multiple consumer tasks. The producers run independently and produce
queue results to the buffer. The consumers run independently and dequeue
from the buffer and perform work on the item. The producer can block if
the buffer is full and wait for room to become available before producing
more results. Also, the consumer can block if the buffer is empty waiting
on more results to be available to consume.
```

15. We are all finished and ready to try it out. Compile and run the application and you should have a window that looks like the following screenshot:

16. Now, click on the **Encrypt File** button and you should see the following output:

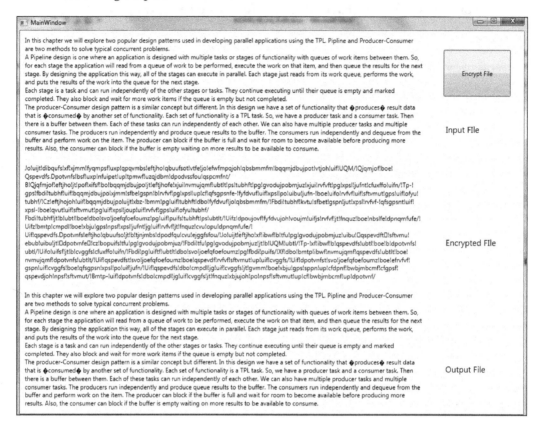

As you can see, the input and output files look the same and the encrypted file looks different. Remember that **Input File** is the text we put in the input data text file; this is the input from the end of stage 1 after we have read the file in to a character list. **Encrypted File** is the output from stage 2 after we have encrypted each character. **Output File** is the output of stage 3 after we have decrypted the characters again. It should match **Input File**.

Now, let's take a look at how this works.

How it works

Let's look at the butEncrypt click event handler method in the MainWindow.xaml.cs file, as this is where a lot of the action takes place. Let's examine the following lines of code:

```
//Create queues for input and output to stages.
int size = 20;
BlockingCollection<char> Buffer1 = new
BlockingCollection<char>(size);
BlockingCollection<char> Buffer2 = new
BlockingCollection<char>(size);
TaskFactory tasks = new TaskFactory(TaskCreationOptions.
LongRunning, TaskContinuationOptions.None);

Task Stage1 = tasks.StartNew(() => Stage.
FirstStage(Buffer1, PipelineInputFile));
Task Stage2 = tasks.StartNew(() => Stage.
StageWorker(Buffer1, Buffer2, PipelineEncryptFile));
Task Stage3 = tasks.StartNew(() => Stage.
FinalStage(Buffer2, PipelineResultsFile));
```

First, we create two queues that are implemented using `BlockingCollection` objects. Each of these is set with a size of 20 items. These two queues take a character datatype.

Then we create a `TaskFactory` object and use it to start three tasks. Each task uses a lambda expression that executes one of the stages methods from the `Stages` class — `FirstStage`, `StageWorker`, and `FinalStage`.

So, now we have three separate tasks running besides the main UI thread. `Stage1` will read the input data file character by character and place each character in the queue `Buffer1`. Remember that this queue can only hold 20 items before it will block the `FirstStage` method waiting on room in the queue. This is how we know that `Stage2` starts running before `Stage1` completes. Otherwise, `Stage1` will only queue the first 20 characters and then block.

Once `Stage1` has read all of the characters from the input file and placed them into `Buffer1`, it then makes the following call:

```
finally
{
    output.CompleteAdding();
}
```

This lets the `BlockingCollection` instance, `Buffer1`, to know that there are no more items to be put in the queue. So, when `Stage2` has emptied the queue after `Stage1` has called this method, it will not block but will instead continue until completion. Prior to the `CompleteAdding` method call, `Stage2` will block if `Buffer1` is empty, waiting until more items are placed in the queue. This is why a `BlockingCollection` instance was developed for Pipeline and producer-consumer applications. It provides the perfect mechanism for this functionality.

When we created the `TaskFactory`, we used the following parameter:

`TaskCreationOptions.LongRunning`

This tells the threadpool that these tasks may run for a long time and could occasionally block waiting on their queues. In this way, the threadpool can decide how to best manage the threads allocated for these tasks.

Now, let's look at the code in `Stage2` — the `StageWorker` method. We need a way to remove items in an enumerable way so that we can iterate over the queues items with a `foreach` loop because we do not know how many items to expect. Also, since `BlockingCollection` objects support multiple consumers, we need a way to remove items that no other consumer might remove. We use this method of the `BlockingCollection` class:

```
foreach (char C in input.GetConsumingEnumerable())
```

This allows multiple consumers to remove items from a `BlockingCollection` instance while maintaining the order of the items. To further improve performance of this application (assuming we have enough available processing cores), we could create a fourth task that also runs the `StageWorker` method. So, then we would have two stages and two tasks running. This might be helpful if there are enough processing cores and stage 1 runs faster than stage 2. If this happens, it will continually fill the queue and block until space becomes available. But if we run multiple stage 2 tasks, then we will be able to keep up with stage 1.

Then, finally we have this line of code:

```
Task.WaitAll(Stage1, Stage2, Stage3);
```

This tells our button handler to wait until all of the tasks are complete. Once we have called the `CompleteAdding` method on each `BlockingCollection` instance and the buffers are then emptied, all of our stages will complete and the `TaskFactory.WaitAll` command will be satisfied and this method on the UI thread can complete its processing, which in this application is to update the UI and data files:

```
            //Display the 3 files.
            using (StreamReader inputfile = new StreamReader(Pipeline
    InputFile))
            {
                while (inputfile.Peek() >= 0)
                {
                    tbStage1.Text = tbStage1.Text + (char)inputfile.
    Read();
                }

            }
            using (StreamReader inputfile = new StreamReader(Pipeline
    EncryptFile))
```

```
            {
                while (inputfile.Peek() >= 0)
                {
                    tbStage2.Text = tbStage2.Text + (char)inputfile.
    Read();
                }

            }
            using (StreamReader inputfile = new StreamReader(Pipeline
    ResultsFile))
                {
                while (inputfile.Peek() >= 0)
                {
                    tbStage3.Text = tbStage3.Text + (char)inputfile.
    Read();
                }

            }
```

Next, experiment with longer running, more complex stages and multiple consumer stages. Also, try stepping through the application with the Visual Studio debugger using the techniques we learned in *Chapter 8, Debugging Multithreaded Applications with Visual Studio*. Make sure you understand the interaction between the stages and the buffers.

Explaining message blocks

Let's talk for a minute about message blocks and the TPL. There is a new library that Microsoft has developed as part of the TPL, but it does not ship directly with .NET 4.5. This library is called the TPL `Dataflow` library. It is located in the `System.Threading.Tasks.Dataflow` namespace. It comes with various dataflow components that assist in asynchronous concurrent applications where messages need to be passed between multiple tasks or the data needs to be passed when it becomes available, as in the case of a web camera streaming video.

The `Dataflow` library's message blocks are very helpful for design patterns such as Pipeline and producer-consumer where you have multiple producers producing data that can be consumed by multiple consumers. The two that we will take a look at are `BufferBlock` and `ActionBlock`.

The TPL Dataflow library contains classes to assist in message passing and parallelizing I/O-heavy applications that have a lot of throughput. It provides explicit control over how data is buffered and passed. Consider an application that asynchronously loads large binary files from storage and manipulates that data. Traditional programming requires that you use callbacks and synchronization classes, such as locks, to coordinate tasks and have access to data that is shared. By using the TPL Dataflow objects, you can create objects that process image files as they are read in from a disk location. You can set how data is handled when it becomes available. Because the CLR runtime engine manages dependencies between data, you do not have to worry about synchronizing access to shared data. Also, since the CLR engine schedules the work depending on the asynchronous arrival of data, the TPL Dataflow objects can improve performance by managing the threads the tasks run on.

In this section, we will cover two of these classes, BufferBlock and ActionBlock.

 The TPL Dataflow library (System.Threading.Tasks. Dataflow) does not ship with .NET 4.5. To install System. Threading.Tasks.Dataflow, open your project in Visual Studio, select **Manage NuGet Packages** from under the **Project** menu and then search online for Microsoft.Tpl.Dataflow.

BufferBlock

The BufferBlock object in the Dataflow library provides a buffer to store data. The syntax is, BufferBlock<T>. The T indicates that the datatype is generic and can be of any type. All static variables of this object type are guaranteed to be thread-safe. BufferBlock is an asynchronous message structure that stores messages in a first-in-first-out queue. Messages can be "posted" to the queue by multiple producers and "received" from the queue by multiple consumers.

The TPL DatafLow library provides interfaces for three types of objects—source blocks, target blocks, and propagator blocks. BufferBlock is a general-purpose message block that can act as both a source and a target message buffer, which makes it perfect for a producer-consumer application design. To act as both a source and a target, it implements two interfaces defined by the TPL Dataflow library—ISourceBlock<TOutput> and ITargetBlock<TOutput>. So, in the application that we will develop in the *Producer-consumer design pattern* section of this chapter, you will see that the producer method implements BufferBlock using the ITargetBlock interface and the consumer implements BufferBlock with the ISourceBlock interface.

This will be the same BufferBlock object that they will act on but by defining their local objects with a different interface there will be different methods available to use. The producer method will have Post and Complete methods, and the consumer method will use the OutputAvailableAsync and Receive methods.

The BufferBlock object only has two properties, namely Count, which is a count of the number of data messages in the queue, and Completion, which gets a task that is an asynchronous operation and completion of the message block.

The following is a set of methods for this class:

	Name	Description
	Complete	Signals to the IDataflowBlock that it should not accept nor produce any more messages nor consume any more postponed messages.
	Equals(Object)	Determines whether the specified object is equal to the current object. (Inherited from Object.)
	GetHashCode	Serves as the default hash function. (Inherited from Object.)
	GetType	Gets the Type of the current instance. (Inherited from Object.)
	LinkTo	Links the ISourceBlock<TOutput> to the specified ITargetBlock<TInput>.
	ToString	Returns a string that represents the formatted name of this IDataflowBlock instance. (Overrides Object.ToString().)
	TryReceive	Attempts to synchronously receive an available output item from the IReceivableSourceBlock<TOutput>.
	TryReceiveAll	Attempts to synchronously receive all available items from the IReceivableSourceBlock<TOutput>.

Referenced from http://msdn.microsoft.com/en-us/library/hh160414(v=vs.110).aspx

Here is a list of the extension methods provided by the interfaces that it implements:

	Name	Description
	AsObservable<T>	Creates a new IObservable<T> abstraction over the ISourceBlock<TOutput>. (Defined by DataflowBlock.)
	AsObserver<T>	Creates a new IObserver<T> abstraction over the ITargetBlock<TInput>. (Defined by DataflowBlock.)
	LinkTo<T>(ITargetBlock<T>)	Overloaded. Links the ISourceBlock<TOutput> to the specified ITargetBlock<TInput>. (Defined by DataflowBlock.)
	LinkTo<T>(ITargetBlock<T>, Predicate<T>)	Overloaded. Links the ISourceBlock<TOutput> to the specified ITargetBlock<TInput> using the specified filter. (Defined by DataflowBlock.)
	LinkTo<T>(ITargetBlock<T>, DataflowLinkOptions, Predicate<T>)	Overloaded. Links the ISourceBlock<TOutput> to the specified ITargetBlock<TInput> using the specified filter. (Defined by DataflowBlock.)
	OutputAvailableAsync<T>()	Overloaded. Provides a Task<TResult> that asynchronously monitors the source for available output. (Defined by DataflowBlock.)
	OutputAvailableAsync<T>(CancellationToken)	Overloaded. Provides a Task<TResult> that asynchronously monitors the source for available output. (Defined by DataflowBlock.)
	Post<T>	Posts an item to the ITargetBlock<TInput>. (Defined by DataflowBlock.)
	Receive<T>()	Overloaded. Synchronously receives a value from a specified source. (Defined by DataflowBlock.)
	Receive<T>(CancellationToken)	Overloaded. Synchronously receives a value from a specified source and provides a token to cancel the operation. (Defined by DataflowBlock.)
	Receive<T>(TimeSpan)	Overloaded. Synchronously receives a value from a specified source, observing an optional time-out period. (Defined by DataflowBlock.)
	Receive<T>(TimeSpan, CancellationToken)	Overloaded. Synchronously receives a value from a specified source, providing a token to cancel the operation and observing an optional time-out interval. (Defined by DataflowBlock.)
	ReceiveAsync<T>()	Overloaded. Asynchronously receives a value from a specified source. (Defined by DataflowBlock.)
	ReceiveAsync<T>(CancellationToken)	Overloaded. Asynchronously receives a value from a specified source and provides a token to cancel the operation. (Defined by DataflowBlock.)
	ReceiveAsync<T>(TimeSpan)	Overloaded. Asynchronously receives a value from a specified source, observing an optional time-out period. (Defined by DataflowBlock.)
	ReceiveAsync<T>(TimeSpan, CancellationToken)	Overloaded. Asynchronously receives a value from a specified source, providing a token to cancel the operation and observing an optional time-out interval. (Defined by DataflowBlock.)

	Name	Description
	SendAsync<T>(T)	Overloaded. Asynchronously offers a message to the target message block, allowing for postponement. (Defined by DataflowBlock.)
	SendAsync<T>(T, CancellationToken)	Overloaded. Asynchronously offers a message to the target message block, allowing for postponement. (Defined by DataflowBlock.)
	TryReceive<T>	Attempts to synchronously receive an item from the ISourceBlock<TOutput>. (Defined by DataflowBlock.)

Referenced from http://msdn.microsoft.com/en-us/library/hh160414(v=vs.110).aspx

Finally, here are the interface references for this class:

	Name	Description
	IDataflowBlock.Fault	Causes the IDataflowBlock to complete in a Faulted state.
	ISourceBlock<T>.ConsumeMessage	Called by a linked ITargetBlock<TInput> to accept and consume a DataflowMessageHeader previously offered by this ISourceBlock<TOutput>.
	ISourceBlock<T>.ReleaseReservation	Called by a linked ITargetBlock<TInput> to release a previously reserved DataflowMessageHeader by this ISourceBlock<TOutput>.
	ISourceBlock<T>.ReserveMessage	Called by a linked ITargetBlock<TInput> to reserve a previously offered DataflowMessageHeader by this ISourceBlock<TOutput>.
	ITargetBlock<T>.OfferMessage	Offers a message to the ITargetBlock<TInput>, giving the target the opportunity to consume or postpone the message.

Referenced from http://msdn.microsoft.com/en-us/library/hh160414(v=vs.110).aspx

So, as you can see, these interfaces make using the `BufferBlock` object as a general-purpose queue between stages of a pipeline very easy. This technique is also useful between producers and consumers in a producer-consumer design pattern.

ActionBlock

Another very useful object in the `Dataflow` library is `ActionBlock`. Its syntax is `ActionBlock<TInput>`, where `TInput` is an `Action` object. `ActionBlock` is a target block that executes a delegate when a message of data is received. The following is a very simple example of using an `ActionBlock`:

```
ActionBlock<int> action = new ActionBlock<int>(x =>
Console.WriteLine(x));

action.Post(10);
```

In this sample piece of code, the `ActionBlock` object is created with an integer parameter and executes a simple lambda expression that does a `Console.WriteLine` when a message of data is posted to the buffer. So, when the `action.Post(10)` command is executed, the integer, 10, is posted to the `ActionBlock` buffer and then the `ActionBlock` delegate, implemented as a lambda expression in this case, is executed.

In this example, since this is a target block, we would then need to call the `Complete` method to ensure the message block is completed.

Another handy method of the `BufferBlock` is the `LinkTo` method. This method allows you to link `ISourceBlock` to `ITargetBlock`. So, you can have a `BufferBlock` that is implemented as an `ISourceBlock` and link it to an `ActionBlock` since it is an `ITargetBlock`. In this way, an `Action` delegate can be executed when a `BufferBlock` receives data. This does not dequeue the data from the message block. It just allows you to execute some task when data is received into the buffer.

`ActionBlock` only has two properties, namely `InputCount`, which is a count of the number of data messages in the queue, and `Completion`, which gets a task that is an asynchronous operation and completion of the message block. It has the following methods:

	Name	Description
	Complete	Signals to the dataflow block that it shouldn't accept or produce any more messages and shouldn't consume any more postponed messages.
	Equals(Object)	Determines whether the specified object is equal to the current object. (Inherited from Object.)
	GetHashCode	Serves as the default hash function. (Inherited from Object.)
	GetType	Gets the Type of the current instance. (Inherited from Object.)
	Post	Posts an item to the target dataflow block.
	ToString	Returns a string that represents the formatted name of this IDataflowBlock instance. (Overrides Object.ToString().)

Referenced from http://msdn.microsoft.com/en-us/library/hh194684(v=vs.110).aspx

The following extension methods are implemented from its interfaces:

	Name	Description
	AsObserver<TInput>	Creates a new IObserver<T> abstraction over the ITargetBlock<TInput>. (Defined by DataflowBlock.)
	Post<TInput>	Posts an item to the ITargetBlock<TInput>. (Defined by DataflowBlock.)
	SendAsync<TInput>(TInput)	Overloaded. Asynchronously offers a message to the target message block, allowing for postponement. (Defined by DataflowBlock.)
	SendAsync<TInput>(TInput, CancellationToken)	Overloaded. Asynchronously offers a message to the target message block, allowing for postponement. (Defined by DataflowBlock.)

Referenced from http://msdn.microsoft.com/en-us/library/hh194684(v=vs.110).aspx

Also, it implements the following interfaces:

	Name	Description
	IDataflowBlock.Fault	Causes the dataflow block to complete in a faulted state.
	ITargetBlock<TInput>.OfferMessage	Offers a message to the dataflow block, and gives it the opportunity to consume or postpone the message.

Referenced from http://msdn.microsoft.com/en-us/library/hh194684(v=vs.110).aspx

Now that we have examined a little of the `Dataflow` library that Microsoft has developed, let's use it in a producer-consumer application.

Producer-consumer design pattern

Now, that we have covered the TPL's `Dataflow` library and the set of objects it provides to assist in asynchronous message passing between concurrent tasks, let's take a look at the producer-consumer design pattern. In a typical producer-consumer design, we have one or more producers putting data into a queue or message data block. Then we have one or more consumers taking data from the queue and processing it. This allows for asynchronous processing of data. Using the `Dataflow` library objects, we can create a consumer task that monitors a `BufferBlock` and pulls items of the data from it when they arrive. If no items are available, the consumer method will block until items are available or the `BufferBlock` has been set to `Complete`. Because of this, we can start our consumer at any time, even before the producer starts to put items into the queue.

Then we create one or more tasks that produce items and place them into the `BufferBlock`. Once the producers are finished processing all items of data to the `BufferBlock`, they can mark the block as `Complete`. Until then, the `BufferBlock` object is still available to add items into. This is perfect for long-running tasks and applications when we do not know when the data will arrive.

Because the producer task is implementing an input parameter of a `BufferBlock` as an `ITargetBlock` object and the consumer task is implementing an input parameter of a `BufferBlock` as an `ISourceBlock`, they can both use the same `BufferBlock` object but have different methods available to them. One has methods to produces items to the block and mark it complete. The other one has methods to receive items and wait for more items until the block is marked complete. In this way, the `Dataflow` library implements the perfect object to act as a queue between our producers and consumers.

Now, let's take a look at the application we developed previously as a Pipeline design and modify it using the `Dataflow` library. We will also remove a stage so that it just has two stages, one producer and one consumer.

How to do it

The first thing we need to do is open Visual Studio and create a new console application called `ProducerConsumerConsoleApp`. We will use a console application this time just for ease. Our main purpose here is to demonstrate how to implement the producer-consumer design pattern using the TPL `Dataflow` library.

Once you have opened Visual Studio and created the project, we need to perform the following steps:

1. First, we need to install and add a reference to the TPL `Dataflow` library. The TPL `Dataflow` library (`System.Threading.Tasks.Dataflow`) does not ship with .NET 4.5. Select **Manage NuGet Packages** from under the **Project** menu and then search online for `Microsoft.Tpl.Dataflow`.

2. Now, we will need to add two `using` statements to our program. One for `StreamReader` and `StreamWriter` and one for the `BufferBlock` object:

    ```
    using System.Threading.Tasks.Dataflow;
    using System.IO;
    ```

3. Now, let's add two static strings that will point to our input data file and the encrypted data file that we output:

    ```
    private static String PipelineEncryptFile = @"c:\projects\
    EncryptData.txt";
            private static String PipelineInputFile = @"c:\projects\
    InputData.txt";
    ```

4. Next, let's add a static method that will act as our producer. This method will have the following code:

```
// Our Producer method.
static void Producer(ITargetBlock<char> Target)
{
    String DisplayData = "";

    try
    {
        foreach (char C in GetData(PipelineInputFile))
        {

            //Displayed characters read in from the file.
            DisplayData = DisplayData + C.ToString();

            // Add each character to the buffer for the
next stage.
            Target.Post(C);

        }
    }

    finally
    {
        Target.Complete();
    }

}
```

5. Then we will add a static method to perform our consumer functionality. It will have the following code:

```
// This is our consumer method. IT runs asynchronously.
static async Task<int> Consumer(ISourceBlock<char> Source)
{
    String DisplayData = "";

    // Read from the source buffer until the source buffer
has no
    // available output data.
    while (await Source.OutputAvailableAsync())
    {
        char C = Source.Receive();

        //Encrypt each character.
```

```
            char encrypted = Encrypt(C);

            DisplayData = DisplayData + encrypted.
ToString();

        }

        //write the decrypted string to the output file.
        using (StreamWriter outfile =
                new StreamWriter(PipelineEncryptFile))
        {
            outfile.Write(DisplayData);
        }

        return DisplayData.Length;

    }
```

6. Then, let's create a simple static helper method to read our input data file and put it in a `List` collection character by character. This will give us a character list for our producer to use. The code in this method will look like this:

```
    public static List<char> GetData(String PipelineInputFile)
    {
        List<char> Data = new List<char>();

        //Get the Source data.
        using (StreamReader inputfile = new StreamReader(Pipel
ineInputFile))
        {
            while (inputfile.Peek() >= 0)
            {
                Data.Add((char)inputfile.Read());
            }

        }

        return Data;
    }
```

7. Next, we will add a static method to encrypt our characters. This method will work like the one we used in our pipelining application. It will add one to the ASCII numerical value of the character:

```
    public static char Encrypt(char C)
    {
```

```
        //Take the character, convert to an int, add 1, then
convert back to a character.
            int i = (int)C;
            i = i + 1;
            C = Convert.ToChar(i);

            return C;
        }
```

8. Then, we need to add the code for our `Main` method. This method will start our consumer and producer tasks. Then, when they have completed processing, it will display the results in the console. The code for this method looks like this:

```
        static void Main(string[] args)
        {
            // Create the buffer block object to use between the
producer and consumer.
            BufferBlock<char> buffer = new BufferBlock<char>();

            // The consumer method runs asynchronously. Start it
now.
            Task<int> consumer = Consumer(buffer);

            // Post source data to the dataflow block.
            Producer(buffer);

            // Wait for the consumer to process all data.
            consumer.Wait();

            // Print the count of characters from the input file.
            Console.WriteLine("Processed {0} bytes from input
file.", consumer.Result);

            //Print out the input file to the console.
            Console.WriteLine("\r\n\r\n");
            Console.WriteLine("This is the input data file.
\r\n");
            using (StreamReader inputfile = new StreamReader(Pipel
ineInputFile))
            {
                while (inputfile.Peek() >= 0)
                {
                    Console.Write((char)inputfile.Read());
                }
```

```
        }

        //Print out the encrypted file to the console.
        Console.WriteLine("\r\n\r\n");
        Console.WriteLine("This is the encrypted data file.
\r\n");
        using (StreamReader encryptfile = new StreamReader(Pip
elineEncryptFile))
        {
            while (encryptfile.Peek() >= 0)
            {
                Console.Write((char)encryptfile.Read());
            }

        }

        //Wait before closing the application so we can see
the results.
        Console.ReadLine();
    }
```

9. That is all the code that is needed. Now, let's build and run the application using the following input data file:

> In this chapter we will explore two popular design patterns used in developing parallel applications using the TPL. Pipline and Producer-Consumer are two methods to solve typical concurrent problems.
>
> A Pipeline design is one where an application is designed with multiple tasks or stages of functionality with queues of work items between them. So, for each stage the application will read from a queue of work to be performed, execute the work on that item, and then queue the results for the next stage. By designing the application this way, all of the stages can execute in parallel. Each stage just reads from its work queue, performs the work, and puts the results of the work into the queue for the next stage.

10. Once it runs and completes, your output should look like the following screenshot:

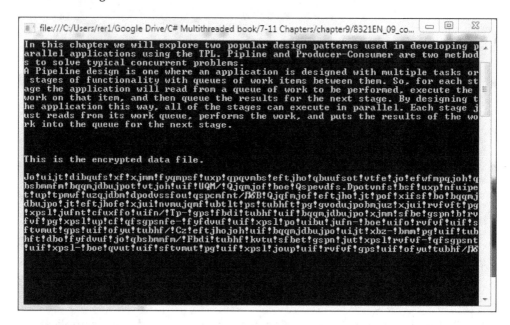

Now, try this with your own data files and inputs. Let's examine what happened and how this works.

How it works

First we will go through the `Main` method. The first thing `Main` does is create a `BufferBlock` object called `buffer`. This will be used as the queue of items between our producer and consumer. This `BufferBlock` is defined to accept character datatypes.

Next, we start our consumer task using this command:

```
Task<int> consumer = Consumer(buffer);
```

Also, note that when this buffer object goes into the consumer task, it is cast as `ISourceBlock`. Notice the method header of our consumer:

```
static async Task<int> Consumer(ISourceBlock<char> Source)
```

Next, our `Main` method starts our producer task using the following command:

```
Producer(buffer);
```

Then we wait until our consumer task finishes, using this command:

```
consumer.Wait();
```

So, now our `Main` method just waits. Its work is done for now. It has started both the producer and consumer tasks. Now our consumer is waiting for items to appear in its `BufferBlock` so it can process them. The consumer will stay in the following loop until all items are removed from the message block and the block has been *completed,* which is done by someone calling its `Complete` method:

```
while (await Source.OutputAvailableAsync())
    {
            char C = Source.Receive();

            //Encrypt each character.
            char encrypted = Encrypt(C);

            DisplayData = DisplayData + encrypted.ToString();


    }
```

So, now our consumer task will loop asynchronously, removing items from the message queue as they appear. It uses the following command in the while loop to do this:

```
await Source.OutputAvailableAsync())
```

Likewise, other consumer tasks can run at the same time and do the same thing. If the producer is adding items to the block quicker than the consumer can process them, then adding another consumer will improve performance. Once an item is available, then the consumer calls the following command to get the item from the buffer:

```
char C = Source.Receive();
```

Since the buffer contains items of type character, we place the item received into a character value. Then the consumer processes it by encrypting the character and appending it to our display string:

Now, let's look at the consumer. The consumer first gets its data by calling the following command:

```
GetData(PipelineInputFile)
```

This method returns a `List` collection of characters that has an item for each character in the input data file. Now the producer iterates through the collection and uses the following command to place each item into the buffer block:

```
Target.Post(C);
```

Also, notice in the method header for our consumer that we cast our buffer as an `ITargetBlock` type:

```
static void Producer(ITargetBlock<char> Target)
```

Once the producer is done processing characters and adding them to the buffer, it officially closes the `BufferBlock` object using this command:

```
Target.Complete();
```

That is it for the producer and consumer. Once the `Main` method is done waiting on the consumer to finish, it then uses the following code to write out the number of characters processed, the input data, and the encrypted data:

```
// Print the count of characters from the input file.
        Console.WriteLine("Processed {0} bytes from input file.",
    consumer.Result);

        //Print out the input file to the console.
        Console.WriteLine("\r\n\r\n");
        Console.WriteLine("This is the input data file. \r\n");
        using (StreamReader inputfile = new StreamReader(Pipeline
    InputFile))
        {
            while (inputfile.Peek() >= 0)
            {
                Console.Write((char)inputfile.Read());
            }

        }

        //Print out the encrypted file to the console.
        Console.WriteLine("\r\n\r\n");
        Console.WriteLine("This is the encrypted data file.
    \r\n");
        using (StreamReader encryptfile = new StreamReader(Pipelin
    eEncryptFile))
        {
            while (encryptfile.Peek() >= 0)
            {
```

```
                    Console.Write((char)encryptfile.Read());
        }


    }
```

Now that you are comfortable implementing a basic producer-consumer design using objects from the TPL `Dataflow` library, try experimenting with this basic idea but use multiple producers and multiple consumers all with the same `BufferBlock` object as the queue between them all.

Also, try converting our original Pipeline application from the beginning of the chapter into a TPL `Dataflow` producer-consumer application with two sets of producers and consumers. The first will act as stage 1 and stage 2, and the second will act as stage 2 and stage 3. So, in effect, stage 2 will be both a consumer and a producer.

Summary

We have covered a lot in this chapter. We have learned the benefits and how to implement a Pipeline design pattern and a producer-consumer design pattern. As we saw, these are both very helpful design patterns when building parallel and concurrent applications that require multiple asynchronous processes of data between tasks.

In the Pipeline design, we are able to run multiple tasks or stages concurrently even though the stages rely on data being processed and output by other stages. This is very helpful for performance since all functionality doesn't have to wait on each stage to finish processing every item of data. In our example, we are able to start decrypting characters of data while a previous stage is still encrypting data and placing it into the queue.

In the Pipeline example, we examined the benefits of the `BlockingCollection` class in acting as a queue between stages in our pipeline.

Next, we explored the new TPL `Dataflow` library and some of its message block classes. These classes implement several interfaces defined in the library — `ISourceBlock`, `ITargetBlock`, and `IPropogatorBlock`. By implementing these interfaces, it allows us to write generic producer and consumer task functionality that can be reused in a variety of applications.

Both of these design patterns and the Dataflow library allow for easy implementations of common functionality in a concurrent manner. You will use these techniques in many applications, and this will become a go-to design pattern when you evaluate a system's requirements and determine how to implement concurrency to help improve performance. Like all programming, parallel programming is made easier when you have a toolbox of easy-to-use techniques that you are comfortable with.

Most applications that benefit from parallelism will be conducive to some variation of a producer-consumer or Pipeline pattern. Also, the BlockingCollection and Dataflow message block objects are useful mechanisms for coordinating data between parallel tasks, no matter what design pattern is used in the application. It will be very useful to become comfortable with these messaging and queuing classes.

Now, we will move back to data parallelism in the next chapter, and this time, we will explore explicit data parallelism using PLINQ.

10
Parallel LINQ – PLINQ

In this chapter, we will learn about declarative data parallelism using **Parallel Language Integrated Query (PLINQ)**. In *Chapter 7, Data Parallelism*, we discussed data parallelism using the `Parallel` library and the `Parallel.For` and `Parallel.ForEach` loops. PLINQ is a parallel version of LINQ to Objects. **LINQ to Objects** allows for LINQ queries on in-memory data collections such as `List` and `DataTable` that implement the `IEnumerable` or `IEnumerable<T>` interface. Unlike a sequential LINQ, PLINQ tries to use all of the processors in the computer it is running on by dividing the data collections into segments and creating a task to process each segment of the data collection. PLINQ and the **Common Language Runtime (CLR)** are smart enough to evaluate the query and determine if it will benefit from a multithreaded execution. If not, then it will run sequentially like a normal LINQ. It is the best of both worlds. .NET figures out whether it can gain performance improvements by operating concurrently or not and makes the decision for you.

The parallel extension methods were added to the `System.Linq` namespace in .NET 4.5. It includes extension methods for all standard LINQ operators as well as some extra ones for parallel operators. Almost all of the PLINQ methods are implemented in the `System.Linq.ParallelEnumerable` namespace.

The topics that will be covered in this chapter are as follows:

- Executing a PLINQ
- Ordering in PLINQ
- Merging in PLINQ
- Canceling a PLINQ
- Understanding performance improvements in PLINQ

Executing a PLINQ

Now, let's take a look at a basic PLINQ and syntax. We will use three different methods to perform the PLINQ and then examine the results. The first will use the ForAll method of the ParallelQuery class. The next one will use the AsParallel method of the LINQ library on the Enumerable collection. The final way will use the standard LINQ method syntax.

We will then display the results of the three queries in three listboxes and also display the time it took to execute each query.

How to do it

Let's start by opening up Visual Studio and creating a new WPF application project named WpfPLINQQuery. Once this project is open, let's perform the following steps:

1. In the MainWindow.xaml file in design mode add three button controls and name them btnMethod1, btnMethod2, and btnMethod3. Set the Content property of each to Execute Method 1, Execute Method 2, and Execute Method 3, respectively. Next, create a click event handler for each in the MainWindow.xaml.cs file and name these three methods btnMethod1_Click, btnMethod2_Click, and btnMethod3_Click, respectively.

2. In the btnMethod1_Click event handler method, place the following code:

```csharp
private void btnMethod1_Click(object sender, RoutedEventArgs e)
    {
        IEnumerable<int> collection1 = Enumerable.Range(10,
500000);

        //Start the timer.
        Stopwatch sw1 = new Stopwatch();
        sw1.Start();

    //Method 1 - This uses a ForAll method and an empty
    //delegate method.
        ParallelQuery<int> PQ1 = from num in collection1.
AsParallel()
            where num % 5 == 0
            select num;

    PQ1.ForAll((i) => DoWork(i));

    // Use a standard foreach loop and merge the results.
        foreach (int i in PQ1)
        {
            lb1.Items.Add(i);
        }
```

```
//Stop the timer.
sw1.Stop();

tbTime1.Text = sw1.ElapsedMilliseconds.ToString();

}
```

3. In the `btnMethod2_Click` event handler method, place the following code:

```
private void btnMethod2_Click(object sender, RoutedEventArgs e)
{
        IEnumerable<int> collection2 = Enumerable.Range(10,
500000);

        //Start the timer.
        Stopwatch sw2 = new Stopwatch();
        sw2.Start();

        // Method 2 - Use a standard ToArray method to return
//the results.
        int[] PQ2 = (from num in collection2.AsParallel()
                where num % 10 == 0
                select num).ToArray();

        // Use a standard foreach loop and merge the results.
        foreach (int i in PQ2)
        {
            lb2.Items.Add(i);
        }

        //Stop the timer.
        sw2.Stop();

        tbTime2.Text = sw2.ElapsedMilliseconds.ToString();
}
```

4. In the `btnMethod3_Click` event handler method, place the following code. Also, let's add three listboxes and name them `lb1`, `lb2`, and `lb3`.

```
private void btnMethod3_Click(object sender, RoutedEventArgs e)
{
        IEnumerable<int> collection3 = Enumerable.Range(10,
10000);

        //Start the timer.
        Stopwatch sw3 = new Stopwatch();
        sw3.Start();
```

```
// Method 3 - Use the LINQ standard method format.
ParallelQuery<int> PQ3 = collection3.AsParallel().
Where(n => n % 10 == 0).Select(n => n);

// Use a standard foreach loop and merge the results.
foreach (int i in PQ3)
{
    lb3.Items.Add(i);
}


//Stop the timer.
sw3.Stop();

tbTime3.Text = sw3.ElapsedMilliseconds.ToString();

}
```

5. Then add three textboxes and name them `tbTime1`, `tbTime2`, and `tbTime3`. Also, clear their `Text` properties.

6. In the `MainWindow.xaml.cs` file, we will need to add a `using` statement so that the `Stopwatch` class is available to us. So, add the following statement at the top of the file with the rest of the `using` statements:

```
using System.Diagnostics;
```

7. Then we need to add an empty method to serve as our delegate for the lambda expression. We will call it `DoWork`. Add it to the bottom of the `MainWindow` class with the following code:

```
static void DoWork(int i)
    {
    }
```

8. That is all the code we need to add to our `MainWindow.xaml.cs` file. Our `MainWindow.xaml` file should now contain the following code:

```
<Window x:Class="WpfPLINQQuery.MainWindow"
        xmlns="http://schemas.microsoft.com/winfx/2006/xaml/
presentation"
        xmlns:x="http://schemas.microsoft.com/winfx/2006/xaml"
        Title="MainWindow" Height="759.12" Width="725.431">

    <Grid>
        <ListBox x:Name="lb1" HorizontalAlignment="Left"
Height="557" Margin="38,78,0,0" VerticalAlignment="Top"
Width="150"/>
        <ListBox x:Name="lb2" HorizontalAlignment="Left"
Height="557" Margin="285,78,0,0" VerticalAlignment="Top"
Width="150"/>
```

```
        <ListBox x:Name="lb3" HorizontalAlignment="Left"
Height="557" Margin="526,78,0,0" VerticalAlignment="Top"
Width="150"/>
        <Button x:Name="btnMethod1" Content="Execute Method
1" HorizontalAlignment="Left" Height="43" Margin="38,26,0,0"
VerticalAlignment="Top" Width="150" Click="btnMethod1_Click"/>
        <Button x:Name="btnMethod2" Content="Execute Method
2" HorizontalAlignment="Left" Height="43" Margin="285,26,0,0"
VerticalAlignment="Top" Width="150" Click="btnMethod2_Click"/>
        <Button x:Name="btnMethod3" Content="Execute Method
3" HorizontalAlignment="Left" Height="43" Margin="526,26,0,0"
VerticalAlignment="Top" Width="150" Click="btnMethod3_Click"/>
        <TextBox x:Name="tbTime1" HorizontalAlignment="Left"
Height="28" Margin="38,684,0,0" TextWrapping="Wrap"
VerticalAlignment="Top" Width="150"/>
        <TextBox x:Name="tbTime2" HorizontalAlignment="Left"
Height="28" Margin="285,684,0,0" TextWrapping="Wrap"
VerticalAlignment="Top" Width="150"/>
        <TextBox x:Name="tbTime3" HorizontalAlignment="Left"
Height="28" Margin="526,684,0,0" TextWrapping="Wrap"
VerticalAlignment="Top" Width="150"/>

    </Grid>

</Window>
```

Now our project is completed. Let's build and run the project. The program should look like this when it runs:

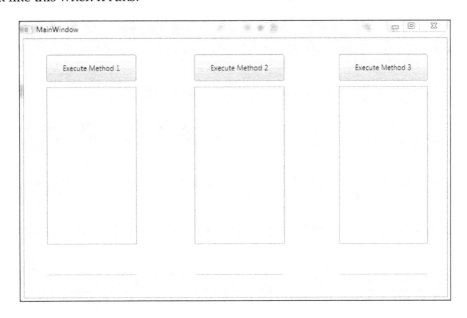

Now, let's click on the **Execute Method 1** button. We should see results like the following:

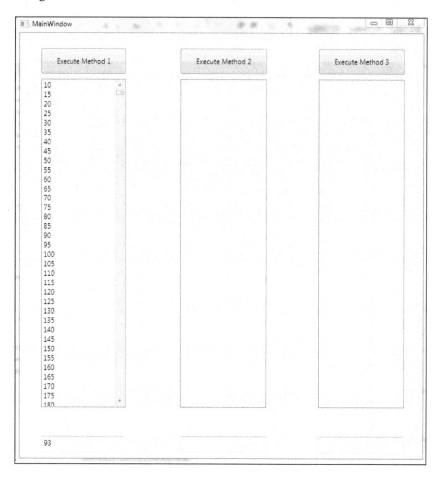

Now, let's click on the next two buttons, **Execute Method 2** and **Execute Method 3** and see what the program looks like:

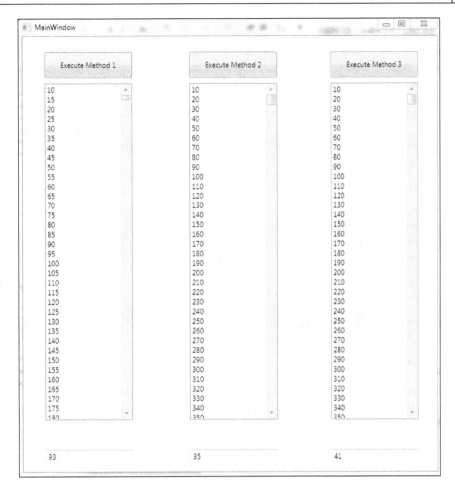

As you can see, we executed the PLINQ parallel query using three different methods and the results are different each time. The first thing you'll notice if you scroll through the results is that the numbers in the listbox are not ordered. The next thing you will notice is that the runtime of each is not exactly the same. Granted, the first one will take longer to display because we divide by 5 instead of 10, so there are more results. But the query itself should take roughly the same time. You can play with this by moving the command to stop the Stopwatch object.

Now let's examine how this works.

How it works

In this project, we performed a PLINQ parallel query using three different methods. In the first one, we defined a `ParallelQuery` object using this line of code, but didn't execute it yet:

```
ParallelQuery<int> PQ1 = from num in collection1.AsParallel()
                         where num % 5 == 0
                         select num;
```

We add the `AsParallel` method to the `IEnumerable` collection with the following command:

```
collection1.AsParallel();
```

This tells .NET to try and execute this query concurrently if it determines that it will improve performance. We can force .NET to operate this query concurrently using the parallel extension method `WithExecutionMode(ParallelExecutionMode.ForceParallelism)`.

Then we actually ran the query using the `ForAll` method of the `ParallelQuery` class. We did this using the following command:

```
PQ1.ForAll((i) => DoWork(i));
```

To use this command, we need to pass it a lambda expression. We are just using a lambda expression that passes a delegate to a method that does nothing. We do not need to do work in the delegate method because we are doing all of the work in the parallel query.

In the second method, we create a parallel query that executes when the command is processed and returns an array. This command is as follows:

```
int[] PQ2 = (from num in collection2.AsParallel()
                   where num % 10 == 0
                   select num).ToArray();
```

> Notice that here we have added the `ToArray()` method to the results of the query. By implementing the parallel query this way we ensure that the query is executing during this command. In the first method, we create the query but do not execute it until the `ForAll` command is executed.

In the final method, we use the LINQ method syntax. Here is the statement that performs the query using this syntax:

```
ParallelQuery<int> PQ3 = collection3.AsParallel().Where(n => n % 10 ==
0).Select(n => n);
```

Here we return a `ParallelQuery` object instead of an array.

Also, notice that in all three methods the results are not returned in order. We will see later in the chapter how to ensure the order of the results if that is necessary. For now, we are just trying to run a parallel query. We will let .NET determine how to run the query (concurrently or sequentially), and in whatever order.

Ordering in PLINQ

Now, what if the order of our results matters? In a lot of cases, we will want the results to come back in a certain order. Let's examine how we can accomplish this.

There are several methods contained in the parallel extension methods of the `IEnumerable` interface. The two we use the most are `AsOrdered()` and `AsOrderedBy()`. These two methods guarantee order preservation in the results of the parallel query. This does add some cost and overhead.

Let's take our project from the last section and update it to return the ordered results.

How to do it

Let's open up our `PLINQQuery` project and make the following changes:

1. Change the parallel query statement in the `btnMethod1_Click` method to look like the following by adding the `AsOrdered` method to the query:

   ```
   ParallelQuery<int> PQ1 = from num in collection1.AsParallel().
   AsOrdered()
                   where num % 5 == 0
               select num;
   ```

2. Now, make a similar change to the statement in the `btnMethod2_Click` method. Make its parallel query statement look like the following:

   ```
   int[] PQ2 = (from num in collection2.AsParallel().AsOrdered()
                   where num % 10 == 0
               select num).ToArray();
   ```

3. Finally, let's make a similar change to the `btn3Method_Click` method and its query statement:

```
ParallelQuery<int> PQ3 = collection3.AsParallel().AsOrdered().
Where(n =>             n % 10 == 0).Select(n => n);
```

That is all of the changes; seems simple enough. Now, let's build and run our application. You should get a program that looks like the following screenshot:

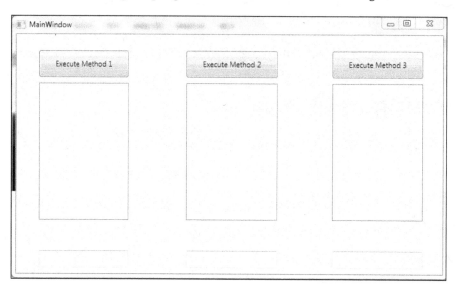

Now, let's click on each of the three buttons to run all the three queries. Your program should now look like the following screenshot:

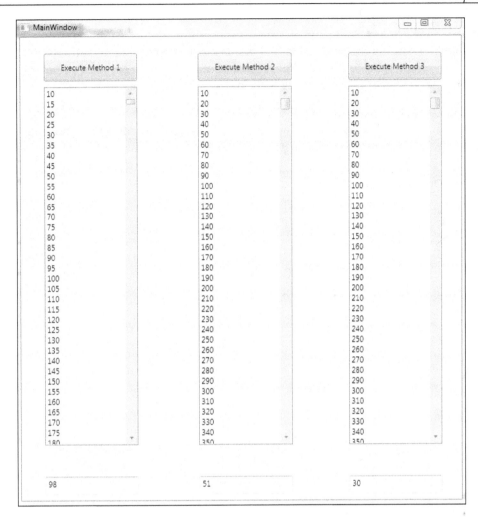

As you can see, the results are now ordered. This is a simple example; however, in a more complex example, you will also see that the runtimes are longer. As you would expect, ordering the results will slow down the query processing.

Also, did you notice that if you execute the queries in the application in a different order you will see that typically the first one takes longer than the last one? There are two explanations for why the last one to run is usually faster. .NET has run the query, so it has also taken time to determine the best execution method. Also, if it chooses to run the query concurrently, it has already taken the overhead of creating the tasks in the threadpool.

How it works

The change from the first project to this one is a simple one. We just added the `AsOrdered()` method to the parallel extension method, `AsParallel()`, that we execute against the `IEnumerable` collection.

This forces .NET to order the results. We can also order the results with the `OrderBy` query syntax. It should be noted that `OrderBy` is done sequentially, not in parallel. The following screenshot explains items in the query itself that will order the results:

◢ Query Operators and Ordering

The following query operators introduce order preservation into all subsequent operations in a query, or until AsUnordered<TSource> is called:

- OrderBy

- OrderByDescending

- ThenBy

- ThenByDescending

The following PLINQ query operators may in some cases require ordered source sequences to produce correct results:

- Reverse<TSource>

- SequenceEqual

- TakeWhile

- SkipWhile

- Zip

Referenced from http://msdn.microsoft.com/en-us/library/dd460677(v=vs.110).aspx

Merging in PLINQ

We have learned how to perform a parallel query and how to order the results. Now, let's examine merging with our parallel queries.

When a parallel query is performed, the .NET CLR partitions the source collection so that several tasks can work sections of the collection concurrently. Once this is completed, the results need to be merged into a result collection for processing. Depending on the query operators used, the results can be merged in different ways. Query operators that dictate a new order on the result collection will buffer all items from the separate threads before merging them together again. Other query operators are partially buffered, while the query operator, `ForAll<TSource>`, is not buffered. It produces all items from all tasks as soon as they are processed.

The `WithMergeOptions<TSource>` method can tell PLINQ how to perform the merging process of a concurrent query.

If a query cannot perform the merge option specified, .NET will ignore it. So, you can see that .NET treats merge options as suggestions and will not throw an error if the merge option is not compatible; it will just ignore it. Likewise, if you do not specify a merge option, .NET will select one for you. So, you can use a merge option if you have determined that a specific merge is best for your performance or just let .NET decide for you. This is one of the beautiful things of the TPL. It handles a lot of the thinking for you when it comes to common concurrent issues.

The different options with which the parallel merge can be set up are listed in the following screenshot:

- **Not Buffered**

  The NotBuffered option causes each processed element to be returned from each thread as soon as it is produced. This behavior is analogous to "streaming" the output. If the AsOrdered operator is present in the query, **NotBuffered** preserves the order of the source elements. Although **NotBuffered** starts yielding results as soon as they're available., the total time to produce all the results might still be longer than using one of the other merge options.

- **Auto Buffered**

  The AutoBuffered option causes the query to collect elements into a buffer and then periodically yield the buffer contents all at once to the consuming thread. This is analogous to yielding the source data in "chunks" instead of using the "streaming" behavior of **NotBuffered**. **AutoBuffered** may take longer than **NotBuffered** to make the first element available on the consuming thread. The size of the buffer and the exact yielding behavior are not configurable and may vary, depending on various factors that relate to the query.

- **FullyBuffered**

  The FullyBuffered option causes the output of the whole query to be buffered before any of the elements are yielded. When you use this option, it can take longer before the first element is available on the consuming thread, but the complete results might still be produced faster than by using the other options.

Referenced from http://msdn.microsoft.com/en-us/library/dd997424(v=vs.110).aspx

The following are the parallel query operators that support merging:

Operator	Restrictions
AsEnumerable<TSource>	None
Cast<TResult>	None
Concat	Non-ordered queries that have an Array or List source only.
DefaultIfEmpty	None
OfType<TResult>	None
Reverse<TSource>	Non-ordered queries that have an Array or List source only.
Select	None
SelectMany	None
Skip<TSource>	None
Take<TSource>	None
Where	None

Referenced from http://msdn.microsoft.com/en-us/library/dd997424(v=vs.110).aspx

How to do it

Now, let's go back to our project and try changing our program to use the NotBuffered, AutoBuffered, and FullyBuffered merging options.

To do this, let's open our PLINQQuery project and change the parallel query statement in the btnMethod1_Click method to look like the following:

```
ParallelQuery<int> PQ1 = from num in collection1.AsParallel().
AsOrdered().WithMergeOptions(ParallelMergeOptions.NotBuffered)
            where num % 5 == 0
            select num;
```

Now, let's build and run the program and click on the **Execute Method 1** button. You should see the following results:

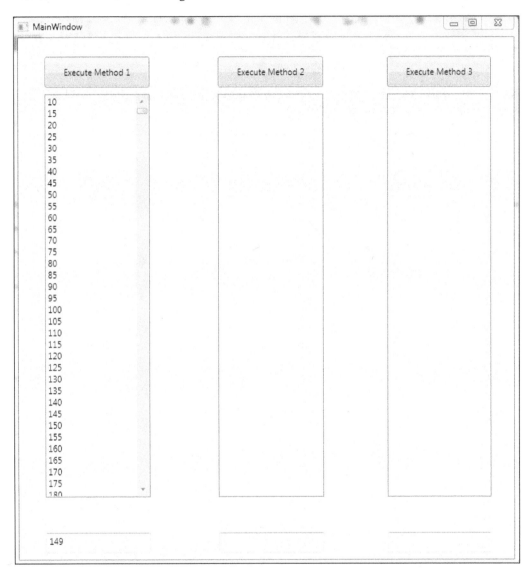

Now, let's try to use the `AutoBuffered` method. To do this, in the `btnMethod1_` `Click` method, change the parallel query statement to the following:

```
ParallelQuery<int> PQ1 = from num in collection1.AsParallel().
AsOrdered().WithMergeOptions(ParallelMergeOptions.AutoBuffered)
                        where num % 5 == 0
                        select num;
```

Now, build and run the program again. Click on the **Execute Method 1** button and you should get the following results:

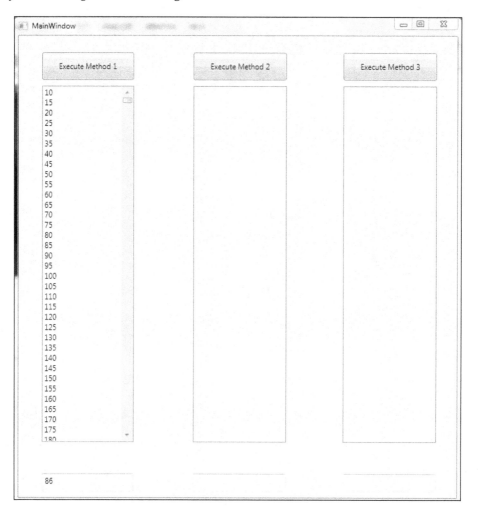

Now, let's make one final change to the parallel query in this method to use the `AutoBuffered` option. Change the `btnMethod1_click` method to have the following parallel query statement:

```
ParallelQuery<int> PQ1 = from num in collection1.AsParallel().
AsOrdered().WithMergeOptions(ParallelMergeOptions.FullyBuffered)
                where num % 5 == 0
                select num;
```

Now, let's build and run this application one final time and click on the **Execute Method 1** button. The results should look like the following screenshot:

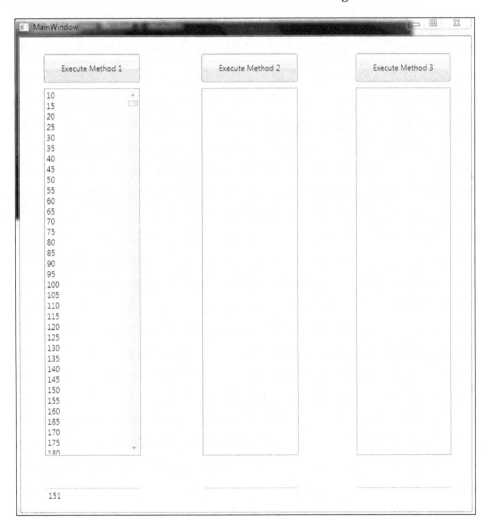

How it works

As you can see, to dictate to .NET on how to merge the results of a buffered query is as easy as calling the WithMergeOptions() parallel extension method; just like ordering the results is as easy as calling the AsOrdered() parallel extension method.

But you will also notice that the best results come from using the AutoBuffered or no-merge option. Even though PLINQ gives you these options to dictate how the parallel query is merged, if we let .NET determine how to do it, the results are often far better.

For complex examples, it might be beneficial to tell .NET how to merge the results, but often it is best to let the CLR determine this itself. This is one of the benefits of using PLINQ and the TPL—a lot of the complex work and thinking are handled for you. You can concentrate your coding time on the functionality and not the performance.

Canceling a PLINQ

Canceling a parallel query is very similar to canceling a task using TPL. First, we create a cancellation token and then we issue a cancel request to the cancellation token. This will create an operation cancellation exception. Then when we execute our parallel query, add the parallel extension method WithCancellation(), and pass it the cancellation token. Then, finally, we catch the operation cancellation request and process it.

The .NET framework does not pass a single OperationCanceledException into a System.AggregateException; the OperationCanceledException must be processed in a separate catch block.

How to do it

Now, let's open our PLINQQuery project again and this time we will add a Cancel button and work with the btnMethod2_Click event handler method:

1. First, add a new button control to our MainWindow.xaml.cs file and set its Content property to Cancel and name the control btnCancel.

2. Next, we need to add a using statement for the Threading namespace so we can create a cancellation token object. Add the following using statement:

   ```
   using System.Threading;
   ```

3. Next, let's create a cancellation token at the top of our `MainWindow` class with the following statement:

```
CancellationTokenSource cs = new
CancellationTokenSource();
```

4. Now, let's add a `btnCancel_Click` click event handler method for our **Cancel** button. It should have the following code:

```
private void btnCancel_Click(object sender,
RoutedEventArgs e)
    {
        cs.Cancel();
    }
```

5. Also, let's change our `IEnumerable` collection to have 500,000 items, so it will run longer and give us a chance to cancel the operation:

```
IEnumerable<int> collection1 = Enumerable.Range(10,
500000);
```

6. Finally, let's change the `btnMethod2_Click` event handler to have the following code for the parallel query:

```
try
    {
        // Method 2 - Use a standard TOArray method
to //return the results.
PQ2 = (from num in collection2.AsParallel().AsOrdered().
WithCancellation(cs.Token)
                where num % 10 == 0
                select num).ToArray();
    }
    catch (OperationCanceledException ex)
    {
        lb2.Items.Clear();
        lb2.Items.Add(ex.Message);
        return;
    }
```

Now, let's build and run our program. Click on the **Execute Method 2** button and immediately click on the **Cancel** button. You should see the following output in your application:

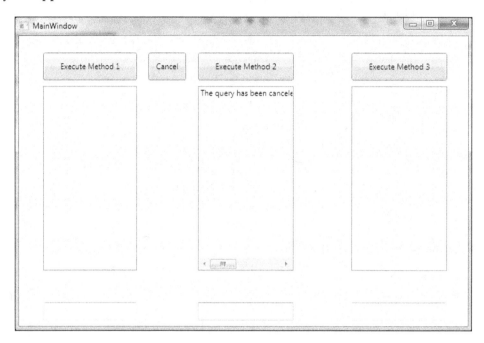

You can see that we have canceled the parallel query before its completion. Now, let's now take a look at how it was performed.

How it works

We performed this very simply. First, we created a cancellation token to use with this command:

```
CancellationTokenSource cs = new CancellationTokenSource();
```

Next, we created a **Cancel** button. and when it is pressed, we execute the Cancel() method of the cancellation token object. This is done here:

```
private void btnCancel_Click(object sender, RoutedEventArgs e)
    {
        cs.Cancel();
    }
```

Finally, in our parallel query, we add the `WithCancellation()` method
and pass it the cancellation token. Then we add a `catch` block and catch any
`OperationCanceledException` exceptions:

```
        try
        {
                // Method 2 - Use a standard TOArray method to return
   the //results.
                PQ2 = (from num in collection2.AsParallel().
   AsOrdered().WithCancellation(cs.Token)
                           where num % 10 == 0
                           select num).ToArray();
        }
        catch (OperationCanceledException ex)
        {
            lb2.Items.Clear();
            lb2.Items.Add(ex.Message);
            return;
        }
```

That is all there is to it.

Understanding performance improvements in PLINQ

We have seen how we can implement PLINQ queries and specify ordering, merging,
and parallel execution options. We have also seen how to execute a PLINQ with the
`ForAll()` method and as a `foreach` loop. All of these factor into the performance
of the query. It is also important to examine how .NET decides to partition a source
data collection when it decides to execute a PLINQ in parallel. Remember, a PLINQ
executed in parallel is just a LINQ where a data collection is partitioned into groups
and a task is created to process the `Where` action of the query on each partition of
data. The following diagrams depict the differences between LINQ processing and
PLINQ processing.

The following diagram shows the process of the LINQ:

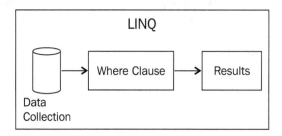

The following diagram shows the process of PLINQ. Notice how the data is partitioned and the Where clause is executed concurrently on each partition:

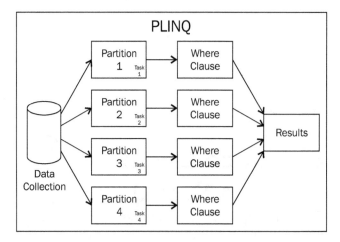

Also, when we perform a query using a ForAll versus a foreach loop, the processing is different. We can determine which of these are the best methods, usually by finding out whether or not the order of the results matter. If the order of the results is important, then foreach is the better processing method because the results are merged after the loop processes. Using the ForAll loop, the whole query is processed on each data partition individually so that there is no merging of the results in the correct order. You can place the AsOrdered method on the IEnumerable collection for the query, but it then basically buffers all results to merge them so you lose the performance gains the ForAll loop gives you. The following diagrams depict the differences in the way each of these is processed.

First, we'll have a look at the `ForAll` processing:

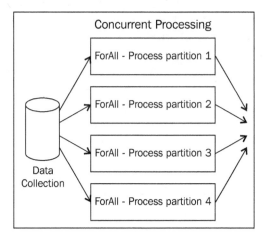

Second, let's look at the process of the `foreach` processing. Notice in the following diagram that the merge happens before the `foreach` loop processing, so the `foreach` processing is done sequentially:

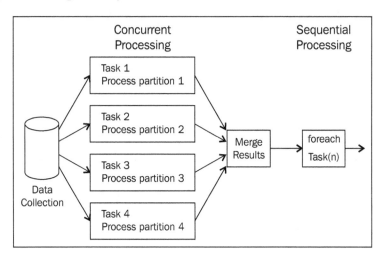

Now, let's take a look at the algorithms PLINQ (or more aptly the .NET CLR) uses to partition a data collection into groups for parallel processing. .NET uses four different algorithms to partition data based on the collection and the query. The following screenshot details the first two algorithms:

1. **Range Partitioning** – This is a pretty common partitioning scheme, similar to the one that I described in the example above. This is amenable to many query shapes, though it only works with *indexible data sources* such as lists and arrays (i.e. IList<T> and T[]). If you give PLINQ something typed as IEnumerable or IEnumerable<T>, PLINQ will query for the IList<T> interface, and if it's found, will use that interface implementation with range partitioning. The benefits of these data sources is that we know the exact length and can access any of the elements within the arrays directly. For the majority of cases, there are large performance benefits to using this type of partitioning.

2. **Chunk Partitioning** – This is a general purpose partitioning scheme that works for any data source, and is the main partitioning type for *non-indexible data sources*. In this scheme, worker threads request data, and it is served up to the thread in chunks. IEnumerables and IEnumerable<T>s do not have fixed Count properties (there is a LINQ extension method for this, but that is not the same), so there's no way to know when or if the data source will enumerate completely. It could be 3 elements, it could be 3 million elements, it could be infinite. A single system needs to take all of these possibilities into account and factor in different delegate sizes, uneven delegate sizes, selectivity etc. The chunk partitioning algorithm is quite general and PLINQ's algorithm had to be tuned for good performance on a wide range of queries. We've experimented with many different growth patterns and currently use a plan that doubles after a certain number of requests. This is subject to change as we tune for performance, so don't depend on this. Another important optimization is that chunk partitioning balances the load among cores, as the tasks per core dynamically request more work as needed. This ensures that all cores are utilized throughout the query and can all cross the finish line at the same time vs. a ragged, sequential entry to the end.

Referenced from http://blogs.msdn.com/b/pfxteam/archive/2009/05/28/9648672.aspx

The details of the other two algorithms are as follows:

3. **Striped Partitioning** – This scheme is used for SkipWhile and TakeWhile and is optimized for processing items at the head of a data source (which obviously suits the needs of SkipWhile and TakeWhile). In striped partitioning, each of the n worker threads is allocated a small number of items (sometimes 1) from each block of n items. The set of items belonging to a single thread is called a 'stripe', hence the name. A useful feature of this scheme is that there is no inter-thread synchronization required as each worker thread can determine its data via simple arithmetic. This is really a special case of range partitioning and only works on arrays and types that implement IList<T>.

4. **Hash Partitioning** – Hash partitioning is a special type of partitioning that is used by the query operators that must compare data elements (these operators are: Join, GroupJoin, GroupBy, Distinct, Except, Union, Intersect). When hash-partitioning occurs (which is just prior to any of the operators mentioned), all of the data is processed and channeled to threads such that items with identical hash-codes will be handled by the same thread. This hash-partitioning work is costly, but it means that all the comparison work can then be performed without further synchronization. Hash partitioning assigns every element to an output partition based on a hash computed from each element's key. This can be an efficient way of building a hash-table on the fly concurrently, and can be used to accomplish partitioning and hashing for the hash join algorithm. The benefit is that PLINQ can now use the same hash partitioning scheme for the data source used for probing; this way all possible matches end up in the same partition, meaning less shared data and smaller hash table sizes (each partition has its own hash table). There's a lot going on with hash-partitioning, so it's not as speedy as the other types, especially when ordering is involved in the query. As a result the query operators that rely upon it have additional overheads compared to simpler operators.

Referenced from http://blogs.msdn.com/b/pfxteam/archive/2009/05/28/9648672.aspx

As you can see from the previous screenshot, PLINQ partitions the source data collection based on the type of data and the type of query. This is all part of the logic that .NET performs so we do not have to. Just like determining if a query should be run concurrently or sequentially, it also determines if concurrent is the best way to partition the data.

As we also saw, based on whether or not you need the results ordered either a `ForAll` or a `foreach` statement can yield better performance.

Summary

In this chapter, you learned how to change an ordinary LINQ to Objects query into a concurrent PLINQ. You also learned how to order results, merge results, and cancel queries. PLINQ makes it very easy to concurrently process queries on any memory data collection that supports IEnumerable.

It is also important to remember that PLINQ only supports LINQ to Objects and not the other forms of LINQ such as LINQ to SQL or LINQ to XML.

PLINQ is as easy to implement as adding a parallel extension method to a source data collection in a LINQ query — it is really that simple. Then .NET can determine if the query will have better performance running concurrently by partitioning the data collection into pieces, and if so, how to partition it. You as the programmer do not have to worry about any of this through your source code. PLINQ is really a no-brainer when performing a LINQ query because if .NET cannot improve performance making the query concurrent, it will just run the query sequentially.

In the next chapter, we will examine the new async and await keywords and how to easily implement asynchronous methods.

11
The Asynchronous Programming Model

In this chapter, we will be learning about the new `async` and `await` keywords provided in .NET 4.5, along with the **Asynchronous Programming Model** (APM). The `async` and `await` keywords are .NET's latest method for making asynchronous and multithreaded programming simple for the developer. These new keywords make using the `BackgroundWorker` component harder to justify. The `async` keyword makes it seamless to turn an ordinary method into an asynchronous method that runs on a separate thread. Then you can continue processing in the main thread. When you are ready to wait for the results of the asynchronous method, you can then use the `await` keyword in your main thread to block until the method returns.

The Asynchronous Programming Model uses the `IAsyncResult` interface to accomplish the same type of design. In this design pattern, you create a delegate and then use the `BeginInvoke` and `EndInvoke` methods of the delegate to start the method and wait on it to complete. You can also use the `IAsyncResult` interface that is returned by the `BeginInvoke` method to poll to see if the asynchronous method has completed, or set a `wait` handle for the asynchronous method to complete.

These two methods give us easy ways to implement functionality similar to the `BackgroundWorker` component that is used so heavily in Windows Forms applications and earlier versions of .NET. This functionality is especially useful in desktop applications when we do not want the main thread of the application to block. There are few things worse in desktop application design than having a user click on a button and the whole user interface freezes while some function is being performed.

Let's start by looking at the Asynchronous Programming Model and how to use this design pattern to run a method in a thread separate from the main thread. Then we will have the main thread wait on its results.

In this chapter, we will cover the following topics:

- The Asynchronous Programming Model
- Using an `AsyncCallback` delegate method
- The `async` and `await` keywords

Introduction to the Asynchronous Programming Model

The Asynchronous Programming Model is used by .NET classes to implement asynchronous designs. One example is the `BeginRead` and `EndRead` methods of `FileStream`. This allows the `FileStream` class to implement an asynchronous file read. The `StreamReader` and `StreamWriter` classes also have asynchronous methods. They implement this functionality using the `IAsyncResult` interface. In your customer classes, you can also implement this interface to allow you to have asynchronous functionality.

The naming convention when using this interface is to prefix your method names with `Begin` and `End`. So, you would name one `BeginMyMethod` and the other `EndMyMethod`. The first method is the one you execute asynchronously. The second method is what you call to block your main thread when you want to wait on the `Begin` method to end and have it also return the results.

Now, let's look at an example using the `BeginRead` and `EndRead` methods of the `FileStream` class. This same technique can be implemented using your own classes and implementing the `IAsyncResult` interface. You do not have to prefix your method names with `Begin` and `End`, but it is a good programming practice to follow the naming convention so that future developers using your classes will intuitively understand how they operate.

How to do it

First, let's open up Visual Studio and create a new console project called
FileReadAsync. Then, let's perform the following steps:

1. Add two using statements for the IO and Threading classes, as shown here:

    ```
    using System.Threading;
    using System.IO;
    ```

2. Now, let's add the following code to the Main method:

    ```
    public static void Main()
        {
            byte[] FileData = new byte[1000];

            FileStream FS = new FileStream("c:\\projects\\
    InputData.txt", FileMode.Open, FileAccess.Read,  FileShare.Read,
    1024, FileOptions.Asynchronous);

            Console.WriteLine("To start async read press
    return.");
            Console.ReadLine();

            IAsyncResult result = FS.BeginRead(FileData, 0,
    FileData.Length, null, null);


            // Work being done while we wait on the async //read.
            Console.WriteLine("\r\n");
            Console.WriteLine("Doing Some other work here. \r\n");
            Console.WriteLine("\r\n");

            //Calling EndRead will block the main thread //until
    the async work has finished.
            int num = FS.EndRead(result);


            FS.Close();
    ```

```
            Console.WriteLine("Read {0}  bytes from the file.
\r\n", num);
            Console.WriteLine("Is the async read completed - {0}.
\r\n", result.IsCompleted.ToString());
            Console.WriteLine(BitConverter.ToString(FileData));

            Console.ReadLine();
    }
```

3. Then, finally, we need to add a file called `InputData.txt` to `C:\projects`. This will be the file that we read asynchronously. It can contain any text that you would like; for our example, the `InputData.txt` file looks like the following screenshot:

Now, let's build and run our application. You should see a screen like this:

The program is waiting on the user to click on the return button; once the button is clicked, it will execute the asynchronous read of the data file. Once you click on return, you should see the following results:

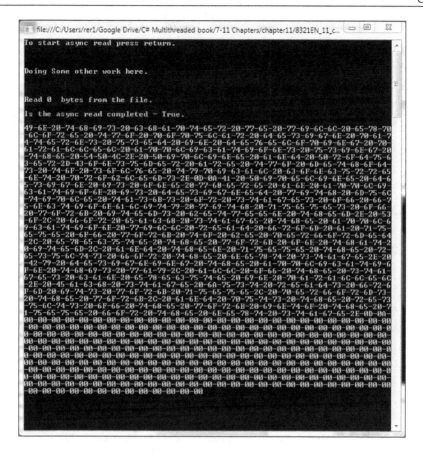

If you click return again, the application will finish and exit. So, let's look at how this works.

How it works

This is a very simple example of an existing .NET class, `FileStream`, that implements the Asynchronous Programming Model with the two methods, `BeginRead` and `EndRead`. If you look at the method definition for the `BeginRead` method, you will see that it implements the `IAsyncResult` interface:

```
public override IAsyncResult BeginRead(
    byte[] array,
    int offset,
    int numBytes,
    AsyncCallback userCallback,
    Object stateObject
)
```

You can also view the method definition for the `EndRead` method as follows:

```
public override int EndRead(
    IAsyncResult asyncResult
)
```

Now, let's look at your example project. In the following lines of code, we set up the `FileStream` object called `FS`:

```
FileStream FS = new FileStream("c:\\projects\\InputData.txt",
FileMode.Open, FileAccess.Read,
            FileShare.Read, 1024, FileOptions.Asynchronous);
```

Here we are declaring a new `FileStream` object with parameters that define the file to stream, the mode to open, the access to read, and the option to read asynchronously.

Then we initiate the read operation asynchronously with the following code:

```
            IAsyncResult result = FS.BeginRead(FileData, 0, FileData.
Length, null, null);
```

We then do some other work while the read operation is happening asynchronously on another thread. This "other" work is represented by the following three `Console.WriteLine` statements:

```
            // Work being done while we wait on the async read.
            Console.WriteLine("\r\n");
            Console.WriteLine("Doing Some other work here. \r\n");
            Console.WriteLine("\r\n");
```

Now, we block the main thread and wait on the `async` write to complete using this statement:

```
            //Calling EndRead will block the main thread until the
async work has finished.
            int num = FS.EndRead(result);
```

This statement will complete when the read is complete and return the `IAsyncResult` object and the number of bytes read. We then write these results to the console using the following statements:

```
            Console.WriteLine("Read {0}  bytes from the file. \r\n",
num);
            Console.WriteLine("Is the async read completed - {0}.
\r\n", result.IsCompleted.ToString());
```

We examine the `IsCompleted` method of `IAsyncResult` to make sure the read has completed even though we know it has because we blocked waiting on the `EndRead` method. We did this to preview another design pattern for the Asynchronous Programming Model, which we will not demonstrate in this chapter — the polling method. Instead of calling the `EndRead` method to block the main thread waiting on the `Main` method to complete, we can create a loop and periodically check the `IsCompleted` property of the `IAsyncResult` object returned by the `BeginRead` method. This is handy if we want to show a progress update throughout the read operation.

A third way to implement the Asynchronous Programming Model involves using a delegate method for processing when the read operation has completed.

Using an AsyncCallback delegate method

We have seen how we can use the APM design pattern that is implemented in the `FileStream` class to perform an asynchronous read and then wait on the results. We also mentioned how we can poll to see if the asynchronous read has completed instead of blocking the main thread. Now, we will see how we can execute a delegate method when the asynchronous read has completed.

Using this method, we do not have to block the main thread waiting or perform the work of polling the `IsCompleted` property to see when the read has completed. We simply execute the `BeginRead` method and pass it a delegate method. We then go on our way and, when the read completes, the delegate method will be executed.

Let's look at the method header for the `BeginRead` method of the `FileStream` class. The following is the method definition:

```
public override IAsyncResult BeginRead(
    byte[] array,
    int offset,
    int numBytes,
    AsyncCallback userCallback,
    Object stateObject
)
```

You will see that the fourth parameter passed to this method is an `AsyncCallback` delegate. In our previous example, we passed a null value for this parameter when we called this method. This time let's use a delegate method.

How to do it

Let's open Visual Studio and create a new console application called
`FileReadAsyncWithDelegate`. Once this has been created, we will perform
the following steps:

1. Add two `using` statements for the `IO` and `Threading` classes, as shown:

    ```
    using System.Threading;
    using System.IO;
    ```

2. Next, let's add the following code to the `Main` method of our application:

    ```
    public static void Main()
        {

            FileStream FS = new FileStream("c:\\projects\\
    InputData.txt", FileMode.Open, FileAccess.Read,
            FileShare.Read, 1024, FileOptions.Asynchronous);

            Console.WriteLine("To start async read press
    return.");
            Console.ReadLine();

            IAsyncResult result = FS.BeginRead(FileData, 0,
    FileData.Length, ReadComplete, FS);


            // Work being done while we wait on the async //read.
            Console.WriteLine("\r\n");
            Console.WriteLine("Doing Some other work here. \r\n");
            Console.WriteLine("\r\n");


            Console.ReadLine();
        }
    ```

3. Before the `Main` method, we need to declare a static byte array so that it is
    available to both the `Main` method and our new delegate method. Add the
    following statement before the `Main` method.

    ```
    private static byte[] FileData = new byte[1000];
    ```

4. Then, we need to add our delegate method. Add the following code for our delegate method:

```
private static void ReadComplete(IAsyncResult AResult)
        {
                // Write out the id of the thread that is //performing
the read.
                Console.WriteLine("The read operation is being done on
thread id: {0}.",
                        Thread.CurrentThread.ManagedThreadId);

                // Get the FileStream out of the IAsyncResult object.
                FileStream FS = (FileStream)AResult.AsyncState;

                // Get the results from the read operation.
                int num = FS.EndRead(AResult);

                // Make sure to close the FileStream.
                FS.Close();

                //Now, write out the results.
                Console.WriteLine("Read {0}  bytes from the file.
\r\n", num);
                Console.WriteLine("Is the async read completed - {0}.
\r\n", AResult.IsCompleted.ToString());
                Console.WriteLine(BitConverter.ToString(FileData));
        }
```

That is all the code we will need for this example. We do still need our `InputData.txt` file in `C:\projects`. It should still be there from when we created it in the last exercise.

Now, build and run the application and you should see the following:

Then press return and the application should display the following results:

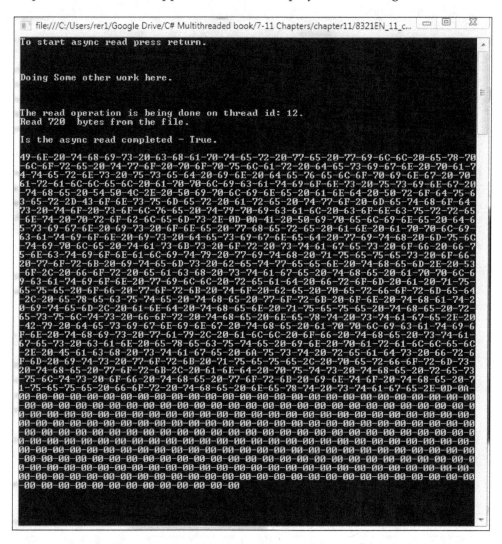

You will see that the results look almost identical to the results from the previous exercise. This is true. But how we achieve them is very different. This time, instead of blocking the main thread that is waiting on the read to complete, we initiated a delegate method on a separate thread and waited there for the read to complete and then display the results. Let's look at how we did it.

How it works

First, let's look at our `Main` method. This time it is more streamlined and does less work. It essentially just creates the `FileStream` object and calls the `BeginRead` method and passes it a delegate method. That is it. Then it goes about its business. It does not wait on the read to complete, does not process the results, and does not close the `FileStream` object. The following code shows this:

```
public static void Main()
{

        FileStream FS = new FileStream("c:\\projects\\InputData.
txt", FileMode.Open, FileAccess.Read,
        FileShare.Read, 1024, FileOptions.Asynchronous);

        Console.WriteLine("To start async read press return.");
        Console.ReadLine();

        IAsyncResult result = FS.BeginRead(FileData, 0, FileData.
Length, ReadComplete, FS);


        // Work being done while we wait on the async read.
        Console.WriteLine("\r\n");
        Console.WriteLine("Doing Some other work here. \r\n");
        Console.WriteLine("\r\n");


        Console.ReadLine();
}
```

The key here is the following statement:

```
IAsyncResult result = FS.BeginRead(FileData, 0, FileData.Length,
ReadComplete, FS);
```

Now, instead of the fourth and fifth parameters being `null`, we pass a delegate method and the `FileStream` object to this method. This allows the `Main` method to then go about its business.

Now, let's look at where the work is now being done—the delegate method, `ReadComplete`:

```
private static void ReadComplete(IAsyncResult AResult)
{
        // Write out the id of the thread that is performing the
read.
```

```
            Console.WriteLine("The read operation is being done on
    thread id: {0}.",
                Thread.CurrentThread.ManagedThreadId);

            // Get the FileStream out of the IAsyncResult object.
            FileStream FS = (FileStream)AResult.AsyncState;

            // Get the results from the read operation.
            int num = FS.EndRead(AResult);

            // Make sure to close the FileStream.
            FS.Close();

            //Now, write out the results.
            Console.WriteLine("Read {0}  bytes from the file. \r\n",
    num);
            Console.WriteLine("Is the async read completed - {0}.
    \r\n", AResult.IsCompleted.ToString());
            Console.WriteLine(BitConverter.ToString(FileData));
        }
```

The first thing you will notice is that the `AsyncCallback` delegate definition requires a method that returns no value and receives an `IAsyncResult` parameter as input.

We then get the `FileStream` object state using the following statement:

```
    FileStream FS = (FileStream)AResult.AsyncState;
```

Then, we wait on the read to complete and get the results using this statement:

```
    int num = FS.EndRead(AResult);
```

And finally, we process the results using these statements:

```
            Console.WriteLine("Read {0}  bytes from the file. \r\n",
    num);
            Console.WriteLine("Is the async read completed - {0}.
    \r\n", AResult.IsCompleted.ToString());
            Console.WriteLine(BitConverter.ToString(FileData));
```

That is all there is to it. We have spent the last two sections of this chapter looking at three ways to implement the APM:

- Call the `Begin` method name, perform some action, and then block using the `End` method name until the asynchronous action is finished

- Call the `Begin` method name, continue processing, and periodically check the `IsCompleted` property of the `IAsyncResult` object to know when the asynchronous operation is completed

- Call the `Begin` method name to initiate the asynchronous operation and then implement a delegate method on a separate thread to wait on the asynchronous operation and process the results

For the rest of the chapter, we will explore the new `async` and `await` keywords that were introduced in .NET Version 4.5.1.

The async and await keywords

In .NET 4.5, Microsoft introduced the `async` and `await` keywords that made it very easy for developers to implement asynchronous functionality in their methods. Adding the `async` keyword to the method header tells .NET's CLR to run this method in a separate thread in the threadpool if it determines that the following two conditions are met: first, that running it in a separate thread will increase performance, and second, the `await` keyword is used in the method. An `async` method will either return void, `Task`, or `Task<TResult>`. Also, the naming convention is to postfix any methods that use the `async` keyword with `Async`. So, the method name should be `MyMethodAsync`. That is all there is to it. The implementation is similar to the APM but does not use the `IAsyncResult` interface or implement it.

The design pattern for using this method is for your program to run a method that uses the `async` keyword by running it in a separate task. It is then free to continue on. If the `async` method does not have a return value, then the main thread can just continue on. If there is a return value that the `Main` method cares about or wants to know when the asynchronous operation has completed, it can wait on the asynchronous task to complete and view the results. In the asynchronous task, the method will perform functions on its own thread and then call the `await` keyword when it wants to wait on some action to complete.

To demonstrate the use of these two new keywords, we will rewrite our previous application to read a file asynchronously using the `async` and `await` keywords. Let's get started.

How to do it

First, let's open Visual Studio and create a new console application called
`FileReadUsingAsync`. Once we have this project created, perform the following steps:

1. Add two `using` statements for the `IO` and `Threading` classes, as follows:

    ```
    using System.Threading;
    using System.IO;
    ```

2. Next, let's add the following statements to the `Main` method:

    ```
    static void Main()
        {
            Console.WriteLine("The ID of the Main method: {0}.
    \r\n",
                Thread.CurrentThread.ManagedThreadId);

            //Wait on the user to begin the reading of the //file.
            Console.ReadLine();

            // Create task, start it, and wait for it to //finish.
            Task task = new Task(ProcessFileAsync);
            task.Start();
            task.Wait();

            //Wait for a return before exiting.
            Console.ReadLine();
        }
    ```

3. Next, we will create the `ProcessFileAsync` method that will run inside
    the task we created in the `Main` method. This method will implement the
    async keyword and run asynchronously. Add the following code to create
    this method:

    ```
    static async void ProcessFileAsync()
        {
            // Write out the id of the thread of the task //that
    will call the async method to read the file.
            Console.WriteLine("The thread id of the
    ProcessFileAsync method: {0}. \r\n",
                Thread.CurrentThread.ManagedThreadId);

            // Start the HandleFile method.
            Task<String> task = ReadFileAsync("C:\\projects\\
    InputData.txt");

            // Perform some other work.
    ```

```
            Console.WriteLine("Do some other work. \r\n");

            Console.WriteLine("Proceed with waiting on the read to
complete. \r\n");
            Console.ReadLine();

            // Wait for the task to finish reading the //file.
            String results = await task;
            Console.WriteLine("Number of characters read are: {0}.
\r\n", results.Length);

            Console.WriteLine("The file contents are: {0}. \r\n",
results);
        }
```

4. Now, this method will call another `async` method that will actually open the file and read the contents. This method, `ReadFileAsync`, will have the following code:

```
static async Task<String> ReadFileAsync(string file)
        {
            // Write out the id of the thread that is //performing
the read.
            Console.WriteLine("The thread id of the ReadFileAsync
method: {0}. \r\n",
                Thread.CurrentThread.ManagedThreadId);

            Console.WriteLine("Begin Reading file asynchronously.
\r\n");

            // Read the specified file.
            String DataRead = "";
            using (StreamReader reader = new StreamReader(file))
            {
                string character = await reader.ReadToEndAsync();

                //Build string of data read.
                DataRead = DataRead + character;

                //Slow down the process.
                System.Threading.Thread.Sleep(10000);

            }


            Console.WriteLine("Done Reading File asynchronously.
\r\n");
            return DataRead;
        }
```

That is all there is to it. Let's build our application and run it. We should see the following output:

At this point, the application is waiting for us, so we need to press return. Then we will see the following output:

```
The ID of the Main method: 10.

The thread id of the ProcessFileAsync method: 11.
The thread id of the ReadFileAsync method: 11.
Begin Reading file asynchronously.
Do some other work.
Proceed with waiting on the read to complete.
```

Now, we have initiated the asynchronous reading of the file, performed some other work, and are waiting on the file reading to complete. Once it has completed, we should see the following output:

```
The ID of the Main method: 10.

The thread id of the ProcessFileAsync method: 11.
The thread id of the ReadFileAsync method: 11.
Begin Reading file asynchronously.
Do some other work.
Proceed with waiting on the read to complete.
Done Reading File asynchronously.
```

Now, if we press return again we will see the results of the read operation:

file:///C:/Users/rer1/Google Drive/C# Multithreaded book/7-11 Chapters/chapter11/8321EN_11_c...

```
The ID of the Main method: 10.

The thread id of the ProcessFileAsync method: 11.

The thread id of the ReadFileAsync method: 11.

Begin Reading file asynchronously.

Do some other work.

Proceed with waiting on the read to complete.

Done Reading File asynchronously.


Number of characters read are: 729.

The file contents are: In this chapter we will explore two popular design patter
ns used in developing parallel applications using the TPL.
Pipeline and Producer-Consumer are two methods to solve typical concurrent proble
ms.

A Pipeline design is one where an application is designed with multiple tasks or
 stages of functionality with queues of work items between them.
So, for each stage the application will read from a queue of work to be performe
d, execute the work on that item, and then queue the results for
the next stage. By designing the application this way, all of the stages can exe
cute in parallel. Each stage just reads from its work queue,
erforms the work, and puts the results of the work into the queue for the next s
tage.
.
```

Finally, if we press return one last time, the application will finish and exit.
So, how did this all work?

How it works

Now, let's examine how this program works. First, take a look at the `Main` method:

```
static void Main()
{
    Console.WriteLine("The of ID the Main method: {0}. \r\n",
        Thread.CurrentThread.ManagedThreadId);

    //Wait on the user to begin the reading of the file.
    Console.ReadLine();

    // Create task, start it, and wait for it to finish.
    Task task = new Task(ProcessFileAsync);
    task.Start();
```

```
        task.Wait();

        //Wait for a return before exiting.
        Console.ReadLine();
    }
```

This is a simple method that creates a new task that executes an `async` method called `ProcessFileAsync`. It then starts the task and waits for it to finish. That is all. So, the `Main` method just spawns a task to do the work.

Now, the `async` method `ProcessFileAsync` is executed in a separate thread from the `Main` method. This is shown by displaying the thread ID number. You will notice from the console output that the `Main` thread ID is different from the thread ID of the task running the `ProcessFileAsync` method. Let's examine this method. The following is the code for us to dissect:

```
    static async void ProcessFileAsync()
    {
        // Write out the id of the thread of the task that will
call the async method to read the file.
        Console.WriteLine("The thread id of the ProcessFileAsync
method: {0}. \r\n",
            Thread.CurrentThread.ManagedThreadId);

        // Start the HandleFile method.
        Task<String> task = ReadFileAsync("C:\\projects\\
InputData.txt");

        // Perform some other work.
        Console.WriteLine("Do some other work. \r\n");

        Console.WriteLine("Proceed with waiting on the read to
complete. \r\n");
        Console.ReadLine();

        // Wait for the task to finish reading the file.
        String results = await task;
        Console.WriteLine("Number of characters read are: {0}.
\r\n", results.Length);

        Console.WriteLine("The file contents are: {0}. \r\n",
results);
    }
```

This method's main objective is to run the `async` method, ReadFileAsync. This is done with the following statement:

```
Task<String> task = ReadFileAsync("C:\\projects\\InputData.txt");
```

We then await this task with the following statement:

```
String results = await task;
```

The preceding statement tells the method to start an `async` task and then wait on it to complete. Since the method it is calling has a return value of Task<String>, the `await task` statement returns a string value. The ReadFileAsync method takes a filename as the input and then returns a string that contains the contents of the file as a string. This method reads the file asynchronously on a separate thread from the main thread.

The heart of the work is done in the ReadFileAsync method. Let's look at this method:

```
static async Task<String> ReadFileAsync(string file)
{
    // Write out the id of the thread that is performing the
read.
    Console.WriteLine("The thread id of the ReadFileAsync
method: {0}. \r\n",
        Thread.CurrentThread.ManagedThreadId);

    Console.WriteLine("Begin Reading file asynchronously.
\r\n");

    // Read the specified file.
    String DataRead = "";
    using (StreamReader reader = new StreamReader(file))
    {
        string character = await reader.ReadToEndAsync();

        //Build string of data read.
        DataRead = DataRead + character;

        //Slow down the process.
        System.Threading.Thread.Sleep(10000);

    }


    Console.WriteLine("Done Reading File asynchronously.
\r\n");

    return DataRead;
}
```

Here, we use the `async` keyword to designate this as an asynchronous method. This method creates a `FileStream` for the filename passed in and then calls the `StreamReader.ReadToEndAsync` method to asynchronously read the file. It uses the `await` keyword in this statement to signal .NET that this is an asynchronous operation:

```
string character = await reader.ReadToEndAsync();
```

By putting in the `wait` statement to slow down the processing a little, you can see the delay in execution between the following write statements:

```
            Console.WriteLine("Proceed with waiting on the read to
complete. \r\n");
            Console.ReadLine();

Console.WriteLine("Done Reading File asynchronously. \r\n");
```

This allows you to see that the main thread is available while the file is being read on a separate thread.

Another point to note is that by using the `async`/`await` programming method or the APM design pattern, we do not have to deal with the underlying code of starting, stopping, and managing threads. This is handled for us by .NET. We just have to write the logic and use the appropriate design pattern.

This is a generic way to easily implement any asynchronous operation that can benefit an application's performance without having to design the entire application for parallelism or concurrency like we did with the producer-consumer or Pipelining design patterns. We can simply code a single task to run asynchronously.

Summary

In this chapter, you have learned two very important ways to make a particular piece of functionality in an application run asynchronously from the main thread of the application. These two ways are the Application Programming Model and the `async`/`await` keywords. These two design techniques allow you to take advantage of the asynchronous execution of a task without designing an application around concurrency. This is especially useful for long-running tasks or tasks that access outside resources. In this way, we do not tie up the main thread of an application while we are waiting for something like a file read, an HTTP GET request, or a database read. These are all tasks whose duration is outside our control and not predictable. It therefore makes sense to perform these kinds of functions asynchronously so that our application's main thread can continue running.

These techniques are very useful when we do not have enough concurrent functionality to design a complete parallel application but have a particular task that can take a long time. These two methods are used in much the way the `BackgroundWorker` component is used and continues to make it obsolete.

The Application Programming Model is a design technique used when you create a class. You can create two methods and name them `BeginMethodName` and `EndMethodName` that implement the `IAsyncResult` interface. Then you can use them to start an asynchronous operation and, if needed, block the main thread waiting on the asynchronous operation to complete. This technique is used in many .NET classes such as the `FileStream`, `StreamReader`, and `StreamWriter`. But it can also be used by you when designing your classes.

The `async` and `await` keywords are a simple way to designate in a method's signature that it is meant to be performed as an asynchronous operation. The `async` keyword designates the method as an asynchronous method and the `await` keyword is used within the method to wait on a statement to complete before its method completes. This technique can be implemented within a class or as static methods within an application or helper class. These two techniques give the .NET developer two more tools in their toolbox to implement concurrent functionality.

Throughout this book, we have explored many ways to implement concurrent and asynchronous functionality in .NET. This includes techniques that have been around from .NET 1.0 to techniques introduced in the latest .NET 4.5. They range from simple asynchronous methods that do not allow blocking a main UI thread to objects for designing complete concurrent applications, to objects for processing sets of data concurrently. There are many ways and techniques to perform multithreaded functionality in .NET depending on the requirements of your specific application or task.

Now that you know all of what .NET has to offer, never waste an opportunity in your development to maximize the use of your computing hardware or its responsiveness by sticking to a single-threaded approach.

Index

D

data
  sharing, between threads 86-95
data parallelism, on collections
  with Parallel.ForEach command 189-197
deadlock 214
delegate 157, 158

E

encryption program 73
error handling
  threads, using 131-136
event wait handles 126
exceptions
  handling, in parallel loops 201-206
Exclusive OR (XOR) operations 78
execution cores 16

F

faulted task 180
Filter Image function 24
Find All References function 221
Flag column, Threads window 216
Flags column, Tasks window 218
Floating Point Unit (FPU) 10
ForEach overloads
  Action<TLocal> function 207
  ForEach<TSource, TLocal> datatype 207
  Func<TLocal> function 207
  Func<TSource, ParallelLoopState, TLocal,
    TLocal> function 207
  IEnumerable<TSource> collection 207
Front Side Bus (FSB) 17

G

GetBrightness() method 112
GetHue() method 112
GetSaturation() method 112
Gustafson's law 31, 32

H

hardware
  examining 18-20
hardware thread 14
heavyweight concurrency 71, 128
hyperthreading 13-15

I

Icons column, Tasks window 218
ID column, Tasks window 218
ID column, Threads window 216
image processing application
  used, for pipelining 107-112
input-processing-output (IPO) 8
inter-processor bus 29
IsAlive method 113
IsBusy() function 67

L

lambda expressions 157, 158
lightweight concurrency 71
LINQ to Objects 271
Load Image function 24
Location column, Tasks window 218
Location column, Threads window 216
lock condition 214

M

machine cycle 21
Managed ID column, Threads window 216
managed thread 216
merging, in PLINQ 282-288
message blocks
  examining 255, 256
mono-processor systems
  about 8
  single processing core 9
multicore 16
multiple BackgroundWorker components
  working with 58-66
multiple core processors 13

Thank you for buying
C# Multithreaded and Parallel Programming

About Packt Publishing

Packt, pronounced 'packed', published its first book, *Mastering phpMyAdmin for Effective MySQL Management*, in April 2004, and subsequently continued to specialize in publishing highly focused books on specific technologies and solutions.

Our books and publications share the experiences of your fellow IT professionals in adapting and customizing today's systems, applications, and frameworks. Our solution-based books give you the knowledge and power to customize the software and technologies you're using to get the job done. Packt books are more specific and less general than the IT books you have seen in the past. Our unique business model allows us to bring you more focused information, giving you more of what you need to know, and less of what you don't.

Packt is a modern yet unique publishing company that focuses on producing quality, cutting-edge books for communities of developers, administrators, and newbies alike. For more information, please visit our website at www.packtpub.com.

About Packt Enterprise

In 2010, Packt launched two new brands, Packt Enterprise and Packt Open Source, in order to continue its focus on specialization. This book is part of the Packt Enterprise brand, home to books published on enterprise software – software created by major vendors, including (but not limited to) IBM, Microsoft, and Oracle, often for use in other corporations. Its titles will offer information relevant to a range of users of this software, including administrators, developers, architects, and end users.

Writing for Packt

We welcome all inquiries from people who are interested in authoring. Book proposals should be sent to author@packtpub.com. If your book idea is still at an early stage and you would like to discuss it first before writing a formal book proposal, then please contact us; one of our commissioning editors will get in touch with you.

We're not just looking for published authors; if you have strong technical skills but no writing experience, our experienced editors can help you develop a writing career, or simply get some additional reward for your expertise.

Parallel Programming with Python

ISBN: 978-1-78328-839-7   Paperback: 128 pages

Develop efficient parallel systems using the robust Python environment

1. Demonstrates the concepts of Python parallel programming.

2. Boosts your Python computing capabilities.

3. Contains easy-to-understand explanations and plenty of examples.

OpenCL Parallel Programming Development Cookbook

ISBN: 978-1-84969-452-0   Paperback: 302 pages

Accelerate your applications and understand high-performance computing with over 50 OpenCL recipes

1. Learn about parallel programming development in OpenCL and also the various techniques involved in writing high-performing code.

2. Find out more about data-parallel or task-parallel development and also about the combination of both.

3. Understand and exploit the underlying hardware features such as processor registers and caches that run potentially tens of thousands of threads across the processors.

Please check **www.PacktPub.com** for information on our titles